PLEASURES OF THE BELLE EPOQUE

Toulouse-Lautrec, *Moulin de la Galette*
(Art Institute of Chicago): detail.

Pleasures of the Belle Epoque

ENTERTAINMENT
& FESTIVITY
IN
TURN·OF·THE·CENTURY
FRANCE

CHARLES REARICK

YALE UNIVERSITY PRESS · NEW HAVEN AND LONDON

Published with assistance from the Amasa Stone Mather, 1907 Memorial Fund.

Designed by Sally Harris
and set in Goudy Old Style type by Rainsford Type, Ridgefield, CT.
Printed in the United States of America by
Murray Printing Company, Westford, Massachusetts.
Color sections printed by Eastern Press, New Haven, Connecticut.

Library of Congress Cataloging in Publication Data

Rearick, Charles, 1942-
Pleasures of the belle époque.
Bibliography: p.
Includes index.
1. Leisure—France—History.   2. Amusements—France—
History.   3. France—Popular culture—History.
4. France—Social conditions.   I. Title.
GV79.R43 1986   306'.48'0944   85-40468
ISBN 0-300-03230-7

The paper in this book meets the guidelines for
permanence and durability of the Committee on
Production Guidelines for Book Longevity
of the Council on Library Resources.

10 9 8 7 6 5 4 3 2 1

TO MARY

"Paris . . . la capitale même du royaume des Plaisirs."
—Camille Debans, *Les plaisirs et les curiosités de Paris* (1889)

"L'amusement prend une telle place dans l'existence et
jusque dans les parties les plus sévères de l'existence,
qu'on est à se demander s'il n'est pas pour beaucoup en
train d'en devenir le fond, et si nous ne finirons pas
par n'être plus qu'un peuple qui s'amuse."
—Frédéric Passy, "Les fêtes foraines et les administrations municipales" (1883)

CONTENTS

List of Color Illustrations   viii

Acknowledgments   ix

Introduction   xi

1 A Time for Festivity   1

2 The Right to Be Lazy and to Enjoy   25

3 Bohemian Gaiety and the New Show Business   53

4 The Music Halls: A New Democratic Culture?   81

5 The World's Fairs and Other Extravaganzas   117

6 The Rhythms of Modern Life   147

7 The Spectacles of Modern Life   167

8 Dancing on a Volcano   197

Conclusion   217

Notes   223

Selected Bibliography 235

Index   237

COLOR ILLUSTRATIONS

Seurat, *A Sunday Afternoon on the Island of the Grande Jatte*, 1884–86 (Art Institute of Chicago) *facing page 16*

Monet, *Rue Saint Denis*, June 30, 1878 (Musée des Beaux-Arts, Rouen) *facing page 17*

Toulouse-Lautrec, *Moulin de la Galette* (Art Institute of Chicago) *facing page 48*

Seurat, *The Circus*, 1890–91 (Cliché des Musées Nationaux, Paris) *facing page 49*

Chéret, Jardin de Paris, poster (Musée de la Publicité, Paris) *facing page 112*

Horloge poster (Musée de la Publicité, Paris) *facing page 113*

Chéret, Moulin Rouge, poster (Musée de la Publicité, Paris) *facing page 144*

Vulliemin, Peugeot poster (Musée de la Publicité, Paris) *facing page 145*

Page references for black and white illustrations are indicated in bold face in the Index.

ACKNOWLEDGMENTS

Some of the people who helped me are unaware of their decisive role. In 1978 at a historical conference in Rhode Island, Eugen Weber, for example, tossed to me the idea of combining my interest in festivals with the subject of entertainment. Later at a couple of points, the interest that Susanna Barrows took in my work helped move this project toward completion. The continuing moral support of H. Stuart Hughes has also been important.

A number of my colleagues at the University of Massachusetts offered much appreciated encouragement and advice—among them, Gerald McFarland, Mario DePillis, and Robert Griffith. Ronald Story read a draft of the full manuscript and made excellent suggestions, including the idea of having maps prepared.

My student Allan Potofsky also read the manuscript and thoughtfully responded to it in detail. So did graduate student Mary Lewis, whose pointed and sometimes humorous comments helped improve an early draft. Robert Kentor and Odile Hullot helped me puzzle my way through some difficult questions and translations. Discussions with Rosalind and Gary Williams made my visits to Boston-area libraries more pleasant. Among others who helped me find answers were Miriam Levin and William Markey.

In Paris, Professor Gérard Vincent graciously received me and helped me contact some of his colleagues. Among them were Anne and Jacques Gournay, who helped in my research for illustrations, and Professor Madeleine Rebérioux, who discussed the universal expositions and workers' leisure with me. At the Musée de Montmartre, Mariel Frèrebeau-Oberthür offered her expertise on Montmartre cabarets, and at the Musée de la Publicité I had the good fortune of chancing upon Alain Weill, who shared some of his knowledge of posters and music halls. Over several years M. and Mme. Jean Chagnaud-Forain have generously given me encouragement and insights into turn-of-the-century France, to which they afforded me a privileged access through the home and works of artist Jean-Louis Forain.

As the work moved into the publishing phase, Dean Murray Schwartz of the University of Massachusetts supplied funds for defraying the costs of illustrations. At the press, Cecile Watters and Jay Williams have been expert and patient in the final editing. Sally Harris artfully designed the book and the complex layout of illustrations. Charles Grench has played a creative role as editor, making suggestions about the form of the book and illustrations, for example, even before the writing began. I am grateful to each of these people and to such others as librarians and family members. I wish to thank all who helped. One other must be named, one who has made innumerable contributions since I began this study—my wife Mary, to whom the book is dedicated.

INTRODUCTION

The French have long attracted admiration for their reputed capacity to enjoy life, a joie de vivre associated with good wine and good food, wit, sensuality, and sociability. Perhaps no period in France's history is more identified with those qualities than the three decades before the First World War, a period that has become known as *la belle époque*. The French of that period did not recognize it as such a "beautiful" era and did not name it. They, like historians now, knew too much about it. Not until the twentieth-century nightmares of world war and depression gripped France did the prewar years look particularly fortunate. Since the Second World War the phrase *belle époque* has gained enough acceptance to appear as an encyclopedia entry and in numerous book titles. *

Books recalling the epoch as *belle* are now common; many have regaled readers with anecdotes of scintillating banquets and exuberant fêtes enjoyed by the rich and by artistic Bohemians. A few even tell of worker amusements. At Maxim's, at the Chat Noir, or in Belleville *assommoirs*, laughter mingled with music, as wine, absinthe, or champagne flowed freely. Presumably people enjoyed themselves.

To descriptions of such scenes, historians commonly counterpose accounts of France's problems in the period: bitter labor and political conflicts, anarchist attacks, threats to the parliamentary Republic, poverty and economic crises, and fierce battles over the Church. In that larger context, the belle époque does appear to be a myth, as it has often been called. Yet at times and in certain places and for some people, there were festive moments that lay at the source of the generalized memory of the belle époque. The good times to be examined here are celebrations and entertainments. Those to

*Even books in languages other than French; for example, Raymond Rudorff's *Belle Epoque: Paris in the Nineties* (London: Hamilton, 1972) and Willy Haas's *Die Belle Epoque* (Munich: Verlag Kurt Desch, 1967).

be highlighted were new and much acclaimed ones that were apparently most pleasing to many people, representing a range of social classes. This is a history best known through its illustrations, which include enduring art by Renoir, Toulouse-Lautrec, Chéret, and Seurat.

Toulouse-Lautrec alone is reminder enough that the entertainments were not always cheering. Joyless gaiety was well known to the belle époque. For historians the question of how the enjoyments and the depressing problems of the age were interrelated is a thorny one. Popular entertainments are often viewed simply as escapes from the problems, as safety valves for discontents. But it may be that leisure times were alloyed with unease and difficulties—as the entire period so clearly was. In fact, the present study brings out many responses to entertainment that were hardly in the dulcet C-major too often associated with "places of pleasure." What limits did the problems put on enjoyment? In what ways did amusements satisfy and in what ways did they fail to satisfy? In search of answers, this study not only describes and analyzes amusements but also notes varied responses to them and how both changed over time. The pleasure seekers' testimony (incomplete as it is) and the statistics of rising or declining admissions receipts are both helpful. Yet they may still not be enough to explain the shifts in public preferences. Why did dance halls and panoramas fade and why did cinema grow so rapidly? To answer these questions, one might further ask if the entertainments were responses to changes outside the sphere of leisure— changes in people's work, for example. Conversely, it may be that the new entertainments were altering the way people thought and acted outside their strictly leisure time.

This study explores such questions and proposes some answers, certainly leaving many possibilities for future contributions. This large subject of people's leisure and fun has long suffered from the dominant bias toward work and politics; the particulars are a slighted part of French history, interesting in themselves. But the aim here is neither to survey amusements encyclopedically nor to chronicle particular ones; there are already books on the circus, on music halls, on the cinema. My interest is in broad changes and fundamental questions about modern popular culture—particularly a turn-of-the-century culture of entertainments immediately recognizable as modern. Four of my chapters pursue these questions by focusing on one leading new form of entertainment per chapter; the conclusions reached in each apply beyond the specific case. To see what festivity meant in France, a spotlight is placed on the nation's most successful modern celebration. To consider commercialization, we go to Montmartre and to a cabaret called the Chat Noir. For the question of how democratic the emerging culture was, we go to the music halls. For observations on the new technology and blockbuster spectacles, a visit to the Paris world's fairs is appropriate. The rest of the book takes a more direct, wide-angle view of the big scene of change: four chapters (the second and the last three) survey mentalities, time patterns, and social relations as they showed up both in the society at large and in its entertainments. Throughout, the aim is to understand a transition to the modern by examining cultural conditions of public pleasure. That transition entailed gains and losses, conflicts, hopes and anxieties, which, if not universal, certainly go beyond the confines of belle-époque French history.

From this perspective, a rousing event stands out as an opener: a celebration in 1880 that shows much about France's emerging national civilization. To understand that celebration calls for understanding traditions not only of reveling, but also of conflicts that were political and, as continued in chapter 2, more basically cultural. To begin with 1880 is more than to settle on a point of departure that is chronologically neat, a clear-cut first. For its importance in French experience and thought, there is nowhere better to begin than with a fête—as a lived reality and an ideal.

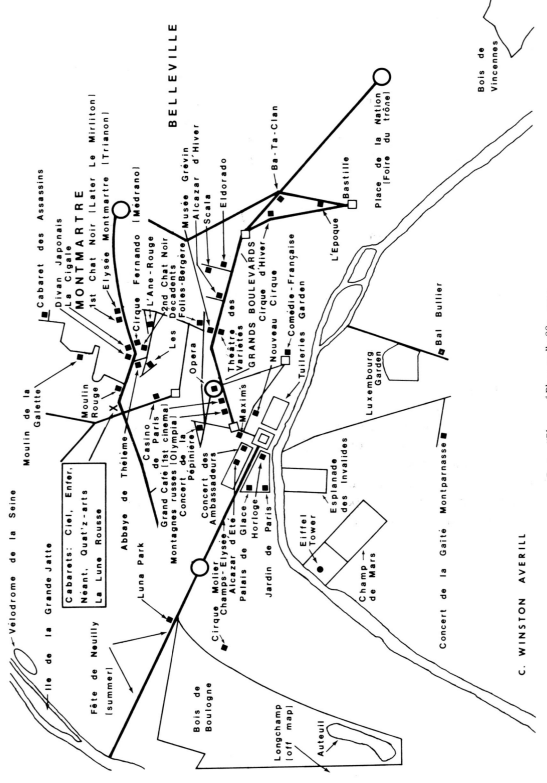

Paris—"Places of Pleasure," 1880–1914

C. WINSTON AVERILL

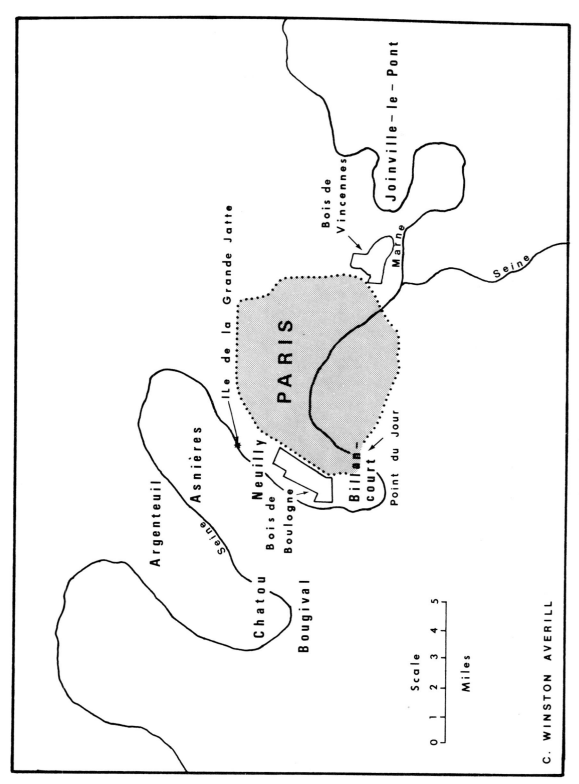

"Places of Pleasure" in the Environs of Paris

C. WINSTON AVERILL

1

A Time for Festivity

Scenes of the landmark national fête of July 14, 1880. The first page of *L'Illustration* on July 24 was devoted to a panoramic collage of public activities on the first national celebration of Bastille Day in modern France. At the top: fairground amusements on the l'Esplanade des Invalides. On the sides: drinking and visiting around tables set up in the middle of Paris streets, flags and garlands interlacing all around, open-air dancing in the rue Réaumur and the Place de la Bourse (at the bottom). Center: people wearing liberty caps and tricolor cockades reveling in the brilliant decor of festive lanterns, garlands, and flags.

A warm, sunny day, it was a holiday unlike any other. Not even a rainstorm in the evening could spoil it. In Paris it had begun with a volley of cannon shots at 8 A.M.; in the country, several hours earlier, villagers had awakened to fanfares of rifle fire and ringing church bells; firecrackers and band music followed. Streets were bedecked with flags and bunting, and in some places banners, garlands, and triumphal arches as well. Parts of central Paris became a gala stage set, a sparkling mosaic of red, white, and blue. At night, gas lamps and electric lights and Venetian lanterns brought a rare cheering radiance to main streets and squares. Fireworks from six locations emblazoned and bombarded the night sky. No one could take July 14, 1880, as just another day.

Through most of France, people gathered to do what they had not done regularly for a decade: to celebrate. They drank and sang, played games, heard speeches and concerts, watched parades, and danced into the night with an apparently untroubled enjoyment. Paris boulevards and squares teemed with merry promenaders even past midnight, and similar crowds reveled in most provincial towns. For color and sociable pleasure-taking, scenes of that day are as essentially "belle-époque" as the more familiar impressionist paintings of leisured people in dance halls, boating parties along the Seine, and richly hued gardens. The 14th of July 1880 may be said to have opened the belle époque.

"The civil fête has been the most unanimous, the most intense, the most brilliant republican demonstration possible to foresee," exulted the normally restrained daily *Le Temps*. In fact, there was no unanimity. The first modern Bastille Day, like other celebrations and entertainments of the era, met with indifference from some and active opposition from others. Still, the positive response was unquestionably impressive. In Paris and many provincial cities and villages, crowds turned out in large numbers and in unmistakably high

3

spirits. Across France thousands of mayors and other rural functionaries hailed local celebrations in terms similar to those in *Le Temps*. "Joy was in all hearts, the enthusiasm was indescribable," reported the mayor of La Boissière, in a southern area where republican sentiment ran particularly high. "The oldest inhabitants of the city do not recall ever having seen a similar fête, so brilliant and so complete," wrote the police commissioner of Thiers to the subprefect.[1]

Such reports could be discounted by the skeptical as politically biased, since they came from republicans who wanted to find and report popular approval of the Third Republic. But even antirepublican journalists conceded that a considerable part of the population, of course deplorably misguided, took part in the revels. "Paris was an immense spree [*goguette*]," complained the monarchist *Le Français*. "Paris was a cheap dance hall [*bastringue*]," the even more conservative *Gazette de France* noted indignantly. "The night of July 14–15 has been only an immense orgy," the legitimist *Union* lamented. Foreign observers confirmed the more positive republican reports. "Here in Paris," wrote the *Times* of London correspondent, "the fête has been a brilliant success. . . . The *abandon* with which Frenchmen throw themselves into a festival has never been more strikingly exemplified." The *New York Times* reported that the "populace everywhere" joined in with "wholehearted enthusiasm." In Paris and many provincial towns, that July 14 was a high point of collective enjoyment in the belle époque, a day rarely rivaled by subsequent festivals. It was a day by which the era's mushrooming commercial entertainments could be measured and found wanting.

WORKDAYS AND FEAST DAYS

That fête of 1880 was special in a way that no later Bastille Day could be. It was the first time since the French Revolution that all France could legally celebrate the most stirring and epoch-making event of the Revolution: the storming of the Bastille. The story of July 14, 1789, remained vivid in French memories through oral tradition, popular prints, a commercial panorama in Paris, and dramatic histories by Jules Michelet and Louis Blanc, as well as a press campaign by the popular republican leader Léon Gambetta and his associates. Yet through the nineteenth century successive governments had opposed any public demonstration of enthusiasm for the day. Why would rulers anxious about public order want to encourage a memory of bloody revolt? Like its monarchist and Bonapartist predecessors, the government of the Third Republic feared renewed crowd risings, and for almost a decade it too rejected the Bastille commemoration. After less conservative leadership took over in the late 1870s, it adopted the Bastille fête only with reluctance, as a token concession to the strengthening Left.

Never before in modern times had the French gone so long without any regular national celebration. The monarchists who controlled the Third Republic for most of the decade had not been secure enough to settle on a royalist commemoration. Besides, that decade had generally been a time when mourning and national soul-searching seemed more appropriate than celebration. Those were the years of recovery from the Terrible Year of military defeat by the Prussians, followed by bitter and devastating civil war in Paris.

Recovery was far enough advanced by 1878 that the French government could stage a splendid "universal exposition" in Paris to show off regained national wealth and power. To celebrate that world's fair and France's new success, the Republic's monarchist leaders authorized a national fête on June 30. It was timed like a traditional harvest festival, following intense and fruitful labor. Across the land people responded with a surge of decorating and dancing—in an "explosion of long deferred and long awaited joy," recalled journalist Camille Pelletan two years later. "All witnesses can still see a dazzle of garlands and decorative foliage of flags fluttering and flickering in the wind and multi-colored lights with which the night was all flowered as if some incomprehensibly joyous tricolor spring had broken out over the city." The brilliance of that tricolor decor lives on for posterity in two well-known Monet paintings. When *Le Temps* sought to praise July 14 two years later, it resorted to the phrase "a glorious new edition of the day of June 30, 1878."[2]

After the success of June 30, calls for regular fêtes intensified. But a festive June 30 was not to be repeated. The day lacked a richness of historic meaning and symbolism that could have made it reverberate through the years; neither the celebration nor the fair represented a turning point decisive enough to produce annual sequels. No such new and arbitrary date could stir passions

5

the way revolutionary *journées* could, and no journée had advocates as insistent as those for July 14. Finally in 1880, only days before the actual anniversary and after years of republican journalist clamor and weeks of parliamentary politicking, French lawmakers passed the law establishing July 14 as *the* national holiday.

Unlike June 30, the new holiday was to be celebrated every year henceforth. In the past, repetition over the generations had given traditional fêtes, like old proverbs, an ingratiating familiarity, a timeworn comfortableness that was a part of their strength. But would that be the case in modern society? Could a new fête day secure enduring popularity by being fixed and repeated annually? There was much reason for doubts in a period when many traditional fêtes were falling into decay, along with the work routines and magical beliefs undergirding them. Change was becoming so much a way of life that repetitive annual celebrations no longer promised to satisfy, an editorialist for *Le Temps* had argued in 1878. Fixed feasts implied "stagnation in social life" and "immobility in conception." Better would be a "new method" of "seizing occasions" that would command enough interest to spark a genuinely spirited national celebration. The legislators ignored the analysis of modern society and the proposal the prominent historian Michelet had also made nearly a decade before.[3] Yet they instituted a fête that was in its debut one of those occasions not fixed long in advance. The first official modern Bastille Day occurred as a conceptually rich novelty, a timely release from routine. Like the Republic itself, it represented fresh possibilities of joy and fraternity not yet limited by experience nor dulled by overfamiliarity.

The timing of Bastille Day within the year was also favorable in some important ways. No major religious or traditional holiday came close enough to it to divert festive energies and resources. The closest was a monarchist celebration of Saint Henri, but Bastille Day upstaged that rival by coming one day before. There was good reason for that summer lull in the traditional festive calendar. July was a time of heavy agricultural labor in peasant France and no time to call farm workers to consume and play. Church and folkloric holidays had long been concentrated in less demanding seasons. In 1880 and for years thereafter, rural workers who were unsympathetic to the Republic often skipped the new civic fête, especially its daytime activities, not just for political reasons but also because of the need to continue pressing field work. Country people in many villages sought to move the festivities to Sunday, both to combine it with religious ceremony and to avoid losing a workday. Yet republican peasants, with the same crops and exhausting field labor, found it possible to take a day off or to join in dancing late into the night. The mid-July timing was inconvenient but not prohibitive.[4]

No such discomfiture with timing appeared in the cities. For urban people, the holiday was a gift of freedom from normal routine, a day nicely placed in early summer that promised good weather allowing a maximum of outdoor play. The creators of the holiday, urban men, had provided a fête best suited to urban work life. The city, a place of work by inexorable clocktime in shop and office, was also a place where free time was more clearly demarcated and more malleable. There, without regard to nature's cycles or to tradition, free time could readily be created, as well as new entertainments to occupy that time.

DAY OF DELIVERANCE, DAY OF CONCORD

Bastille Day 1880 had the further advantage of occurring when reasons to celebrate seemed multifold and genuine. France was coming out of an economic slump that from 1876 to 1879 had brought the highest prices for necessities during the last thirty years of the nineteenth century. The army that the Germans defeated a decade before had renewed itself as well, a prime cause for many to exult. The most popular spectacle in Paris was the redistribution of flags to the army at Longchamp, marking the military recovery from the shame and humiliation of 1870. A crowd of more than one hundred thousand (three hundred thousand by some accounts) gathered there to cheer the troops. Supporters of the Republic could also cheer the firm establishment of that form of government after ten years of uncertainty and threats of monarchist restoration or Bonapartist takeover. Socialists and anarchists and radicals could celebrate a recovery from the devastation of the Paris Commune, which had ended in the arrest and exiling of thousands of leftist leaders. Just before creating the Bastille Day holiday, the French parliament granted amnesty to the former Communards. In short, the new decade and the new Republic marked a new beginning for France.[5]

The promises of liberty and fraternity that resounded in republican rhetoric

Fireworks at the Carrefour de l'Observatoire,
July 14, 1880. On the night of the Third Republic's first official Bastille Day, the central
symbol of popular liberation was appropriately
the subject of the principal fireworks display
near Paris's Luxembourg Garden. Ten thousand
flares of multiple flashes outlined the ancient
fortress together with the monument later built
on the Bastille site, the July Column topped by
a figure of the "spirit of liberty."

Marianne, the symbol of the Republic,
triumphs, bringing universal suffrage and "the
rights of man." She stands up for the good
working people of France, while their enemies—kings, Bonapartes, and Germans—faint
away, unable to withstand her virtue. This
scene of apotheosis, reminiscent of traditional
religious imagery, was a favorite of the Third
Republic's supporters in the late nineteenth
century. The motif showed up in prints, festivals, statues, and pageantry. (Musée
Carnavalet, Paris)

raised hopes, and the promises of 1789 could again rouse support. At least a Republic identifying with 1789 would not bring back the ancien régime, which to worried peasants meant a restoration of the tithe and the loss of noble and church lands acquired since the Revolution. Further, July 14 could be celebrated, as it was by republican moderates, not just as a day of bloody popular deliverance but also as a day of fraternal unification. By recalling the first peaceful July 14 anniversary, held in 1790, republican orators pointed to a rallying of French revolutionaries from all France in the grand Festival of the Federations, the fête of fêtes, as Michelet hailed it. Such a rite of revolutionary reconciliation had much appeal to moderates in 1880, who were anxious to bring together as many partisan groups as possible behind the young republican government. "What we celebrate today," wrote radical Camille Pelletan in *La Justice*, "is the resurrection of France." Resurrection, reconciliation, liberation, and concord—such were the powerful hopes and myths that republicans professed to find realized in July 14.[6]

In the manner of traditional religious holidays, the celebration combined both official ritual and simple merrymaking. Ardent republicans adorned themselves with red liberty caps or red-white-and-blue hats, ties, sashes, boutonnieres, cockades, and dresses. In Aramon (Gard) and other republican villages, citizens wearing cockades paraded through the streets singing the Marseillaise. In the South particularly, they planted liberty trees as the 1789 revolutionaries had done. In Saint Hippolyte-Caton (Gard), citizens placed crowns and fascicles of flags on liberty trees planted during the earlier revolutions, to cries of "Vive la République!" In the cities they dedicated statues of a classical woman, nicknamed Marianne, who symbolized the Republic; in the villages, they paid homage to busts of the Republic, busts in some cases carried through the bourg like saints' effigies and then enshrined in the town hall. Eventually republican villagers acquired emblems from commercial firms in Paris, but in the early years makeshift local creations were pressed into service. In Ars (Ile de Ré), for example, "an artist of our little village made a statue for the public square," reported the mayor to the prefect in July 1881. Communal officials marched there on July 14 to "pay homage to the Republic." Awaiting the cortege was a group of little children dressed in tricolor robes and liberty caps, and one of them—"a charming little girl"—

"made some patriotic remarks ringing with emotion," according to the may-
or's report. Monsieur Edouard Martineau, pharmacist and donor of the statue,
also spoke movingly. The homages continued with republican toasts at "a
democratic punch" and at fraternal banquets. For enthusiastic partisans such
acts of devotion to the Revolution and to the Republic were the high points
of the day.[7]

Although the ceremonies generally attracted a politicized minority of
inhabitants, a far larger number joined in amusements that lacked political
motifs. The young and energetic scrambled up a greased pole (*mât de cocagne*)
to snatch a prize. Others played *boules and quilles* and competed in races of
all sorts: swimming, simple footraces, races with competitors carrying pots
on their heads, races on stilts and skates, wheelbarrow and sack races, races
of bulls and donkeys. Toward the end of the century, bicycle races were
popular, especially in the cities. In some towns crowds gathered to watch
the ascent of a balloon, a popular spectacle since the end of the Old Regime.
In Paris and provincial garrison towns, military parades, which consistently
drew large crowds, were widely cheered spectacles—patriotic rites that pleased
Bonapartists, royalists, and republicans alike, until the Dreyfus affair and
the rise of an antimilitarist Left around 1900. In the evening the crowds
generally grew larger with more people leaving work, and aided by wine,
spirits rose. Dancing was the main entertainment. "The population appeared
a little indifferent during the day," the mayor of Mareuil-sur-Lay (Vendée)
reported frankly in 1880, but "it assembled in the evening." It was after 11
o'clock when the happy mayor concluded his report ". . . and the violin is
again asked back."[8] More formal finales were concerts and fireworks (in the
more prosperous communities) and often a torchlight retreat. In central
France, traditional bonfires, *feux de joie*, blazed from hilltops. Thus with
minimal expenditures, common people gave themselves simple entertainments, especially dancing and races, that allowed for maximum participation
and a lively spectacle for everyone interested.

Almost all the events were free. The banquets were kept at low cost, but
even the few francs charged were beyond the means of the poor. To them
went special doles of bread, wine, and sometimes meat. Though the rich
and conservative bourgeois shunned the games and dancing, crowds of artisans, laborers, peasants, and shopkeepers did participate in all but the most

Schoolboy rifle battalions paraded and occupied
a central place in the official programs of Bastille Days in the 1880s. Like gymnastic societies
of the same period, the rifle teams were organized in a spirit of anti-German militancy and
were often led by devoutly republican school-
teachers. These premilitary youth organizations
were applauded by crowds charged with the
same nationalist zeal that made the Longchamp
military review the climactic popular event of
Bastille Day. (Musée Carnavalet, Paris)

A night dance, July 14, 1881, in the Impasse
du Maine. In the plebeian 14th arrondissement,
popular merrymaking, drinking, and dancing
reached heights of exuberance with some participants also ardently paying tribute to the Republic. Historian Rosemonde Sanson has
counted eighteen Bastille Day balls in Paris in
1880 and seventy-two in 1881; the number
continually increased through the prewar years.
The wine merchant, whose store is in the background, was an important supplier of tables,
chairs, and decorations as well as the essential
popular drink.

antirepublican areas. Such participation made Bastille Day a truly popular fête rather than simply a staged spectacle.

Clearly the republican organizers of the holiday wanted to make the Republic more attractive by offering people some fun under republican auspices. Their great rival was not so much royalty, with its regal pageantry, as the Roman Catholic Church, with its widely followed fêtes. In the competition for popular favor, Bastille Day was a way of making the Republic less austere and less abstract. It was a way of teaching the people, more than a fifth of them still illiterate (over half in some backward areas), new values and a new identity. Marianne, the personification of the Republic, was taking the place of Mary, and democratic participation was to supplant the orchestrations of elites.[9] Alongside the ballot for every man and the new republican laic schools created in 1881–82, the new civic fête was a step in the creation of a secular democratic culture to rival the older culture of Catholic and royal France.

FESTIVE COMMUNITY: HOPES AND PROBLEMS

Since the great Revolution, advocates of such fêtes as Bastille Day had held out many hopes couched as expectations, but nothing shows better their capacity to hope against hope than their view that those celebrations could make economic and social differences vanish: the country's wounds would heal from time to time in a day of joyous unanimity. As we have seen, republicans insisted that their day of July 14, 1880, had indeed been one of those miraculous occasions. Using Michelet-style rhetoric of democratic faith, even *Le Temps* boldly reported the incredible: "The whole population of all classes and all nuances took an active and joyous part."[10] One of the proofs of unanimity commonly adduced was the minimal one of an absence of disturbances and fights. France had suffered from so much bloody conflict over the past century that a gala day of concord appeared to the hopeful as a magnificent achievement heralding a joyously fraternal France. In a land of notorious class consciousness, distrust, antagonism among social groups, and inequalities, a festival was a sorely needed medicine, if not a cure. Such was the hope of republicans not wanting to redistribute wealth or even to give small governmental aid to the poor.

Reconciliation through fêtes presupposed the voluntary participation of the community. Republicans prided themselves on establishing liberty and a democracy that would have nothing to do with the coercion and manipulation characteristic of Napoleonic festivals and elections. Republicans wanted to organize festivals, but they also wanted popular participation that was spontaneous and voluntary. In practice, they struck a compromise. Government leaders notified local authorities of the new law and urged them to make preparations and to do everything possible to enhance the celebration. Then the central government provided subsidies to boost local resources for the purchase of such paraphernalia as flags, lanterns, and fireworks. Finally, the government required local reports from municipal councils, even in tiny villages, to see that the observances had been correct. Local mayors and civil servants were clearly under pressure to celebrate. Names of those who boycotted the event were forwarded to Paris authorities, and in some cases punitive actions were taken. Some mayors were suspended from their functions, and some even removed from office. But for most ordinary citizens, participation in dancing or games was voluntary. In no earlier regime had so many people, particularly in rural villages, joined in government-sponsored celebration. The festivities of 1880 opened a new era of popular national recreation in France, authorized, but not carried out, by a democratic central government.

The state had long played a role in creating and organizing festivals, especially in the capital. Under the kings and Bonapartes, the birthday of the ruler and his marriage occasioned so-called national celebrations that were, in fact, confined to the large cities. What was distinctive about Bastille Day 1880 was how little power the state exercised in planning and directing local revels throughout the land. The legislation creating the holiday was so late in passage that the central authorities had little time to formulate extensive orders or to implement them. The Ministry of the Interior offered only small subsidies to the towns and villages of France—commonly ten or fifteen francs to villages, and one hundred or two hundred francs to towns. * The state imposed no uniform program; it confined itself to urging local

*In the period before the First World War, 5 francs equaled $1.

15

authorities to follow "local usages." Bastille Day 1880 was truly national and modern, stemming from a single source of secular authority, but the state was far from playing the homogenizing "culture industry" role of later media producers.

Yet, contrary to the republican dream, local festivals did not arise spontaneously from all the people. Leaders and organizers emerged from groups of people most in touch with national politics and ideological thinking. These were usually educated local functionaries—the village mayor, the schoolmaster, the tax collector, the informal political groups often centered in a village café, the kind of people who read newspapers and had some independence, economic and intellectual, from village priests and antirepublican notables. They often contributed money as well as time and effort. A public collection in a "republican café" in Aigues-vives (Hérault), for example, produced two hundred francs for July 14, 1880; the other half of the festival fund came equally from the mayor's personal contribution and from public money voted by the municipal council. In Piré, a particularly antirepublican Breton town, the schoolmaster and "several patriots" defied the hostile mayor and the majority: they "installed flags, brought up a cannon, assembled faggots for a feu de joie," and bought a small fireworks package. Bypassing the elected local government, such republicans sought authorization and subsidies directly from the prefect and usually got some backing.[11]

Local organizers, like the Paris leaders, did not control and organize to the point of repressing individual and unofficial initiatives. In some outlying quarters of the capital, firecrackers began going off as early as July 6, and already by that date in the second arrondissement police reported a "great number of windows decorated." In response to numerous requests, on July 11 the Petite République gave the recipe for feux de Bengale for individuals wanting to make their own fireworks. Especially in the 1880 celebration, much that happened appears to have come freely from the grass roots. What organizer would schedule a patriotic speech to be given after midnight, as in Thiers, where a stationer's extemporaneous oratory "warmly moved the crowd"? Other unsolicited contributions flowed from local commercial interests. A week before the festival, tricolor flags, rosettes, and streamers were on sale throughout Paris. A craftsman of the Rue Charlot made Venetian lanterns in the form of the Bastille. On the outer boulevards, fire-eaters,

Georges Seurat's *A Sunday Afternoon on the Island of the Grande Jatte* (1884–86). Sunday idlers took tranquil respite along the Seine, many of them remaining unengaged, separate spectators. (Art Institute of Chicago)

Monet, *Rue Saint Denis*, Paris June 30, 1878. This impressionist masterpiece by Monet conveys better than any written document how spectacularly colorful some streets became during the Republic's fêtes. Monet painted two such streets during the 1878 fête, both between the Halles and the *grands boulevards*, an area of textile workers and merchants and facilities for flag making. (Musée des Beaux-Arts, Rouen) (Giraudon/Art Resource, N.Y. © S.P.A.D.E.M., Paris/V.A.G.A., New York, 1985)

peddlers, acrobats, and magicians—age-old fun fair (*fête foraine*) regulars—
came out in force to amuse the holiday strollers.[12]

In the country, peasants fell back on old customary amusements such as
the *tir de l'oie*: blindfolded, they threw sticks at a suspended goose to see
who could be the first to knock off the bird's head.[13] Middle-class moral and
political leaders, republican as well as monarchist, generally disapproved of
that kind of blood sport, and indeed it had been outlawed in France at mid-
century; but on Bastille Day, in the spirit of festive liberty, with the normally
forbidden now exceptionally permitted, such popular recreations went
uncensured.

Participation in the festivities varied considerably according to class and
region. In Paris the workers' quarters stood out as the most enthusiastic:
participation in decorating and dancing was clearly greatest in Belleville and
the faubourgs Saint Denis and Saint Gervais. Worker and student groups
were the most common pilgrims to the Place de la Bastille, singing the
Marseillaise and the "Chant du départ." In the richer quarters, the Champs
Elysées and Saint Germain, windows went undecorated, shutters remained
closed, and an exceptional quiet reigned. Such boycotting of Bastille Day
no doubt expressed political disapproval, but it was also a result of well-to-
do Parisians' preference for living it up in ways other than dancing and
drinking in the street, a preference that republican visions of fraternal gaiety
did not take into account.

In the provinces, similar social and economic differences were evident,
along with political resistance. The strongest enthusiasm for Bastille Day
came out in areas traditionally leftist since the Revolution, such as the
Mediterranean countryside from Toulon to Narbonne. There many small
and independent peasants, in close contact with townsmen of democratic
persuasion, kept alive resentment of privileged elites and the Church. Even
in that leftist stronghold, however, scattered antirepublican villages refused
to celebrate. In Murviel, a "veritable nest of reaction," wrote the schoolmaster M. Causse, "the labors of the fields were not suspended . . . and in
the evening at 9 o'clock everyone was in bed." Regions that had opposed
the Revolution, like Britany and the Vendée, were, in 1880, full of municipal councils and peasants who refused to acknowledge the holiday. Everywhere better-off inhabitants opposed to the Republic were conspicuously

absent from the fête. The "rich" in industrial Thiers, for example, not only left their unlighted houses "in mourning," reported the police to the sub-prefect; as employers, they also threatened their workers with dismissal if work did not continue as usual. Some workers heeded the warning. In Chéméré (Britanny) the local priest told schoolchildren that if they took part in games on the holiday they could not take communion. A defiant town council in Challans (Vendée) refused to vote any money for the special day, "considering that the taking of the Bastille has been a deplorable event, of which it is not suitable to revive the memory."[4] The government could not let that defiance stand. The prefect annulled the council decision, granted 250 francs for a celebration, and saw that the money was spent for games, decorations, and a distribution of bread. More commonly, municipal councils pleaded poverty and did nothing when politically unsympathetic. Bastille Day, like election day, was a time of political decision making, and in the early decades of the celebration, France showed itself deeply divided.

As Eugen Weber has shown so well, much of France up to the end of the nineteenth century was still not integrated into a national civilization but remained a patchwork of heterogeneous local cultures. The national cele-bration of Bastille Day took on the varied coloring of that patchwork. People danced the farandole in the Gard and old Breton dances in Finistère. In Saint Gilles and other towns in the South, they watched bull races and took part in bull runs. In Laroque (Hérault) the town council granted citizens the pleasure of fishing in the river where it was normally prohibited. A festival day was a time to reverse the normal order. In Morlaix, Britanny, "something very rare" occurred on July 14, a police official reported: "very few men were drunk." In the river Charente near Jarnac, villagers competed by chasing a duck released from a boat until someone caught it, thereby winning the contest and the duck. In Gâvres off the Breton coast they raced two-sailed fishing boats on the revolutionary holiday, when the village finally joined in the celebration in 1893. Communes with strong religious or an-tirepublican traditions tried to make Mass the central event of the day; sometimes they succeeded in the early years, but the prefects generally dis-approved and eventually stopped the practice. The amount and kind of political ceremony, amusements, and conflicts all varied widely according to local custom and political sentiment. The national fête, decentralized in execution, accommodated a great diversity of parochial traditions.[15]

FROM FÊTE TO HOLIDAY

In the subsequent history of the Third Republic, propitious timing, popular good feelings, and grass-roots initiatives only rarely worked their magic again. The regular repetitiveness of July 14 activities that *Le Temps* had warned against did undermine their appeal, it appears, especially in Paris. Organizers, sensing the thirst for novelty, searched for a new special event or *clou* each year for most of the 1880s. But usually they chose to highlight stiff ceremonial devised for the dedication of a statue, a public building (Paris's new Hôtel de Ville in 1882, for example), or a completed boulevard. Their potential for inventiveness seems to have been sapped in part by their great fear of the people in crowds.[16] Another inhibitor was their ingrained attachment to traditional ceremonial forms, such as pseudoclassical allegory that made for ponderous tableaux vivants and parade floats. In the end they failed to come up with new activities capable of exciting and involving a large share of the population.

Further, the reasons for celebration faded over the years. Once the Republic had been seen by its partisans as a beautiful Goddess "so high in the sky"—a cult ideal that aroused devotion particularly among the young, wrote Professor Ernest Lavisse in 1905. But since the Republic had been firmly established, he noted, youth no longer wanted to hear of it.[17] Prefects and local officials made the same observation about the general population. As the Republic became the all-too-flawed government in control, many felt less and less like rejoicing in its "triumph." The Republic became less a regime of promise and more a routine institution beset with difficulties and failings.

July 14 "is no longer a symbolic fête, a republican fête," declared the daily *L'Eclair* in 1898; "it is a popular, traditional fête, established in people's way of life." Outside such islands of exceptional fervor as the workers' Belleville, the day became simply a holiday for dancing and drinking in the open air. "Allons, enfants de la patrie, le jour . . . de boire est arrivé" (the day to drink

A dozen years after its first celebration of Bastille Day, the leaders of the Third Republic
were still working the theme of its "triumph,"
here represented in a pseudoclassical parade
float on September 22, 1892, the centennial of
France's First Republic. The 1892 celebration
did *not* evoke an enthusiastic popular response.
(Musée Carnavalet, Paris)

Popular rejoicing. Swiss-born artist Théophile Steinlen, who moved to Paris in 1881, captured a holiday's fullness of intimate yet public sociability. The "little people," whom he cherished, dominate here, as they did most street celebrations. Steinlen's work depicts well the easy laughter, dancing, and relaxed enjoyment that many experienced on civic holidays *without* regard to the political significance of the days. (Musée Carnavalet, Paris)

has arrived), sang a clutch of drunken revelers in a Heidbrinck cartoon of 1888.[18] When the historic relevance of the day dimmed, there was little else to give it significance. Bastille Day was not integrated into a large block of memorable days, like the holy season from Ash Wednesday to Ascension. Nor was it closely tied to a natural seasonal change or to a turning point in the work year of urban people. For the farming population, of course, seasonal and work timing continued to be generally unfavorable.

Only exceptional milestones, such as the centenary of the 1789 Revolution, could revive enthusiastic demonstrations for the day and its revolutionary meaning. But in 1889 the government worked against such demonstrations; threatened by malcontents grouped around General Boulanger, it played down revolutionary precedents and for the first time in the Third Republic did more to dampen the celebration than to encourage it. Periodic resurgence of nationalism was a more frequent and sure stimulant of Bastille Day fervor. In the 1890s the new alliance with Russia occasioned widespread rejoicing—first when Russian naval officers and sailors visited France (1893) and then much more in 1896, when the Czar himself came. On the eves of the First and Second World Wars, too, nationalistic sentiment rose to feverish peaks, with huge crowds wildly cheering their military and their country. In 1919 a jubilant crowd turned out to release feelings of relief and joy over the "victory" of parading *poilus*.

In other years, sadness and worry and political disenchantment stifled the impulse to celebrate. Vineyard failures (caused by phylloxera in the 1880s), poor harvests, the assassination of President Carnot in late June 1894, tensions over the Dreyfus affair and over anticlericalism as republican policy, and growing antimilitarist feeling on the Left in the early twentieth century— all took a toll on Bastille Day celebrations.

Divisive protests had been a part of the holiday from the beginning. Opponents of the Revolution and the Republic had not only boycotted the day's official activities but had also flown Bourbon white flags, put up antirepublican signs, and occasionally attacked celebrators and the tricolor. Priests tried to stop republicans from ringing church bells and decorating parish buildings. Such conflicts often raged through the holiday period and added a kind of entertaining drama to quiet village life. In Saligny (Allier) in 1880, for example, the priest took down a flag that had been placed on the rectory door; twice municipal authorities replaced the flag, and twice it was taken away by the curé, who finally broke the staff, ending that round in the conflict. In Piré (Brittany) the stalwart republican schoolmaster who had taken charge of preparations in 1892 found his flags and fireworks confiscated by servants of the "reactionary" mayor; when the schoolmaster tried to light the bonfire in the evening, he was beaten by those same hirelings. In Saint André du Bois (Gironde) "enemies of the government [somehow] burned down the liberty tree."[19] Socialists defiantly flew red flags in the larger towns, and anarchists unfurled their provocative black banners. Both denounced the celebration as a bourgeois farce; for such revolutionaries, important Bastilles remained to be stormed before real liberty could be enjoyed. All too clearly, a festival like Bastille Day was a product of reason and will, not a tradition with roots lost in distant time. Opposing wills and ideologies readily contended over such a legacy of revolt. The fraternal consensus that republicans had dreamed of eluded them on the national holiday as on other days.

After the early years, decorating tended to devolve more upon officials, café owners, and shopkeepers, for the government did less and spent less for the holiday. The national subsidy progressively dropped from the high of 500,000 francs in the early 1880s to only 200,000 francs by 1892. Ordinary citizens also did less. Most noticeable by the 1890s was the reduced number of Venetian lanterns in windows. In the richer quarters, the municipal authorities provided the special lights, whereas in the popular quarters the café and wineshop proprietors did the most decorating by way of attracting holiday business. In Paris, neighborhood cohesiveness as well as republican enthusiasm was on the wane. By the 1890s the community of celebrators declined as increasing numbers of shopkeepers, clerks, and even workers left the city for country outings. For similar reasons, carnival revels also waned.[20] Like the Third Republic itself, the national fête of July 14 was not able to command sustained enthusiasm or to live up to its early promise. Bastille Day 1880 was not only a beginning of the belle époque; it was also a climax rarely again reached.

Yet, more of such festive peaks occurred in the period before 1914 than subsequently. The necessary conditions were not simply a sense of freedom, peace, and prosperity. In 1880 and other early years, the civic fête was able to tap strong patriotic feelings that had long been frustrated. And in a time of rapid liberalization and inchoate official programming, it was loosely enough conceived and executed that a multitude of street-fair (fête foraine) entertainments and traditional games flourished as well. More generally, the peaks occurred when the memory and myth of a liberating victory seemed most real and relevant, because of either a change just undergone or one believed imminent. At those times, it appears, celebrators actually lived out widely shared dreams of a great fête. They both witnessed and experienced their own social life more intensely, more clearly than normally. In community they participated in celebrating themselves and their common triumphs and hopes. They united the freedom of play and rejoicing with the ordering of meaning-laden ritual and spectacle. Here the best potential of festival and entertainment can be seen.

This is not to say that the belle époque was a period when joy and festivity flowed forth ineluctably—not even when political and economic conditions were at their best. For celebrations were no longer givens, handed down by respected tradition, successfully observed in all but the worst of times. Occasions for public gaiety were carefully organized by some and opposed by others; and more than before they were vulnerable to shifts of opinion and mood, taste, and competition. Civic celebrations, music halls, street fairs, and religious feasts were now subjects of lively debate.

Criticism of amusements was not new. What was new was the variety of competing alternatives, the proliferation of new leisure activities by a wide range of organizers for motives of ideology and profit. From the state and a host of private persons and interested political groups came ideas for new fêtes, new sporting events, new amusements, a new popular theater.[21] From entrepreneurs big and small came new forms of commercial entertainment and barrages of advertising to promote them. A new leisure culture was in the making. What was general in the period showed up clearly in the creation of the July 14 fête: a conscious effort to break with a traditional culture now judged too austere or too elitist.

2

The Right to be Lazy
and to Enjoy

Chéret's fun-loving nymph was particularly appropriate for advertising the *Courrier français*, a paper devoted to pleasure, especially pleasure from a male point of view. Chéret created similar female images to advertise products like Saxoléine kerosene (1895–96). Jules Roques's *Courrier français* was an early and strong promoter of Chéret. (Collection du Musée de la Publicité, Paris)

The republicans who gave France such a memorable first modern Bastille Day were hardly setting out to inaugurate a new era of leisure and fun. No nineteenth-century political leader did. The "land of Cockaigne" flickered still only in the minds of scattered dreamers like Charles Fourier who were never in power. The republican leaders who instituted the new festival shared the century's dominant values of work, discipline, and productivity. Léon Gambetta, Henri Martin, Georges Clemenceau—these were middle-class men who attributed their rising fortunes to work, discipline, education, and talent, a way of life they took to be the way of promise for all the French. Recreation was a need, they recognized, but only an occasional need to restore people primarily bound to hard work. Like Michelet, they could call for occasional fêtes, but they also professed with him: "Work is my god; it conserves the world."[1]

Middle-class spokesmen, priding themselves on their diligent work habits, preached their vision of virtue as though the rest of the French were wallowing in laziness and sloth. Their books on morality and their civic manuals castigated idleness (*l'oisiveté*) as "the mother of all vice." August Montagu's *Manuel politique du citoyen français* summed up the matter succinctly: "Work ennobles, idleness debases."[2] Bourgeois educators like Ernest Lavisse promoted the virtue of work in storybooks for children and in textbooks used in the new public schools. The three great world's fairs of the belle époque—in 1878, 1889, and 1900—were other means of propagandizing the value of work; moralizing speeches made explicit what the acres of displayed products represented.

To whom was such moralizing directed? No doubt in part to the middle classes themselves, particularly youth and those who had not yet arrived. But clearly the work ethic was also urged upon workers and peasants who were being "civilized" under bourgeois tutelage. Of course, French workers had long nurtured their own versions of that ethic. Artisans like the youthful Michelet and his printer father had prided themselves on their industrious as well as skilled exertions. Though peasants complained about hard work, understandably, they too respected it as a virtue and made it a point of personal pride. Characteristically they behaved as though dominated by "an instinct of irresistible work," observed André Siegfried.[3] Behind that "instinct" lay age-old anxiety about survival and hunger together with new hopes of improving their lot by producing more and acquiring more land. In the late nineteenth century, the easing pressure of necessity as a goad makes some of the bourgeois preaching understandable, and so does the middle-class awareness of tough foreign competition from the productive Germans and British. The propertied and the political leaders representing them also worried about socialist and anarchist ideas undermining the people's readiness to labor. Finally, there were the new industrial workers and the urban poor without craft skills to be given the gospel of work. The propertied particularly feared and worried about such people, believing them to be the source of crime and rebellion and a menace to the country's economic future.

Some of the concern also reflected awareness that France was entering a new era of greater consumption and amusement for the many. The prodigious quantity of alcohol consumed toward the turn of the century was just one notorious part of the change. In the belle époque the French not only drank more than ever in their history but also drank more as a social pastime—in "by far the most drinking places of any country in the world," Michael Marrus has found. By 1900 Paris had an all-time high number of cafés—27,000, which, together with wineshops and cabarets, gave it more drinking places (11.25 for every thousand residents) than any other major city in the world.[4]

The years from 1880 to 1914 also saw the debuts in France of modern sports such as English football (rugby and soccer) and bicycle racing as spectator and participant recreations. Those same years brought the French not only their annual civic fête and the Tour de France but also the Musée Grévin (wax museum), the Moulin Rouge, and the cinema. After 1880 entertainment places proliferated in the cities—especially in the newer forms such as café-concerts, music halls, and after 1900, film theaters. Already by the turn of the century the capital boasted four wax museums, sixteen cycling tracks, and several ice-skating rinks—all unknown before 1880. Although officially recorded admission receipts did not include all entertainments or the same ones consistently through the years 1879–1913, the amounts that were counted showed a dramatic increase: they tripled while the population of greater Paris did not quite double. Spectacle receipts for the 1870s and 1880s, consisting largely of theater admissions, fluctuated the most, reflecting ups and downs of the general economy and an elastic demand. Yet many of even those early figures reached unprecedented heights, surpassing those of almost all the years of Second Empire "gay Paris." From 1893 on, with fuller official recording of the café-concert and music hall business, the Paris statistics showed a very steady and steep growth of entertainment grosses— from 32,669,084 francs in 1893 to 68,452,395 francs in 1913. That is, receipts more than doubled while the population of Paris grew by only 18 percent and that of greater Paris by 32 percent.[5]

A similar pattern of change occurred in lesser cities. France's leading winter resort, the fast-growing city of Nice, added such entertainment facilities as casinos, skating rinks, and dance halls only in the late nineteenth century, thereby closing an era of quiet sun-and-air tourism. The most popular new attraction there was an annual modern carnival, created by a city festival committee, with a showy "Battle of the Flowers" (from 1876 on) as the climax. On a smaller scale, many of France's some 130 spas, or *villes d'eaux*, became "places of pleasure" in the same period for a clientele that was more mixed socially than before; the kinds of entertainments popular in Paris, as well as gambling casinos, became a central part of life at the spas. Even in ordinary small towns across the countryside, new commercial centers of leisure—cafés and cabarets—were spreading to the point of becoming commonplace, replacing older gathering places of sociability such as village *veillées* (evening socializing) in barns and farmhouses.[6]

Still, the period before World War I was far from being an era of mass leisure. Long weekends and month-long vacations were still a half century away, as was serious talk about a future "civilization of leisure." In the nineteenth century the French were not engaged in a great debate about "the leisure problem," as the contemporary English were. Popular leisure—

or hours free from work—was still too scant. It was not until 1892 that work in industry was legally limited to eleven hours a day for women and adolescents. For men, the twelve-hour day was legal until 1904, and it was only in 1906 that employers were required by law to give their workers one day off a week—a law meant primarily for retail clerks. For domestic and agricultural workers, there was no legal limit or protection. Poor people worked as long as they could or had to work. Yet in the 1880s enough upper- and middle-class people and some workers were patronizing commercial entertainments that a debate about enjoyment of life began to simmer. It was not posed in modern terms of work and leisure, but rather was encrusted in hoary moral terms of suffering versus happiness and work versus laziness. The two sides clashed as stark antitheses.

"We are not in this world to be happy, but to be virtuous. Our lot here below is not rest, but struggle," replied a conservative in 1884 to what he took to be republican promoters of a new hedonism. In fact, republicans generally were just as concerned as monarchists with morality and order, even though they spoke more of liberty. Some expected the Republic to purify

"Yes, papa, all day long, it's against the rules for us to sit down."

"Do as we do—ditch them! [plaques-les!]"

This cartoon by Jean-Louis Forain appeared on the front page of the *Courrier français*, August 5, 1888.

Tensions and conflict over work discipline were rife in this period when working people faced tighter controls at work and sermons on the work ethic even during festivals. Yet they also heard more and more beckoning calls to enjoy commercial entertainments.

morals that had been corrupted by Bonapartist license. But by the mid-1880s there was reason to believe that morality in public life was far from improving. Articles and books on the "moral crisis" afflicting France appeared not just as the fin de siècle approached but as the Republic began to make changes in the name of liberty. One reason for conservative concern was that the liberty cherished by republicans was taking the form of new laws permitting divorce and relaxing press censorship in the early 1880s. To conservative moralists, the Republic was unleashing unprecedented license: divorce, pornography, alcoholism, nudity on stage, egoism, all seen as ever worsening symptoms of sickness and decline, or "decadence"—a term that became a shibboleth in the period. By the turn of the century, conservatives could also cite medical findings that seemed to corroborate their alarms. The frantic quest of pleasure was producing "nervous fatigue, sickness, neurasthenia," maintained Jules Delvaille in 1905, citing Dr. Angelvin's new book on neurasthenia, *Mal social*.[7] Such jeremiads poured forth throughout the belle époque and indeed continued beyond the life of the Third Republic. Each new liberty and amusement was confirmation of the traditionalist's worst fear: the floodgates were being opened.

On the other side, crusaders for pleasure sallied forth against the retrograde enemy. The opposition showing itself still strong, the proponents of change assumed a combative style. Resolute publicists strived to propagate a sympathy for pleasure that can be called the belle-époque spirit. They pointed their lances at a religious and bourgeois culture that worshipped work, prudence, and respectability. Their revolt against what Freud would call repression rose with the changes that brought France its first modern celebration of Bastille Day in 1880. As republicans triumphed over monarchist and clerical forces, as their rhetoric of liberty overshadowed the rhetoric of penitent submission, as political liberties increased, and as now amnestied revolutionaries returned, old revolutionary dreams of a still fuller freedom and happiness revived, and youthful spirits grew more assertive. What one can call a struggle to *create* a belle époque ensued.

Some of the crusaders proclaimed new rights, a historic way of signaling the dawn of a new era. "The right to be lazy," first asserted in 1883, found a brilliant advocate in Paul Lafargue, a doctor by training and a Marxist revolutionary by vocation. Two years later, "the right to integral passion" and "the liberty of the body" were asserted by Georges Chevrier, editor of the *Revue indépendante*. A few years later the Russian anarchist Kropotkin laid claim to a "droit à l'aisance"—a right to good living, which included abundant leisure—in writing translated into French in 1892.[8] Those voices adopted the forms of political rhetoric out of France's great revolutionary tradition. They demanded new rights and liberties in a revolution against bourgeois civilization. Their manifestos issued the call for rebellion against spirit-dampening constraints. If manifestos and declarations of rights had been potent weapons in battles against reactionary governments, why not also in the struggle for joy and pleasure?

"The right to be lazy"—*le droit à la paresse*—was the title of a caustically witty tract by Lafargue published in the year of Marx's death. No one in the belle époque delivered a more forceful and biting attack on the work ethic and the misery of workers in capitalist industry. "The unbridled work to which [the proletariat]... has given itself up since the beginning of the century is the most terrible scourge that has ever struck humanity," charged Lafargue. It was "the cause of every intellectual degeneration, every organic deformation," the source of "all individual and social miseries." Toiling longer hours than prisoners condemned to forced labor or Antilles slaves, French workers had become "besotted [*abrutis*] by the dogma of work." Murderous overwork had become their vice, a perverted passion, so much had they been taken in by bourgeois moralists and economists. Not only were workers killing themselves by overwork, but they also were "vegetating in abstinence," refraining from claiming the fruits of their labor. That "double madness," furthermore, was resulting in overproduction and economic crises that entailed massive unemployment and suffering for those unfortunates who gave too much of themselves; meanwhile "the capitalist class has found itself condemned to idleness and forced enjoyment," nonproductivity and overconsumption.

The way out of this plight was not to condemn the capitalists to ten or twelve hours a day in the forges and mills; that threat only intensified class hatreds and prolonged the problem. Rather Lafargue insisted that work be prohibited or at least reduced to three hours a day. In "the regime of laziness" the capitalists would be rescued from the "work of overconsumption and waste with which they have been overwhelmed," and the proletarians would be free to return to their "natural instincts" and to practice the "virtues of laziness." First workers must "trample under foot the prejudices of Christian, economic and freethinking morality," and then they could lead the good life of leisure recognized by Greek wisdom and practiced by primitives before the enslaving encroachment of capitalism. Their three hours of work would produce enough: even the recent experience of English industrialists showed the productive practicality of reducing work hours and "multiplying paydays and holidays." After three hours work, everyone in Lafargue's utopia could "loaf and carouse the rest of the day and the night."

This tract of 1883 proclaimed a new era in revolutionary hopes and goals. In 1848 the most progressive and socially conscious revolutionaries were demanding "the right to work" for France's poor and unemployed. That right to work, Lafargue now contended, was only "the right to misery." In 1789 revolutionaries had demanded general "rights of man," including rights to property and freedom of commerce, which to Lafargue were only "rights of capitalist domination." Lafargue's revolutionary idea of freedom was the liberation of workers' "joys and passions" in leisure.[9]

For his part, Lafargue did not wait for a triumphant proletarian revolution before enjoying the good life. Heir to a fortune of 161,000 francs from his mother and later hundreds of thousands more from Engels, he lived like a gentleman in fine country houses near Paris. He loved to feast and to socialize, if not "to loaf and to carouse." And so he did, at least until his capital was nearly depleted in 1911. Unable to face the prospect of spending his old age in deprivation, Dr. Lafargue gave himself a fatal injection on November 26, 1911. "I kill myself before pitiless old age, which carries away the pleasures and joys of existence one by one, paralyzes my energy, breaks my will," he explained in a last letter. The same day he also killed his wife, Laura, daughter of Karl Marx.[10]

Lafargue's attack on the work ethic and the inequality of pleasures continued in the cartoons of Steinlen, Poulbot, Widhopff, and Forain. A typical socialist view of Bastille Day observances was Steinlen's drawing showing a destitute girl exclaiming about the decorations: "Oh, Papa! How beautiful the fête would be, if we had something to eat." Widhopff characteristically expressed a more acerbic humor; early in 1900 the *Courrier français* carried a drawing showing an old man in ragged clothes turning out his empty pocket and gesturing toward the Universal Exposition while remarking, "Fortunately there's the Fair." In revolutionary tracts, syndicalist Emile Pouget carried on Lafargue's ironic critique of work in capitalist industry. His pamphlet of 1914, *L'Organisation du surmenage* (The Organization of Overwork—a play on Louis Blanc's pre-1848 tract *The Organization of Work*) brought the tradition up to date with a frontal attack on the efficiency system of American engineer Frederick Winslow Taylor.[11]

A second source of argument against work and austerity was the Enlightenment view of humanity: people are simply earthly creatures intended by nature to pursue happiness and pleasure. In this view the prime enemy was the Church with its otherworldly ascetic teachings. Lafargue's references to the sensual and happy natives of Polynesia belonged to this tradition, and so did Georges Chevrier's calls for "liberty of the body." Around the turn of the century Anatole France and André Gide (especially in the latter's *Nourritures terrestres*) carried on the Enlightenment's battle in forceful tracts and speeches. Anatole France delivered his apology for joy on occasions like the dedication of a People's University called Emancipation:

A long religious tradition which still weighs on us teaches that privation, suffering and sorrow are desirable goods and that there are special merits attached to voluntary privation. What imposture! Don't listen to the priests who teach that suffering is excellent. It is joy that is good![12]

Anticlericalism and insistent sensuality played important roles in the creation of the belle-époque spirit.

GALLIC AND INCOHERENT GAIETY

In a century with a strong historical consciousness, virtually all debates involved references to a model located in the past; the fin-de-siècle debate over work and leisure was no exception. One prominent model of leisure throughout French history had been the aristocracy. Nobles had enjoyed great prestige in part because of their privileged abstinence from demeaning work and their abilities to enjoy such leisure pursuits as hunting and riding. At the end of the nineteenth century a noble like Toulouse-Lautrec's father could devote his days to hunting and indulge in such eccentric pleasures as eating truffles soaked in milk and pitching a camel-hair tent in front of the Albi cathedral; he had the leisure to gaze whenever he wished at the church his forefathers had built. Such people lived free of moral compunctions about being nonproductive and frivolous. But the new apologists for leisure did not turn to them for a model; the nobility, so patently self-promoting and so long on the defensive, had little luster left for advocates of change; perhaps too its favored activities such as hunting did not seem well suited for the increasingly urbanized and democratic modern France.

The most important historic source of inspiration was a Gallic past. That dawn of French history was little known, but certain clichés about the Gauls ranked among the fundamentals of educated Frenchmen's folklore. In an era of intense anti-German feeling and persistent anti-English prejudice, promoters of a belle-époque spirit contended that the French were by nature and inheritance Gauls blessed with an unsurpassed capacity to enjoy this world's delights. The French had only to return to their own sources and to expel foreign poisons such as repressive Christian morality, the German pessimism fashionably represented by Schopenhauer, Anglo-Saxon prudery, and English humor. To laugh was now considered not so much a characteristic of humanity as an endangered and essentially *French* trait. Exponents of this view included leading Bohemian artists and poets of the 1880s, such as Emile Goudeau who, with his fellow Latin Quarter youth, founded the fun-loving literary group that Goudeau named the *Hydropathes* in 1879. Not long after, similar groups formed themselves and adopted other self-mocking names: the Zutistes, the Jemenfoutistes, and the Hirsutes. In 1881 some of the youths followed Goudeau to Montmartre to a new cabaret, the Chat Noir,[13] which came to win more fame than any other—for reasons to be examined in the next chapter.

All these groups were in revolt not only against foreign encroachments but also against a French artistic tradition that was solemn and ponderous. They were breaking with the hieratic effusions of a Hugo and the self-probing suffering of a Baudelaire. Though they avoided explicit political discussion, their revolt can also be seen as a rejection of the moral conservatism fostered by the monarchist and Catholic "moral order" of the 1870s. The youth of 1880 quite consciously followed the example of earlier romantic rebels in provoking controversy and delighting in it. Quoting the Latin Quarter journal *L'Etudiant*, Goudeau's own paper *L'Hydropathe* acknowledged the group's "ambition of reviving the great literary battles of 1830."[14] They spread their rebellious ideas through their own artistic newspapers—*L'Hydropathe* and *Le Chat noir*—and through more general periodicals devoted to pleasure, above all the weekly *Courrier français*.

The prime literary text for the new Gauls was Rabelais, cited particularly for his praise of laughter and his utopia of freedom and pleasure. Georges Chevrier, for one, added to his political slogans the motto of Rabelais's *Abbaye*: 'Fays ce que veulx." A year later, admirers of Rabelais could go to a modern Abbaye de Thélème in the Place Pigalle—where a restaurant-cabaret took on that name. To celebrate its opening on May 22, 1886, luminaries of artistic and literary Paris gathered there to enjoy a "déjeuner gargantuesque." Writers Emile Zola, Aurélien Scholl, and editor Jules Roques were there, and so was Emile Goudeau, of course, along with other Chat Noir habitués such as Caran d'Ache, Adolphe Willette, and Henri Rivière. *Le Courrier français* devoted an entire issue to Rabelais and to the new restaurant.[15] "Today France has returned to the Gauls," proclaimed Mermeix with gargantuan hyperbole. At least the champions of liberty and laughter had "returned" noisily to an anti-Catholic and pre-Catholic past, finding there historic roots for their cause.

Others took up an ahistorical battle cry: "l'incohérence." Its originator was the Hydropath Jules Lévy. The group that rallied to the cry included, predictably, Emile Goudeau. What more direct riposte to classical French values of order and reason could they make? To Lévy, to celebrate "incoherence" was to protest against uniformity and ennui. It was to free the imagination from a stifling orderliness and routine, opening up new springs of amusing creativity. Lévy first put his idea into practice by putting on an exposition of drawings by people who did not know how to draw. The next year, in 1883, the Incoherents opened a much larger, more varied "salon des arts incohérents" to the public; over two thousand persons attended, and the exposition became an annual event. In 1885 and for about a decade thereafter, they also organized a zany costume ball at mid-Lent.[16]

The word and idea *incohérence* quickly became fashionable. In 1885 *Le Temps* columnist Jules Claretie observed that the concept seemed uncannily

appropriate for describing the entire age. At the end of that year a revue-vaudeville entitled *Paris incohérent* played at the Tivoli-Folies. In the 1890s John Grand Carteret used the term to characterize one major tendency of fin-de-siècle caricature. The word was also attached to a place of pleasure: from 1884 to 1893 the Concert des Incohérents flourished as a Montmartre café-concert in the Chat Noir mode.[17] As bewildered and threatened devotees of an older order cried "incoherence" at the appearance of every departure from classical structures and establishment conventions, rebels and innovators claimed the title with mocking defiance. Like the red flag on a revolutionary barricade, the word signaled a burst of freedom and disorder.

Establishment artists bristled at the Incoherents' irreverence. Archconservative painter J.-L. Gérome vilified them as "anarchists of art." Goudeau, pessimistically, came close to agreeing when he described the group's spirit as an almost frantic reaction to a particularly burdensome and desperate civilization. In a troubled society, he pointed out, it was not to be expected that amusements would be calm and reasonable. "In dancing on a volcano, gestures can well be sometimes a little epileptic." But Goudeau also defended the Incoherents' antics as healthy fun in protest against "the ridiculous dandies and idiot prostitutes" invading places of pleasure in Paris—Montmartre in particular. Lévy, eschewing such spleen, emphasized his innocent intent to amuse—"The serious besots; gaiety regenerates"—and in the end fell back on the litany of national characters—"Gaiety is the distinguishing characteristic of the French, let's be French."[18] The Incoherents sought to be jesters for an overserious age, for a civilization suffering from bourgeois work pieties and utilitarian exploitation even of leisure. Like the dadaists whom they anticipated, they *played* with incongruities in art and society, transmuting anxieties into waggish jests.

THE MERRY FRENCH AND THEIR CAPITAL OF PLEASURE

The identification of festivity and gaiety with French character recurred throughout the nineteenth century and can be traced back long before. "Fêtes and rejoicings . . . in our France have a recognized importance since they occur much more often than in any other country," asserted the fireworks impresario Ruggieri in his book of 1830; "this is because of the character of

The Incoherents' Ball, an annual Bohemian revel from 1885 to the early 1890s. Drawing by F. Lunel. (Musée Carnavalet, Paris)

our nation, which is without question the gayest of Europe." Foreign visitors, such as Oliver Goldsmith in the eighteenth century and writer Mrs. [Catherine] Gore in 1841, echoed the same belief, the latter summing up with a comparison: "Jacques Bonhomme is, in short, not only by temperament a merrier fellow than John Bull, but is encouraged in his innocent mirth" by public authorities, who provide more festivities than do the British.[19]

To explain French gaiety, observers commonly cited wine, a "cheerful climate," and above all, innate disposition—the Gallic spirit. At the end of the century the distinguished philosopher Alfred Fouillée added his authority to the cliché in a sober essay for the earnest readers of the *Revue des deux mondes*: "So we always have, like our ancestors, the propensity for pleasure and for joy under all its forms, principally the most spontaneous and the most facile." In popular journalism, the observation took on a more chauvinist tone: Henry Maret, editor of *Le Radical*, asserted unequivocally:

> We are the only gay people in the world. It is we who have infected the world with gaiety, this brightness. No, no other people [has done so], no more in the South than in the North; the Spaniard is solemn; the Italian, morose; the Arab, stately. We alone are joyful.[20]

In crusading for gaiety and festive leisure, belle-époque militants fell back on the solid popular current of feeling and tenet of faith, nationalism.

Another tonic to their cause was the growing reputation of Paris as "the gayest of gay cities," as an English guidebook put it in the 1870s. Though the reputation goes obscurely back centuries before, the myth of "gay Paris" in the nineteenth century was most blatantly propagated by guidebooks written for foreigners and Frenchmen alike, particularly at peak times of tourism—in the years of the universal expositions. For those times a new kind of guide appeared during the Second Empire. Unlike the books of Baedeker, Conty, and Joanne, it did not lead visitors through churches and museums, but "only to places where time can be pleasantly spent, and where life is joyous, gay, and free," as an English guide typically promised. Thus Delvau's guide of 1867 treated Paris as "the capital of pleasure," the "city of pleasure and pleasures par excellence." That happy identity was passed on as self-evident truth from Delvau to Debans's guide of 1889—which dubbed Paris "the very capital of the kingdom of pleasures"—to de Lannoy's book of 1900, *La Vie et les plaisirs de Paris*, to mention only a few bearers of the tradition. English guides in the same vein showed no interest in questioning Paris's claim to gaiety; the *Pleasure Guide for Bachelors* (about 1903), for example, presented the city as "the metropolis of pleasure for the whole world." And the American Richard Davis's book *About Paris* (1895) proceeded with the same premise: "Americans go to London for social triumph or to float railroad shares, to Rome for art's sake, but they go to Paris to enjoy themselves."[21]

Provincials and foreigners cramped by traditional or Victorian morals were lured to the French capital with the assurance that it was "the only corner of the world where pleasure is a social necessity" and a "normal state." There they could enjoy the innocent pleasures of strolling and dining or roguishly follow the tips of the perennial English guide *Paris after Dark*, "containing a description of the fast women, their haunts, habits, etc., to which is added a faithful description of the night amusements and other resorts, also all particulars relative to the working of the social evil in the French metropolis," as the fulsome Victorian subtitle had it. In Paris pleasure seekers could find balls that were Cytheras, visit "the temple of Aphrodite"—otherwise known as the Moulin Rouge—and encounter "nymphs of the pavé" who were not besmirched by drunkenness. From the hints of the guidebooks, tourists fabricated a fuller folklore. From the Mabille dance hall sprang the legend that "all Parisians after their daily labor dance the cancan all evening," as Albert Wolff noted in 1882.[22] Seven years later the Moulin Rouge gave rise to a similar tale. Such beliefs about Paris not only fed the later myth of the belle époque; they also contributed to the growth of pleasure businesses in Paris by encouraging pleasure seekers to flock there. The myth and fantasy became self-fulfilling.

Pleasurable Paris was also the modern Babylon, seductive and scandalous. As Maxime du Camp observed early in the 1870s, foreigners—the British particularly—eagerly patronized the city's pleasures and then went away condemning the immorality of which they had partaken:

Back at home, beside their coal fire, in a boredom increased a hundredfold by the sharpness of memories, they readily say: "It's the most immoral city in the world" and do not perceive that they are at least half the reason for the demoralization with which they reproach us.[23]

Visitors who subscribed to the cancan legend, noted Albert Wolff, joined to it the legend of the "loosening of morals in France and the decay of the family by the dissolving quadrille." For such people, to enjoy the pleasures of Paris was to triumph over customary moral scruples, but the triumph was as transient as their stay in the "naughty" metropolis. This moral ambiguity of Paris's claim to joy was no doubt a major reason for the belle-époque militants' preference for the more encompassing, less controversial Gallic claim.

As the remarks of Wolff and du Camp make clear, it was temptingly easy for the French to maintain that stricken consciences and corruption troubled foreigners only. Parisians, according to du Camp, shrugged their shoulders at the visitors' "slanders" and joined in the pleasures as calculating accomplices:

> Since [the Parisian] knows . . . that pleasures attract foreigners and that the foreigners bring money, he takes part, multiplies the places of amusement, enriches himself, and, like the dog who eats the dinner of his master, he takes his part of the cake; he amuses himself as much as he can with the frivolity of his natural character.[24]

Glossing over the existence of unamused, disapproving Parisians was convenient in a time when clerical and conservative forces still enjoyed official favor.

COMBATIVE FUN

In the 1880s and 1890s, champions of pleasure did not stay on the politic tack of decrying censorious foreigners only; they directly assaulted powerful French traditions—religious, moral, and political. With often obvious enjoyment of the conflict, journals of the cultural opposition—for example, the *Chat Noir*, *Courrier français*, and *Revue indépendante*—carried on a running battle against native French prudes, hypocrites, and censors. Their campaign was not at all confined to issuing declarations of rights and sweeping manifestos; they fired salvos at the enemy wherever he appeared, finding cause for battle in everyday events. A small provincial scandal like that of an adulterous police commissioner in Vitré elicited their programmatic scorn for "puritanism"; George Auriol's response to that affair was to ridicule authorities for punishing "a man having the courage of his gauloiserie."[25]

Over the years censors drew the most concerted fire. From the beginning, the Courrier français defiantly published drawings of nudes in modern settings, defending them as more honest than the half-dressed sirens long filling the pages of La Vie parisienne. A half dozen times in as many years, issues of the Courrier français were seized by the police for cartoons or poems deemed "an outrage to public morals," and legal charges were brought against the journal's editors and collaborators. The writers and cartoonists of the journal responded with biting humor. For months after one police action in 1888, cartoonists dedicated their drawings to the minister of justice and caricatured him as a hypocritical lecher tempted by the flesh he tried to ban from public view (see illus.). The Courrier français assumed the roles of both defender of freedom of the press and defender of freedom of art in general. It heaped ridicule on the respectable who were scandalized by sculptures of embracing couples and on the authorities who relegated such art to obscure places in museums. Contributors to the Courrier français regularly attacked censorship of plays and songs in theaters and music halls as well. The editor Jules Roques himself rose to the defense of street performers (forains) under attack in 1888 for creating noise and uncleanliness.[26] Such struggles gave importance to the promotion of pleasure that still seemed too suspect to stand alone. Even the champions of fun implicitly acknowledged the strength of traditional values by allying their cause to more generally shared values, art and liberty.

The most famous and brutal battle occurred in 1893 when artists and models of the Ecole des Beaux Arts and independent ateliers held a costume ball. It was Jules Roques who transformed what had been an artists' private party into a highly publicized semipublic event held in the Moulin Rouge. There artists and models greeted each other with the familiar tu, members of a family en fête, and there they gaily danced and sang through the night. What brought them trouble was a spectacular procession of floats and atelier delegations, announced by painted banners, vying in festive rivalry in a cortege reminiscent of ancient guild parades. The queen of the ball, Cleo-

"The temptation of Saint Ferrouillat." A chorus line of derrières display copies of the *Courrier français* before a "tempted" government authority. Forain and other *Courrier français* cartoonists ridiculed the minister of justice for months after his acts of censorship in 1888. Finally, in February 1889, Ferrouillat resigned. This cartoon by Jean Louis Forain appeared on the front page of the *Courrier français* on August 12, 1888.

The daring costumes worn by art students at a ball in 1893 led to one of the most resounding clashes of the era over the issue of pleasure and morality. The arts ball, held on February 9, scandalized such conservative notables as Senator Bérenger and led to a court judgment against four models and to violent troubles in the Latin Quarter. This drawing by de Berr appeared in the *Courrier français* on February 26, 1893.

Dessin de DE BER.

patra, nearly nude under a large net, appeared in the company of Olympian deities and slaves, Vercingetorix, Ceres, and other ancients. Reported a sensational success, the gala received so much attention that the leading champion of conservative morality, Sen. René Bérenger, president of the League against License in the Streets, lodged a formal complaint with the *procureur*. The organizers and some star models, for whom nudity was a condition of work as well as pleasure, were charged with perpetrating an outrage to public morals and were brought before a tribunal. They lost and were fined one hundred francs each—with the sentence suspended since the offenders had no previous record. The condemnation aroused protests and fights with the police and troops in the Latin Quarter. The battles ended with one youth killed. With new bitterness the writers and artists heaped their scorn and contempt on *Père le Pudeur*, Bérenger. What they denounced as Anglo-Saxon puritanism or English discipline won, as usual, only a Pyrrhic victory. The Bal des Quat' *z*' Arts continued each year, enhanced by the publicity as a particularly daring and merry fling.[27]

Montmartre became the bastion of pleasure from which attacks were launched on the dull and somber guardians of workaday order. At the Chat Noir in the 1880s, cabaretier Rodolphe Salis adopted the revolutionary language of Sieyès to promote the cause: "What is Montmartre? Nothing. What should it be? Everything." Such overblown declamation aside, Salis fought crucial but mundane battles regularly, like contending with the police when they tried to curtail piano playing in the cabaret. He and his entertainers also had to struggle against censors, who weekly exercised veto power over their songs. The Montmartre entertainers fought back by mocking the government, the ruling bourgeoisie, the censors, and the police.[28]

Aristide Bruant was one of the most combative, celebrating the outlaw and the prostitute and jeering the propertied and the moralizers. His cachet was to insult the bourgeois in person even as they came into his cabaret as paying customers, addressing them as *mon cochon* (pig) and *tas de salauds* (bunch of bastards). His audience laughed, but he was not purely jesting. "I revenge myself by treating them that way," he confessed, reflecting bitterness about his own youthful suffering in poverty. Bruant's critical attacks sprang from a keen social conscience that was unleavened by hope. Few of the Montmartre satirists and singers were socialists or politically engaged in any other grouping; yet many of them kept up steady fire on the privileged and the exploiters. "Montmartre was a permanent *fronde*," recalled Jules Bertaut.[29] It was a fronde open enough to all that even the privileged could temporarily join in the festive freedom of the cultural outsiders. Mockery and playful bullying leveled all into a temporary community rarely experienced elsewhere.

In retrospect the Montmartre revolt can be seen as only a part of a larger fin-de-siècle struggle for fantasy, more natural enjoyment, liberty, and social justice. Lafargue, Goudeau, Bruant, and such politically engaged figures as Emile Zola of course did not work together formally, but even in the late nineteenth century some could see the unity of their causes.

No one summarized the interconnected larger battle better than the writer Paul Adam in a *Revue blanche* article in 1896. Looking back over the last quarter of the century, he could see such different figures as Clemenceau, Zola, Catulle Mendès, and Jean Lorrain as heroic rebels struggling against "the armies of Suffering." Around 1880, recalled Adam, "a new liberty took flight, and with its fresh wing threatened the camp of Suffering." In politics, society, literature, and art, champions of the new liberty refused the ethic of sacrifice and demanded "the right to license and enjoyment." In an age of positivist philosophy, critical and skeptical minds no longer accepted old precepts of virtue that "experience shows to be always unobserved." Paul Adam had himself fought against established moral constraints; his novel *Soft Flesh* was condemned as pornographic in 1884, and he had served several months in prison. But Adam did not recount recent events as discrete personal battles; he elevated them to the mythic level of titanic forces, "planetary energies [that] exalted themselves against the lie of virtue and the dogma of the acceptance of *douleur*." And he did not hesitate to claim imminent victory for the "current energy" favoring life, happiness, and enjoyment for all. Adam already saw "gigantic results. . . . It suffices to read the newspapers of 1870 and to compare their spirit to that of today's papers, toward this end of the century, to see the enormous change that has taken place in the mentality of the world."[30]

The difference is indeed clear to anyone making such a comparison. He could also have pointed to the franker eroticism introduced into sculpture by Rodin and into literature by Anatole France, Guy de Maupassant, and Pierre Loti. For freedom of expression in literature and songs, the clearest breakthrough came in 1906, when the office of censorship was finally eliminated.

But outside the arts, it is difficult to find the parallel victories or "progress" for public gaiety and Rabelaisian laughter. Mardi Gras and July 14 fêtes hardly showed the happy change that Adam favored. In Paris the "English" mode of phlegmatic *pince sans rire* did not yield to the charades of Goudeau and Lévy. By 1890, Georges Brandimbourg reported with regret, it had become "chic" *not* to laugh but "to gaze on the greatest farce impassively."[31] Was the straight face simply un-French phlegm or melancholy, as was commonly explained? Or was it not still another form of rebellion—against too obvious clowning and the too common "vulgar" reaction to joking? Such questions of ambiguity and complexity rarely troubled partisans of pleasure or Cassandras of decadence. They looked for a routing of the "Armies of Suffering" or of the legions of license. Both sides shared a Manichaean sense of cosmic conflict underlying the freer humor and pleasure of the turn of the century.

To have fun often did entail rebellion, the Paris literary and artistic libertarians understood well. In the rural villages republican authorities trying to encourage July 14 revels proceeded with the same understanding. In the Vendée, for example, they viewed the number of people participating in dancing as an index of rebellion against priests.[32] Further, the rebellion itself was part of the fun. At least it appears so for the Paris artistic and literary set; for country youths flocking to dances and cafés there is less evidence. But we may note here that their traditional enjoyments had often involved mocking and aggressive thrusts at authority—in carnival, the fête of fools, and charivari. By the turn of the century, those outlets were disappearing or fading from rural life, partly because of attacks on them by order-keeping authorities, partly because young people were adopting new forms of recreation and sociability. Youth's flight to the cafés and July 14 dances perhaps fulfilled some of the old carnival function in reversing normal submission to workaday routines and nay-saying authorities.

Toulouse-Lautrec, *Moulin de la Galette.* Originally a true working windmill high on the
Butte of Montmartre, the Moulin de la Galette
was a popular dance hall in the decades around
1900. Although it was quite unglamorous compared to the Moulin Rouge and distant from
the center of Paris, it was invariably listed in
guidebooks as one of the pleasure capital's
bright spots.

Renoir painted a springtime scene of the
cheeriest open-air socializing and dancing there
in 1876. In 1889 Toulouse-Lautrec, who frequented the place on Sunday afternoons and
drank the usual mulled wine, painted this more
somber view of pensive, isolated individuals
waiting on the sideline against a backdrop of
dancing workers, clerks, dressmakers, and a few
top-hatted visitors. (Art Institute of Chicago)

Seurat, *The Circus,* 1890–91. In his last and
unfinished painting, Seurat featured the leading
attractions of the traditional, almost intimate,
one-ring circus (here Montmartre's Cirque Fernando) and depicted spectators of various social
ranks and moods—with ennui and distraction
as evident as delight. (Cliché des Musées Nationaux, Paris)

In Paris, the prime symbol of gaiety, the cancan,* also symbolized revolt. Identified with the lower classes since revolutionary times, the dance both attracted and disturbed other classes, whose government and police tried to restrain its irreverent kick from going too high. Much of the humor of the period, too, was aggressive, feeding on social disaffection. In Paris by the mid-1880s some 250 satirical periodicals were on sale in the kiosks—an unprecedented tide.[33] Their stock-in-trade was mockery of authority, marriage, bourgeois "respectability" and hypocrisy, pretension and power. Priests, the bourgeois, and the military figured as fools unaware of their own ridiculousness, blind to the transparent gap between their public postures and their all too human shortcomings.

Not all the conflict was with external foes. Individual amusers also struggled against inner constraints and sadness. Such notable wits as Georges Feydeau, Anatole France, and Alphonse Allais were known to their intimates to be fundamentally triste, convinced that life is hard and depressing but determined to provoke laughter as an essential palliative. Much belle-époque gaiety can be understood only in relation to deep-rooted melancholy. Emile Goudeau, for example, suffered years of lonely despair (désespoirs solitaires, he called them), unemployment, and hunger as an unknown young provincial in Paris in the 1870s. Son of a successful sculptor in Périgueux, he had been educated by priests in a seminary; he broke with those identities but could not find a teaching post to support his primary interest, literature. In Paris finally he found a boring job as a minor clerk in the Ministry of Finance. After hours he tried to salvage himself in comic relief and in the 1880s succeeded in gaining some recognition as a bittersweet poet and organizer of artistic escapades. He chose to engage in buffooneries and to maintain "disdain for all," he explained in his memoirs, as the alternative to resigning himself to a "stoic death of poverty." He further admitted that playing the role of the "cool jester" (blagueur à froid) gave him "the aplomb"

---

*The French of the period more commonly used the terms le quadrille naturaliste and le chahut for wild, high-kicking dances that in music-hall form foreigners came to know as "the French cancan."

Writer André Warnod noted that the cancan emphasized more the lifting of the skirt, and the chahut more the lifting of the legs.

the timid provincial sorely needed. "It was a terrible and joyous epoch," he concluded.[34]

We do not have such self-revelation to help us understand most other organizers of merriment in the period. One of the most important and personally obscure of them was Joseph Oller (1839–1922), who founded more leading pleasure institutions in fin-de-siècle Paris than anyone else: the parimutuel for horse races (1867), the Nouveau Cirque (1886), the Montagnes Russes (1887)—an amusement park centered on a roller coaster— the Moulin Rouge (1889), and the music hall Olympia (1893) were among his creations. Like the Isola brothers, who owned and managed a string of establishments almost as impressive, he came to Paris from outside France and quickly outdid Parisian insiders. Perhaps it was because he was from a prominent Catalan family, solidly established in business and local government in Spain, that he did not publicly declaim about promoting French pleasure and national tradition. With self-effacing diligence, he founded one pleasure business after another, apparently taking pleasure in the conception and creation and then losing interest.[35]

A costume ball sponsored by the *Courrier français* at the Elysée-Montmartre, June 15, 1884. Cartoonist Heidbrinck depicted in this drawing the kind of riotous gaiety that editor Jules Roques and his newspaper, *Le Courrier français*, promoted through the period. The newspaper's costume balls on a different theme each year occurred annually through 1896.

More than Adam or Goudeau or Lafargue, Oller was representative of the public he helped entertain in that he asserted the right to enjoyment by his actions, not by manifestos. Whereas the literary and ideological militants drew the lines of battle with truculent clarity in the press and courtrooms, Oller and the growing number of clients for his kind of entertainment claimed their rights in everyday life. France's cultural tensions and historic campaigns for liberty—the legacy of the Enlightenment, the French Revolution, and anticlericalism—were bearing fruit in more self-gratifying attitudes toward leisure, most noticeably among the urban middle and working classes. At the same time, it was becoming ever more clearly profitable to exploit those cultural changes commercially. As enterprising newcomers succeeded in selling new entertainments to a growing public, the business possibilities became more alluring to still others.

It is doubtful that the consumers of amusement in this period had much more "free time" than their predecessors; most of them probably did have more disposable income; but what is clearest and most significant is that they had a greater willingness to spend their money and time on entertainment and to risk others' moralistic disapproval. On this point, one area of Paris in particular sings out for our attention. In the rise of Montmartre as the leading belle-époque pleasure district, we can see most clearly the fruitful consequences of a marriage between cultural rebellion and capitalist innovation in entertainment.

3
Bohemian Gaiety and
the New Show Business

The striking facade of the second Chat Noir
on the rue de Laval.

No group so clearly broke with the bourgeois work imperative and immersed itself in amusements, public and private, as did the Bohemian artists and writers of late nineteenth-century Montmartre. They were not just an avant-garde in art and literature but an avant-garde in belle-époque enjoyments. Many of their pleasure haunts became popular with a public that included nobles, bourgeois, and even some better-off workers. The Bohemians rejected and mocked the bourgeoisie; yet bourgeois Frenchmen flocked to their cabarets and applauded their humor. Although the Bohemians gave their allegiance to art, most of them sought and some of them found commercial success that put them among the newest of the nouveaux riches.

Of the many festive communities of fin-de-siècle Bohemia, the most seminal one was the group of students, artists, and poets who organized themselves as the Hydropaths in October 1878. Their principal organizer and first president, Emile Goudeau, chose the name *Hydropathes* because the funny-sounding word, the title of a German waltz he heard in a café-concert, fascinated him with its potential for amusing word play (as did his own name *Goud-eau*: "drop of water" or "taste of water"): the roots of the word could mean persons afraid of water or the contrary, those loving water, or even more imaginatively, water-feet (*hydropattes*). The group so identified with water in fact gave itself to drinking wine with gusto. An initial thirty or so men met in various small Latin Quarter cafés to drink and talk, to recite poetry and to discuss it, while joking and laughing together. Performer-participants included such notables as André Gill, Jules Jouy, Paul Bourget, Paul Arène, François Coppée, and Alphonse Allais, but participation was apparently open to all. The group quickly grew to some two hundred within three months. The attraction was talent performing in a free, sometimes uproarious atmosphere. Nothing was rehearsed or routine, and the unpre-

Henri Rivière's drawings show Bohemian camaraderie flourishing in the first Chat Noir
(above), while decor and the beau monde take
over in the second Chat Noir.

A view of the interior of the Chat Noir. An evening there included drinking, conversing, listening to singers and Salis's witty patter, and watching shadow plays in a profusely artistic setting.

dictable that often happened ranged from hilarious repartee to outbursts of fireworks. Politics did not intrude; the debates of "moral order" monarchists and earnest republicans were part of what the Hydropathes were escaping. What counted for the Bohemians was their talents and sociability. To preserve and disseminate the fruits of both—in the form of poems, caricatures, and news of their activities—the group published a journal L'Hydropathe, the first issue appearing on February 19, 1879.[1]

In December 1881 the group moved to Montmartre. They had accepted the invitation of Rodolphe Salis, owner of a new cabaret named Le Chat Noir, to use his place for their gatherings. Within a month a new journal appeared, Le Chat noir, publicizing the group's members and works. The journal, like the L'Hydropathe, conveyed a sense of the group's free, humorous spirit as well as their warm fraternal ties, reflected in regular biographical sketches that were lighthearted but enthusiastic personal tributes. Le Chat Noir attracted an ever larger group of talented singers, poets, caricaturists, and painters. Artists such as Willette, Steinlen, Caran d'Ache, Henri Pille, and Henri Rivière decorated the cabaret, hung their works there, and illustrated the journal. In turn the performance and artistic gatherings drew a growing number of customers. Bohemian merriment in an antique and artistic decor was beginning to yield profits that owners of earlier artistic cabarets, like Laplace of La Grande Pinte, had not known.

Within a few years, clients became numerous enough that Salis looked for larger quarters. He wanted not only more room but also a location off the Boulevard Rochechouart where he was plagued by fights with neighborhood pimps and toughs. By 1885 the move was set. With a publicity-attracting procession of artists, Salis made a public festival of the exodus to the quieter Rue Laval (soon changed to the Rue Victor Massé). Now the Chat Noir had three floors, the third floor alone holding as many as one hundred people.[2]

With the help of his artistic friends, Salis gave the new place a rich bric-a-brac decor festively different from anything contemporary and bourgeois. The furnishings were a feast of old copper pots, swords, his coat of arms, dark oak antique chairs and tables. The outside sign declared the style to be that of the age of Louis XIII; to observers it seemed either Renaissance or medieval. In any case, the royal rustic interior was extraordinary enough that it could attract curiosity seekers as a museum draws tourists. At the same time, the place resembled an atelier and gallery with paintings and murals covering the walls; Salis, a former art student himself, included some of his own caricatures in the style of Gill. Stained glass windows added further color and beauty to the rich ambiance of art and history.

On this splendidly eclectic stage, Salis performed and directed the shows with a dramatic and comic flair that was masterly. In a luxuriant spirit of parody, he gave rooms and even tiny halls grandiloquent names—*la Salle des Etats, la Salle des Seigneurs, la Salle des Gardes.* The second floor, which consisted of a simple nook and one room, held the Office of the Archives and Disputed Claims Department, the Hall of the Colonies, the Print Room, the Board Room, the Chapel, the Secret Library, the Private Armor Hall, the Newspaper Office, the Administrative Office, the Organ Loft, the Box of Monsieur the President of the Republic, the Theater Library, and the Banquet Hall. The room reserved for an inner group of artists he called the Institut. He dressed his waiters in the uniforms of members of the Académie Française, and he himself stood out with a prefect's uniform of the First Empire on his large frame.

In a deep powerful voice Salis addressed entering customers with archaic courtesy: "This way, my lord. . . . Will you take a seat, Monseigneur? . . . What will you have to drink, your highness?" With such baroque politeness, the "gentilhomme cabaretier" drew customers into the act with flattering personal attention, leavened with enough irony to satisfy those with skeptical humor. In an age when nobility was politically routed and monarchy ousted, and dull bourgeois Jules Grévy was president, the public could find a picturesque change of scene and playful distinction at the Chat Noir. Salis's ironic tone, characteristic of much of the new popular culture, conveyed both a comfortable insouciance and a fresh smartness that constituted an entertaining, not intimidating "something different" for middle- and upper-class amusement seekers. As a refuge from the workaday world, the cabaret imparted the illusions of theater, but with much more spontaneity and interaction between audience and spectacle, clients and performers. Salis was a virtuoso of impromptu banter and wit, as he greeted the customers, introduced the performers, and commented on their songs. When not performing, the artists mingled with the customers; a kind of festive fraternity took the place of rigid roles and hierarchies entrenched in everyday society outside.

The Chat Noir also offered first-rate talent in the performers of songs and poetry. The high quality of the early group drew others there and encouraged them to give their best in forms and tones that were "incoherently" varied, anarchistically individualistic. Aristide Bruant and Jules Jouy sang of prostitutes and pimps, rogues and felons, the hungry and homeless suffering in the reign of the smug bourgeoisie; tenderness toward the poor and the outcast mixed with venomous anti-Semitism and bitter scorn for capitalist exploiters and the clergy. Others sang sentimental romances and patriotic songs. Straight-faced, even melancholic, Alphonse Allais told macabre tall tales; Charles de Sivry played the piano while on occasion Claude Debussy led group singing. Henri Rivière and Caran d'Ache, illustrators, created one of the most appealing and innovative attractions of the cabaret: a shadow theater with colored shadows. Some of their most acclaimed plays were celebrations of the Napoleonic legend—*L'Epopée* and *La Marche à l'étoile*. A dozen hidden poets puffed away at different tobaccos for smoke-filled battle scenes. A shadow play by Robida showed Paris transformed by aerial war. Other plays recreated Biblical legends and the life of Saint Geneviève. In short, the Chat Noir offered a rich potpourri of arts and entertainment that had no equal elsewhere at the time. It was a restaurant; it was a theater; it was a café and a café-concert, all at the same time.

The journal *Chat noir* offered a similar variety—something for the most diverse interests and tastes. "If one leafs through the 15-year run of the journal *Chat noir*," playwright and one-time cabaret performer Maurice Donnay observed, "one sees how eclectic it was, in turn and at once joking, ironic, tender, naturalist, idealist, realist, lyrical, cynical, hoaxing, Christian, pagan, mystic, republican, reactionary, anarchist, chauvinist."[3] Like music halls and circuses of the period, the artistic cabaret flourished by offering a kaleidoscopic variety; it, however, offered them in more intimate forms and settings.

MONTMARTRE FROLICS AND FREEDOM

The Bohemian gaiety represented by Jules Lévy's Incoherents in the 1880s was much more outlandishly eccentric. His inspired idea of an exposition of hopelessly ridiculous drawings was the kind of joke the Bohemians loved, at once wildly imaginative and mocking. It allowed them to amuse themselves as *camarades* against tradition and bourgeois traps, such as the fetish of art and mercenary ambition. In October 1882 when Lévy opened a large show of *arts incohérents* to the public for the first time, it was to benefit victims of a gas explosion. Exhibitors commonly used pseudonyms as incoherent as their displays. Toulouse-Lautrec participated in 1886 and 1889 under the name Tolav-Segroeg, "Hungarian from Montmartre." His entries included "sculptures in bread crumb" and an oil painting on emery paper entitled "Les Batignolles 3½ years before Christ." Others displayed parody paintings and sculptures of swaying inebriated-looking houses, a cardboard sun rising over a bidet, a "Monsieur Vénus de Milo" (armless and bearded), and "The perplexity of an urchin who doesn't know which breast to suckle." Many of the works were satirical jibes at pompous politicians and generals, stingy notaries, garrulous concierges, establishment artists, drunks, and duelers. Like the large satirical press, the Incoherents' exhibits offered levity about characters known to all; presented annually through the 1880s, they met with a strong public response.[4]

The costume balls the Incoherents held each year from 1885 to the late 1890s were occasions of even more participatory gaiety of the absurd. Some revelers showed up in disparate parts of clown suits; large bearded men appeared in ballet tutus or other female garb. Women disguised their bodies as double-six dominoes or coiffed themselves with flowerpots. Incoherent artist Emile Cohl came as an artichoke, comedian Guyon as a poster column, caricaturist Henry Gray as a medieval dandy. They danced, drank, and dined until daylight the next day. With the *Courrier français* as sponsor until it offered its own costume ball beginning in 1888, the Incoherent fête became an annual event popular enough to rival the long-established elegant Opera Ball. "Those evenings," Gabriel Astruc recalled in his memoirs decades later, "a *vent de folie* blew over Paris."[5]

The Incoherents' Ball opened up the freer world of artistic fantasy to a larger public that in the 1890s followed the attractions of the *Courrier français* balls as well as those of the Quat'z' Arts. The *Courrier français* encouraged the same kind of imaginative zaniness in costume that the Incoherents pioneered, but emphasized special themes each year: big babies (1888), naturalism (1890), mysticism (1891), women—with men dressed as such (1892), a hundred years into the future (1893), pagans (1894), virgins (1895), and statues (1896).[6]

The success of the Chat Noir and the artistic balls were reasons for the opening of a new dance hall in Montmartre in October 1889, the Moulin Rouge. In this period the "Butte" became a capital of commercial entertainment. Still resembling a picturesque village, it was a place apart from modernizing Paris; though a village, it was free of the after-dark torpor and stifling morality of provincial villages. Montmartre was an antidote to the pomposity and stiff class rules that reigned elsewhere. In its dance halls and cabarets Parisians could temporarily free themselves from inhibitions of everyday respectability and find normal forms of bourgeois behavior mocked or disregarded. Like costume balls, Montmartre gave visitors the chance to escape their everyday identities; it allowed them contact with a lower world of colorful Bohemians, high-spirited criminals, and old-fashioned workers. The public that had responded well to realism in the novel now could participate in the milieu of the socially marginal by visiting Montmartre cabarets. There middle-class women and men tried to learn the slang of prostitutes, thieves, and workers. There they could taste the forbidden and the freedom celebrated by François Villon and Rabelais. The Montmartre of commercial entertainments became a playground, a permanent local fête, of liberating role playing for the rest of Paris and visitors from beyond.

THE BOOM IN "ARTISTIC CABARETS"

> Nous cherchons fortune
> Autour du Chat Noir
> Au clair de la lune,
> A Mont-mar-ar-tre.
> —Aristide Bruant

What began as small sporadic gatherings for intimates became regular performances with attentive coverage by the press, including the new journals put out by the cabarets themselves. By the late 1880s the Chat Noir was a tourist attraction, even listed in guides for English-speaking visitors. Salis published his own guidebooks for souvenir seekers, the *Chat-Noir-guide* and the *Almanach du Chat Noir*. Famous fin-de-siècle visitors to the cabaret included Pasteur, Renan, General Boulanger, the Rothschilds, the King of Greece, the Prince of Wales, and King Alexander I of Serbia. The visits of such notables brought further publicity and consecrated the place as a tourist destination. In the 1890s the cabaret's fame was so great that Salis could take Chat Noir troupes on profitable tours in the provinces.

The Chat Noir and the balls of the Incoherents soon ceased to be novelties as numerous imitators established themselves in the late eighties and nineties. As early as 1884, *Le Temps* columnist Jules Claretie observed that "gothic cabarets" were "pullulating" in the Pigalle area as a result of Salis's success.[7] The Brasserie de la Chatte Blanche, the Auberge du Chat Blanc, the Chat Botté (founded by Goudeau), and the Chien Noir were only the most obvious imitators. One of the earliest and most successful rivals was a singer who made a reputation in Salis's establishment: Aristide Bruant, who set out on his own and took over Salis's first locale in 1885. Bruant's cabaret Le Mirliton soon achieved a fame rivaling the original, and he too went on lucrative provincial tours. Bruant himself spawned an imitator in 1896, when one of his assistants named Alexandre broke away and set up a new cabaret called Le Bruyant Alexandre. Even Salis's own brother became a rival; after a family quarrel he and his wife established the Ane Rouge in 1889. Another successor that proved successful opened under the name Les Quat'z' Arts in 1893 and established a journal with the same title, edited by Emile Goudeau. The Chat Noir was the prototype of a new kind of café-concert, the commercial "cabaret artistique," which became a permanent part of Montmartre and greater Paris. By 1898 the Paris-Hachette directory listed twenty-four "cabarets-artistiques," a category quite distinct from the older "café-concert" that designated the Eldorado or the new term "music hall," which the Olympia was first to adopt. Provincial versions of the Chat Noir also appeared in the nineties; in places like Brest customers could hear songs of the Butte in the local Caveau de Montmartre and in Montpellier they could see shadow plays as well in the Caveau du Dix.[8]

It was not just the singing, recitations, topical satire, and shadow plays that spread with the vogue of the Chat Noir. It was also the decor. Chat Noir imitators filled their cabarets' walls with paintings and murals playing out the totem animal motif, be it a white cat, a black dog, or a red ass. The Cabaret des Assassins boasted murals by André Gill; the Cabaret de l'Ane Rouge had murals by Willette, Steinlen, and Feure; Le Mirliton showcased drawings and paintings by Steinlen, Lautrec, and Alfred Le Petit. The stage setting of remote times and places was also widely adopted after the Chat Noir's success with an "old France" ambiance. The Abbaye de Thélème, as we have seen, catered to Renaissance-loving sybarites who sat down to Rabelaisian repasts served by mock monks and nuns. The year before, in 1885, the Taverne du Bagne (prison) opened its gloomy doors to Parisians wanting to spend a playful night out on the other side of respectability. Under red lanterns hanging from gallows, visitors were served by garçons in convicts' uniforms with balls and chains around their feet. An entry sign warned, "Abandon all hope you who enter," but another sign inside rejoined, "However, people do come back." The owner, Maxime Lisbonne, had himself come back from prison where he had served time for his participation in the Paris Commune.

A decade later, one could escape this world more completely at the Cabaret du Ciel (heaven): there people went to drink the "ambrosia of the gods"— a one-franc bock—while watching burlesque religious rites and dining in the dazzling white Hall of the Celestial Banquet, served by angels. Or, in the black and red interior of the Cabaret de l'Enfer (hell) next door, one could be served by devils, after entering between the teeth of an enormous devil's mouth. Here customers, greeted as *chers damnés*, heard guitar music played by two of the damned, stewing for "three thousand years" in a large cauldron; they also watched infernal skits in the "den of Satan." In the Cabaret du Néant (nothingness), owned by the same entrepreneur as the preceding two, customers drank "les microbes de la mort" served by undertakers amid caskets and skeletons; in the Hall of Incineration, they watched bodies decompose and skeletons reappear. In such places people could play a role completely different from their usual, or they could just laugh at the surrounding illusion and actors. The theme cabaret took root, making a change of identity and setting easily available at the slightest twinge of ennui—for a price.

One great advantage of the theme cabaret was that such establishments easily attracted attention and publicity, a key to success in the new entertainment business. Salis was a masterful publicity agent for himself, his cabaret, and Montmartre. Three years after he founded his *hostellerie*, he had his death announced in the *Chat Noir*, with the place of rendezvous for his burial to be, of course, his cabaret; when people arrived on the given day, they found a sign over the door announcing *Ouverte pour cause de décès* and inside, as usual, a jovial Salis. On another occasion he wrote an open letter to the *Courrier français* proposing a Villon fête—with the organization meeting to take place at the Chat Noir. He also gained publicity by running for the National Assembly as candidate from Montmartre. The first time, in 1885, his platform included making Montmartre the capital of France. With his customary verve he sloganeered: "Down with all hierarchies, except for one, the intellectual hierarchy. Let the deputies be painters, poets, *romanciers*, sculptors, musicians, artists." In 1889 he called for the secession of Montmartre from Paris and ballyhooed his cause with Barnumesque panache: "Montmartre is the brain of the world. . . . *La butte sacrée* is the granite and formidable breast at which generations smitten with the ideal will drink."[9] This was what contemporaries called *puffisme*, and for Salis, as for Barnum, it worked.

Word of mouth still counted in launching a place like the Chat Noir, but increasingly newspapers exercised the power of building reputations and directing pleasure seekers. Most of the Paris dailies gave little space to the theater and less to cafés-concerts and other newer entertainments. But toward the end of the century new papers emerged to publicize the pleasure world as the primary one. The leading cabarets put out their own papers, following the practice of the Chat Noir. In the late 1890s Bruant was publishing not only *Le Mirliton*, but also a twenty-four-page weekly called *La Lanterne de Bruant*. For the new sports of cycling and automobile racing, the new daily *Vélo* (from 1891) and *Auto* (from 1903) were effective promoters, the latter leaving a particularly notable mark as the organizer of the first Tour de France

Cabarets Heaven and Hell, ca. 1900. On the
Boulevard de Clichy, the white and blue facade
of the Cabaret Le Ciel and the black and red
Enfer next door beckoned the public to come
inside for mock-angelic or diabolic play acting
and amusement. (Phot. Bibliothèque Nationale, Paris)

(bicycle race) for its own inaugural publicity. In addition, new journals such as the *Fin de siècle* and the weekly *Courrier français* covered the whole of Paris entertainments.

Founded by Jules Roques in 1884, the *Courrier français* is perhaps the best expression of the raffish and hedonist belle époque, which it helped to create. Ostensibly a guide to the pleasures of Paris, in fact it sold not just entertainments but also Pastilles Géraudel, hawked as a cure for throat problems afflicting singers, public speakers, and workers on railroads and in mines. Though Roques published a full-page drawing of a very contemporary nude woman labeled *la vérité* on the first page of his first issue, he did not mention his position as publicity agent for the pastilles firm, which was promoted in articles, cartoons, and explicit back-page advertisements in every issue. Roques pioneered the practice of making commercials as entertaining as the accompanying entertainment. Both the pharmaceutical firm and the newspaper flourished. By 1887, the *Courrier français* could boast of being received in 997 Paris cafés.[10]

Posters promoting entertainment also proliferated in the last decades of the century. Technological innovations made possible mechanically produced color lithographs; passage of a law in 1881 permitted much freer bill posting; and at the same time competitive entrepreneurs open to things new were looking for ways of reaching more customers. Consequently, Paris blossomed with large brilliant images covering walls, kiosks, Morris columns, urinals, tramways, and sandwich boards. From every quarter even those who did not read were urged to go see the latest singer or circus act and the Chat Noir. In the new flowering of the streets, a high proportion of the posters were for the entertainment business. One hundred fifty thousand posters went up in 1891 just to announce the new Casino de Paris. Between 1874 and 1893, Maindron shows, fifty-eight different posters blazoned the attractions of the Folies-Bergère.[11] In 1890 Jules Chéret began making his colorful, lively posters for the *Courrier français* as well as for the Casino de Paris, the Folies-Bergère, the Moulin Rouge—and Pastilles Géraudel. Toulouse-Lautrec's genius was put to the same ends; his first Moulin Rouge poster was the direct successor to Chéret's and more than met the high challenge.

Commercial publicity relentlessly pursued Parisians even after they went inside places of amusement. Printed programs and stage curtains in music

Atget photo, "rue l'Abbaye," 1898. Some Paris
walls were, literally, fully covered with colorful
pitches for entertainments. (Phot. Bibliothèque
Nationale, Paris)

halls were covered with pitches for Vin Mariani, the Purgatif Géraudel, and such entertainments as the Musée Grévin. Parisians strolling by an equestrian statue of Joan of Arc might assume it to be a sign for the Hippodrome pantomime, as a couple did in a Lunel cartoon (*Le Courrier français*, September 7, 1890), so ubiquitous was entertainment advertising in the modern Paris. A closely allied art form was the illustration of sheet music and songbooks, which also benefited from the talents of Toulouse-Lautrec and Steinlen. Such publications brought further profit and publicity to cabarets like the Chat Noir.

BOHEMIA AND THE GOLDEN CALF

As the fame of the Chat Noir spread and Salis prospered, he gained a reputation for avaricious profiteering. His associates complained that from the beginning they had been required to pay at Salis's place just as ordinary customers, even when performing. As the cabaret's popularity rose, so did the price of drinks, and Salis continued to pay artists little or nothing. Bruant, notably, performed without salary at the Chat Noir and received money only from the sale of his songs. Adolphe Willette also got nothing for his early works gracing the cabaret's interior, he bitterly charged in his memoirs. Willette was most outraged when he learned that Salis was selling reproductions and forgeries signed "Willette." The angry artist stormed into the cabaret and broke up the first canvas he found. To him Salis was "Malice." The songwriter Xanrof, who also was never paid by Salis, expressed similar grievances. In an interview published in the *Courrier français* (January 11, 1891), he accused the cabaretier of giving others credit for some of his songs and even presenting another singer as Xanrof.[12]

Other proprietors and singers were doing the same—taking songs without payment or credit. Songwriters, singers, and artists were easily exploited, especially beginning ones. While some spoke out bitterly in interviews, a few tried the more difficult tack of getting justice through the courts. When Toulouse-Lautrec found the publisher Jules Roques not paying for drawings used in the *Courrier français* and selling unpublished ones at the Hôtel Drouot auction, the artist took legal action in 1891 and gained some recompense. Bruant took his imitator Alexandre Leclerc to court and won a partial victory:

Leclerc was allowed to wear the boots and red shirt that were Bruant's trademark, but had to replace the large hat with a worker's or chauffeur's *casquette*.[13]

In these contentious relations, the Bohemian world that was so scornful of bourgeois society was mirroring that society and especially its music hall branch of big business. Paulus, one of the highest paid music hall singers, had a career riddled with fights, firings, and lawsuits—one in 1887 resulting in a thirty-thousand-franc fine for his leaving the Concert Parisien (his new director at the Scala paid the fine).[14] Former Chat Noir singer Gabriel Montoya was similarly forced to pay a penalty after breaking an engagement at the Tréteau de Tabarin to sing at the Boîte-à-Fursy. Joseph Oller successfully sued his Moulin Rouge star Le Pétomane for breach of contract when the performer appeared at a street fair. The captains of the new entertainment industry also feuded among themselves outside the courtroom. In 1890, for instance, when Jules Roques helped dancer La Goulue to get a better contract at the Elysée Montmartre, Moulin Rouge director Zidler angrily took revenge by denying Roques entry to the dance hall; Roques's response was to denigrate the Moulin Rouge in a series of articles.[15]

Potential fortunes were at stake. A singer such as Yvette Guilbert could go from Montmartre cabarets to earning one thousand francs a night at the Olympia by 1903. A star singer like Félix Mayol could earn from one to two thousand francs an evening in a leading music hall. By the late 1890s Bruant had moved up to ownership of the music hall Epoque, which reportedly earned thirty thousand francs a year; he presided over a country estate in his native village Courtenay and could tour the provinces for pay of five hundred francs a night plus first-class round-trip train fare. The amount that Salis earned from the Chat Noir is unknown, but by 1896 he was reporting receipts of seventeen thousand francs for just the shadow-theater admissions alone; most of the income over the years came from food and drink. A successful songwriter Vincent Scotto, who wrote over four thousand songs in his career, received two thousand francs for the hit song *Ah! Si vous vouliez d'l'amour!* The much bigger hit *Viens poupoule* brought in fifteen thousand francs.[16] Meanwhile, the singer's friends could be grinding on as clerks in a government ministry—as Goudeau, Xanrof, and other Bohemians did for years—for salaries of only two thousand francs a year or less.

Willette reacted to economic seduction early in the Chat Noir's history by creating a stained glass window showing Parisians worshiping the Golden Calf; his sympathies went out to a far different way of living, expressed in his cartoons as Pierrot, a gentle, naive, and dreaming Pierrot who ends by going off to die penniless and disillusioned. That sad figure expressed a side of fin-de-siècle Bohemian life that glowing images of banquets and jokes have overshadowed. Though not unsuccessful economically and hardly the innocent that he depicted, Willette thought of himself and of his artistic Montmartre as abused and martyred by greedy philistine businessmen like Salis. Willette was agitated by venomous prejudices against the Germans, the English, and Jews, who were pictured as rapacious capitalists of the most villainous sort; he was also tormented by a fear of death.

Something of his dark mood was shared by fellow caricaturist André Gill, described by a friend as a "somber, bitter philosopher"; within five years of that characterization in an early issue of *L'Hydropathe*, Gill lost his sanity and died in an asylum. Humorist Jules Jouy, who also went mad, had a penchant for the "gay macabre" view of life, best expressed in his many songs about executions. Maurice Mac-Nab's humor, similarly, may be best described as "funereal gaiety," as in the following tale told in his greatest hit, launched by singer Kam Hill at the Jardin de Paris:

> A young man just hanged himself
> In the forest of Saint Germain
> For a little tender-hearted girl
> Whose hand was refused him.
> Let's always share the rope,
> It's happiness for the home.

Maurice Rollinat made his fame with such songs as "Buried Alive" and "The Rondo of the Guillotined."[17] Black humor appeared also in music hall and circus acts like those of the Hanlon brothers and George Footit, but not so generally as among the poets and songwriters of Montmartre.

There was much to be gloomy about in the late 1880s and 1890s. Despite the fraternal ideal of the early republicans, poverty and corruption seemed destined to remain open wounds of the Third Republic. In the early 1890s, the very existence of civilized order seemed threatened by anarchist bombings. Conservatives, of course, found the most to be alarmed about, but concern about decline and decadence was not confined to the political Right or to political issues. It also cropped up in reporting on public entertainments. Year after year observers lamented the decline of carnival. False noses, long a source of carnival-time hilarity, were hard to find at the end of the century, noted Aurélien Scholl. Others reported that public dancing was disappearing. So was the widespread rejoicing of early Bastille Day celebrations. Such signs of a vanishing public gaiety were commonly cited particulars in a general lament about the *mal de siècle*.[18]

Was some of the pessimism a pose by then traditional with artists and poets and continued with more or less conscious intention? From the romantics on, André Gide later observed, "joy appeared vulgar, the sign of too good and dumb animal health. . . . Sadness reserved for itself the privilege of spirituality and, therefore, profundity." Whatever part the historic fashion played, it seems small compared to the many other reasons for dejection in Montmartre. Some of it may have resulted from the Bohemians' reaching middle age without having fulfilled youthful dreams in or out of Bohemian life. Goudeau's case lends itself to that interpretation. By 1888 he had moved out of the Left Bank and had quit the Chat Noir; he had found regular work as a journalist, had established a reputation as a talented poet, had invested in his own cabaret, and had written memoirs of his youth. Though he did not feel martyred like Willette, he remained much less successful economically than Salis or Bruant and was dark in mood. The epoch of laughter-loving Bohemia that he had known he now declared "perhaps the last, . . . given that the blackest pessimism today darkens the faces and hearts of twenty-year-olds."[19]

Many of Goudeau's Bohemian peers found themselves stuck in boring low-paying jobs in government offices or suffering from periodic unemployment. They knew the pain of poverty—their own and others' around them, as biting cartoons in the *Chat noir* and the *Courrier français* frequently showed. Sickness and death haunted them. Mac-Nab died at age twenty-nine. Andhré Joyeux, after taking over the Ane Rouge in 1898, committed suicide while suffering a fever the following year before he reached his thirtieth birthday. Singer Gasta (Gaston Galempois) died insane at age thirty; Jouy died at forty-two. Violence, alcoholism, commercial chicanery, and censorship were pervasive threats, when not day-to-day problems. The pressure to produce new songs also weighed heavily on the *chansonniers*. Jules Jouy, one of the most successful, forced himself to write one a day. Even among the most talented, many unsuccessful creations were written for each song that was a hit. As Eugène Lemercier sang sadly of his work:

> To amuse with songs,
> Isn't it a thankless task?
> You write some in a hundred ways
> That you try one evening and then drop,
> But when you put your hand on
> Some that are sure-fire laugh-getters,
> What a sad business:
> For ten years you drivel them;
> What a sad craft
> The craft of the songwriter![20]

The commercial success of cabarets like the Chat Noir also brought disappointments to some. In the early days of the Chat Noir, poets and singers had responded to one anothers' performances and offered criticism in free discussions. Interaction of that sort diminished with the arrival of larger audiences of strangers. That early fertile intimacy could be revived only away from the hurly-burly that Salis promoted. As personalities and ambitions clashed, some sought greater freedom to present their works as they pleased, away from Salis's strong presence. Such was the case of Adolphe Willette, who led one schismatic group to the Auberge du Clou even before Salis's move to larger quarters. For Bruant and Jouy, among others, breaking away brought the chance to earn much more money with their reputation solidly established at the Chat Noir. A few years after Bruant's successful move, a particularly talented splinter group followed his example and moved to a cabaret called the Chien Noir, where they quickly built up a following. In the early 1890s, Goudeau and Fragerolle founded the Chat Botté, and singer Xavier Privas established the Noctambules. So the schisms continued, the troubled progeny of success.

After several years of financial disarray, the Chat Noir closed in 1897, and a broken Salis died. The trajectory taken by his cabaret was part of a similar one taken by Montmartre. After a decade marked by innovation and wit, the 1890s saw the quarter become notorious for flagrant prostitution (of both sexes) in brightly lighted pleasure spots like the Moulin Rouge; a violent and brutal criminality also became commonplace. To be sure, the excitements of sex and danger—the fascinating "terrible odor" of the lower classes there—lured many of higher social standing in quest of private pleasures. But beyond the lights of the Boulevard de Clichy, the quarter's entertainment boom faltered. Symbolically, in 1893 the great old dance hall the Elysée Montmartre closed, partly because of competition from the Moulin Rouge, but partly because Montmartre was losing some of its luster.[21]

In 1892 and 1893, Toulouse-Lautrec, who had favored the area's haunts since the early 1880s, shifted to the entertainments of central Paris: the Folies-Bergère, the Nouveau Cirque, the Petit-Casino, and the city's top theaters. The boulevards and the Champs Elysées were strengthening their already formidable magnetic power. On the Champs Elysées, the Ambassadeurs in 1892 billed Montmartre's own Bruant, boosted by a powerful new Toulouse-Lautrec poster. Attractions such as Oller's Jardin de Paris and his new music hall Olympia (1893) also drew moneyed pleasure seekers to the chic and safer center and west of Paris. For the many in the 1890s, such ascendant music halls as the Eldorado and Scala, Eden-Concert, and the Parisiana were the places to go to hear and see the era's most popular singers and comics. The *grands boulevards* with their brilliant lights and streaming crowds—as Pissarro and others showed us repeatedly—exerted a persistent pull that the *rue des saoules* (drunks) and *boîtes* like the Cabaret des Assassins could not match. After 1900, night restaurants did multiply in Montmartre, and the Tabarin dance hall opened there (1904), extensions of the sexual marketplace already well established in the vicinity. But overall, outside the literary cabarets and the Cirque Médrano, the quarter's public entertainments were not equal to those of the boulevards. After the Chat Noir's "fête of *l'esprit*" (wit, mind), as Louis Chevalier has put it, the quarter became "a pleasure factory."[22]

NOVELTY, PROFIT, AND LOSS

Montmartre's rise as an entertainment district was only one of many booms in the late nineteenth-century pleasure business. Another arose with the institutionalization of July 14: a large manufacturing industry sprang up to produce festive paraphernalia, an industry centered in Paris and employing an estimated eighty thousand workers. Another came with the invention of paper confetti in 1892 for carnival time; the fifty thousand kilos of confetti sold each year was worth 250,000 francs to manufacturers and small merchants in Paris, it was reported in 1894.[23] The artistic cabaret, artists' costume balls, and nudity (really, seminudity) in music hall sketches and revues (from 1894 on) became rages almost as suddenly.

All became formulas that were widely followed. With a bright idea or new attraction, money could be made quickly in fin-de-siècle Paris, but competition was stiff; rival entrepreneurs moved swiftly. Even the Pétomane, who possessed a rare talent for producing farts sounding like the cutting of cloth or like thunder, found himself with a competitor, a woman whom he sued—without satisfaction.[24] Competition seethed not just among entrepreneurs offering the same amusement but among different kinds of amusements. Public interest and preferences, moreover, changed unpredictably; commercial opportunities could fade as fast as they had emerged. In the early 1880s, the obvious growth entertainment was panoramas, but by the end of the decade their boom was over, though the death blow by cinema was not delivered until the early twentieth century. Around 1890 montagnes russes—roller coasters with adjacent cafés and pleasure gardens—began springing up around the capital. At the same time music halls were enjoying an even bigger and more enduring boom, drawing business away from the theaters.

Parisians were hungry for novelty, observers often commented. One measure of that hunger was the market for new songs: in the 1890s Paris "consumed" twelve to fifteen thousand songs a year.[25] Entertainment entrepreneurs were constantly looking for novel possibilities for profits—new songs, new performers, new acts, new kinds of entertainment, new combinations of old forms. Neither the public nor the new show businessmen felt constrained

The windmill facade of the Moulin Rouge was
never more than commercial decoration, like
America's present-day "golden arches." In 1889
the place opened as a dance hall and pleasure
garden that catered to the fashionable. It became a music hall featuring revues only after
renovation in 1903. (Phot. Bibliothèque Nationale, Paris)

The summer garden of the Moulin Rouge about 1890. The elephant to the left, moved there from a world's fair amusement park, contained a small stage where a belly dancer performed. (Phot. Bibliothèque Nationale, Paris)

by set patterns of the past. Gone were such restrictions as the law and the force of tradition that had kept circus clowns from speaking on stage and acrobats from performing except on horses. The end of the nineteenth century was an era of new liberty, a time of experimentation and innovation, a creative liminal "chaos." The cafés-concerts took the high-kicking chahut from the popular balls, and then music halls took over both chahut and songs. In fact, the music halls adopted a little of everything: acrobats from the circus, wrestling from the fêtes foraines, singers from cabarets, and belly dancers from the universal expositions. At Oller's Olympia, customers could even take in a wax museum set up in the basement. Meanwhile in the most celebrated wax museum, the Musée Grévin, spectators were able to watch a rudimentary form of moving pictures several years before the Lumière brothers' invention.

Joseph Oller was the most creative of those offering the new hybrids. In his Nouveau Cirque he hoped to profit from admissions to circus spectacles and at other times from admissions to the enclosed swimming pool there; then he hit upon the idea of using the pool for special aquatic ballets, which became a part of his circus's repertory; the ring could be converted to a pool within an astonishingly few minutes. In 1891 Oller added to his show the singing of the rising star Yvette Guilbert. Although her performance in the spacious building turned out to be much less effective than on a cabaret stage, Oller's readiness to present her there was characteristic of the new experimentation. At his Jardin de Paris, clients could watch the quadrilles of the Moulin Rouge dancers or a belly dancer, listen to a café-concert star, dance, drink, and eat, have their fortune told, or shoot at targets. "One has to be Protean, take on all forms and persist in none," warned Jules Bois in a *Courrier français* column about the Folies-Bergère; otherwise audiences quickly felt "fatigue, ennui and aversion."[26]

The protean Chat Noir had shown the way. Probably no other commercial establishment of the period has been written about as much, primarily because of its assembled talent—literary and artistic—and the prestige of those who flocked there in search of a new frisson. But the Chat Noir was also important as a pioneer in a new world of commercial entertainment into which even Bohemians were drawn. In that world, success went to those who most skillfully used the tools of mass publicity and those who hit upon the right combinations of large common-denominator amusements. In the scramble for profits, creative camaraderie and the festive closeness of audience and performer did not fare well. What came to prevail was a fast-changing, highly competitive marketplace governed by unpredictable fads and, all too quickly, by new *gros bonnets*.

Folies Bergère

Tous les soirs la famille Birmane

4

The Music Halls:
A New Democratic Culture?

The Burman family—poster, ca. 1890. In the late
nineteenth century, the Folies-Bergère featured
anything and everything unusual—with plenty of
attention-grabbing circus and sideshow acts. In
good Barnum fashion, the bearded Burman family
was billed as being of illustrious Burman royal de-
scent. (Collection du Musée de la Publicité, Paris)

"THE LEVELING OF ENJOYMENTS"

A French workingman visiting the Paris Universal Exposition in 1889 could find before him an expanse and variety of amusements that no king or noble had ever commanded. That the common man should have such opportunity was fitting, since one of the purposes of the fair was to mark the centenary of a revolution against privilege and inequality. Anyone could enter that wonderland for half the low official admission of one franc and sometimes for even less, for many holders of twenty entry-packets were competitively hawking their extra tickets. Or if he chose not to go to the fair, the clerk or carpenter could go out on the town and, for a franc or two, hear and see the best professional singers and comics and acrobats in the land. New places of entertainment flourished by serving worker as well as bourgeois, particularly in the center of Paris.

Most numerous and accessible were the cafés-concerts, of which there were an estimated 264 in the capital around the turn of the century. Most of them charged no admission and made money only on drink and food. At the most basic they were simply cafés with a small stage and some singers, providing entertainment for the ordinary price of a beer. The cafés-concerts were the "democratized theater," declared Jules Claretie, journalist and director of the Comédie-Française. They were the "theaters of the poor," noted expert André Chadourne in his book on cafés-concerts.[1] In the last decades of the nineteenth century some of these places broke with the "temple of song" format and became English-style music halls with richly varied programmes and showy theaterlike interiors.

The Folies-Bergère was the most successful and famous of these. Its box-office receipts were consistently the highest of any café-concert or music hall, running about a million francs a year around 1880 and increasing to past the 2 million mark in 1913. In the last decades of the nineteenth century, most of its seats were unreserved and open to anyone paying the two-franc admission. In contrast, theaters sifted customers into finely graded echelons ranging from fifteen-franc front-stage boxes to fifty-centime perches at the back of the fourth balcony. While the Comédie-Française and the boulevard theaters retained a large clientele through the period, they and the popular suburban theaters of melodrama were losing a growing public— less prosperous and less grounded in literary culture—to the cafés-concerts and music halls (and after 1900, the cinemas). The Folies-Bergère, even though charging a relatively high two francs, drew clients from that growing plebeian public as well as from the more moneyed. In the nineteenth century it served not just tourists and the well-to-do, as later, but what one journalist called "a true public" of husbands and wives, provincials and Parisians from skilled worker to aristocrat. In 1879, when writer J.-K. Huysmans gave us a hauntingly beautiful sketch of the place, it was drawing almost 500,000 people a year (estimate based on reported receipts).[2]

Under an ochre and gold ceiling of ruffled and tasseled fabric, amid allegorical statuary and rattan divans, customers could watch a trapeze duo, ballet dances, a juggler, a snake charmer, wrestlers, clowns, and such novelty acts as a kangaroo boxing a man (see illus., p. 88)—or an array of other spectators throughout the well-lighted hall. No matter where one sat or stood, one's ears were filled with a medley of waltzes and polkas and finale chords blaring over the cries of program hawkers and shoeshiners, audience chatter and applause. Everywhere the air was laden with perfume scents and the acrid odors of cigar smoke, beer, and dusty rugs. The miscellany of sensations mixed together as promiscuously as the prostitutes, *mondaines*, and their admirers in the famous *promenoir* (gallery-lounge) with its elegant bar that Manet's painting has immortalized. "It is ugly and it is splendid," concluded Huysmans; "it is of an outrageous and exquisite taste." In the Folies-Bergère as in the Scala or the Eldorado, the "worker, employee, the bourgeois, the *flaneur* of every profession by means of one or two 20–sou coins is as entertained as an emperor of the One Thousand and One Nights at the height of power, magnificence and idleness," asserted the Comte d'Avenel, a scholarly observer who devoted a whole book to the subject of the "leveling of enjoyments" in modern times.[3]

By "enjoyments" d'Avenel meant housing and food as well as entertainments. The "leveling" that he described more systematically than anyone else was commonly assumed to be one of the trends of the age. It was hailed by partisans of the Republic as democratic "progress" and was attacked as "vulgarization" and decadence by conservatives. Except for socialists and anarchists, the French readily assumed that it was taking place or could easily take place. Scholars of our own time refer to such changes as the "democratization of leisure" and the beginnings of "mass culture." All these terms and ideas suggest a process under way; the question that arises is: how much change was in fact taking place? Was a more democratic culture of leisure emerging?

POPULAR CULTURE FOR A DEMOCRACY

It is easy to see why late nineteenth-century observers were so impressed with the leveling going on in France. Politically the nation was an established democracy by 1880 and the first country in Europe with universal manhood suffrage, a rarity on the continent even as late as 1880. With equality stamped on schoolhouses and court buildings, few expected leveling to be confined to the ballot and to primary education. At least since the Second Republic of 1848, republicans working for a fuller democracy had called for doing more than extending the benefits of elite culture to the people. Democratic advocates such as Jules Michelet had proclaimed the need for a new popular culture, one without the religious and hierarchical traditions of folk culture. They envisioned books, concerts, festivals, plays, imagery, and songs for the common people of a nature appropriate to the democratic ideals of the Republic and the revolutionary tradition. At a minimum *democratic* and *popular* meant accessible to all and appealing enough that the most untutored of the French would participate. Some gains of this kind were easy to claim in the late nineteenth century. A spokesman for the Third Republic, Jules Simon, could exult, for example, that the world's fair of 1889 "gives to the poor the enjoyments of luxury and to the ignorant something of the dazzlements of science."[4]

Certainly the government of the Third Republic did make efforts to offer festivities to the people, as we have seen. In fact, it made greater efforts and reached more people than had any preceding government. In proposing the first July 14 celebration in 1880, Deputy Achard had observed correctly that

FOLIES - BERGÈRE

Folies-Bergère Winter Garden. For publicity purposes, the artist has made all the attractions of this pleasure palace (including soliciting women) appear simultaneously. (Collection du Musée de la Publicité, Paris)

The Folies-Bergère was one of the grandest of the music halls, but Chéret exaggerated the size of the hall and showed none but the most fashionable spectators. The poster makes clear what belle-époque observers described from experience: the spectacle was by no means confined to the stage. The poster also suggests some of the rich variety of acts on stage: trapeze artists, ballet, pantomimes, and operettas. (Collection du Musée de la Publicité, Paris)

FOLIES-BERGÈRE
LE PLUS NOUVEAU SPECTACLE
LE KANGOUROU BOXEUR

the Republic had hitherto been in the hands of men who "did not dare face the contact of the popular masses."[5] Achard and other republican leaders taking over from the monarchists prided themselves on making such contact. The festivities of July 14, we have noted, took place even in villages that had never celebrated any political cause; they grew out of initiatives taken by people of lower social status and elicited more popular participation than had Bonapartist or royal fêtes. The world's fairs of the early Third Republic showed even clearer democratic progress. No other spectacle or amusement attracted so many people, each one drawing more than its predecessor: 16 million in 1878—half again more than the one in 1867—32 million in 1889, and over 50 million in 1900. Legions of peasants and small-town provincials made their first trip to the big city to see one of the fairs. The government and the fair organizers kept admission prices low—the admission in 1900 was the same (one franc) as in 1889—and arranged for special bargain train fares so as to encourage provincials to take part.

During the two biggest fairs, the government made its grandest effort to unite all the French in celebration—symbolically—by hosting the people's

Folies-Bergère poster, ca. 1890. Boxing and wrestling (female as well as male) were music hall favorites, and so were animal acts. Here sport and an animal act were combined in several brief rounds of sparring. The fight was tame compared to English boxing matches that were introduced into France at the end of the century. The kangaroo's human opponent, his trainer, had to take care not to injure the valuable animal. (Collection du Musée de la Publicité, Paris) mayors at mammoth banquets. On August 18, 1889, a date with no divisive revolutionary meaning, 13,456 mayors from all corners of France sat down together to feast their way through a half dozen gargantuan courses and 24,437 bottles of wine, or about 2 bottles per person. At least temporary good will and unity were achieved. A similar grand feast brought together 20,777 mayors on September 22, 1900. The tradition of mayors' banquets, like that of annual Bastille Days, goes back to that watershed year 1880, when the Paris municipal council sponsored a July 14 reception for mayors and delegates from all France's communes. "Under the monarchies, the sovereigns of Europe were received; democracy must reserve its best welcome for those elected by universal suffrage," explained council member Engelhard in June 1880.[6] In those early years Europe's monarchs would not even visit republican France, and republicans were left to glory in democratic flourishes signaling a new era of good times for the many.

The developing economy was at the same time providing more amusements for a growing number. As productivity and the standard of living of most people rose, a leveling of enjoyments was apparent in amusements just as it was in food, shelter, and lighting. Most of d'Avenel's account dealt with such results of economic growth. He was willing to admit that wealth was far from being leveled, but he was nonetheless determined to show that real enjoyments were being equalized. Many of the pleasures still confined to the rich, like owning a painting or an automobile, d'Avenel argued, really brought no greater or better satisfaction than the poor person's enjoyment of beauty in a public museum or getting there by bicycle.[7] Obviously the examples he gave were at best debatable, and his argument was clearly tendentious, but one can find *some* recreations that were filtering down to the *nouvelles couches* in the period. In 1893 clients of the Moulin Rouge for a small sum could hear the best and latest Edison phonograph available in France playing the music of a New York orchestra, the greatest singers of the day, and Plébins reciting monologues. At the Fête de Vincennes in April 1901, seamstresses and butchers could, for a mere four sous, take a ride in an automobile.[8]

Or for only a franc they could watch the horse races. Once a sport confined to the rich and aristocratic, the racetracks in the 1890s drew new clients from lower social levels. Up to 40,000 people went to the Paris track on Sundays at the turn of the century, and the greatest part of them walked there and paid the lowest admission of one franc to watch from the standing area, the *pelouse*. In the 1870s Longchamp races, which consistently drew the largest crowds through the entire period, were attended by never more than 200,000 a year on the pelouse; by the 1890s, attendance there was in the 500,000 to 600,000 range. One of the reasons was the establishment of a regular pari-mutuel system of betting, which allowed small bettors without particular expertise a greater chance of winning something; "the people" increasingly indulged in betting alongside counts and millionaires at Longchamp, if not at the more distant Chantilly and Deauville.[9] The growth of racetrack attendance and sums wagered is perhaps the best evidence for democratic leveling of amusements in the belle époque.

Most racetracks, circuses, cabarets, and music halls kept prices relatively low through the nineteenth century. The entertainment entrepreneurs, that is, opted for volume business, their labor costs being little affected, in contrast to restaurant owners whose widely ranging prices strictly separated habitués of soup kitchens from those of Maxim's. At a cabaret like the Ane Rouge or a café-concert like the Alcazar d'Eté in the 1890s one could enter without charge and drink a bock for fifty centimes, only a little more than in an ordinary café. At the circus and in the theaters, a variety of seats and prices was available. One could see the Cirque d'Hiver for as little as half a franc or get the best seat for only two francs, while at the chic Nouveau Cirque, prices ranged from two francs up to five francs in 1900. At the Hippodrome de l'Alma, one paid one franc admission. Entry to the Moulin Rouge in 1900 was two or three francs, depending on the day. Some of the cheapest places of amusement were dance halls; at the Moulin de la Galette in 1898 admission was only twenty-five centimes for women and fifty for men, and ten centimes per couple each time they danced. In contrast, the lowest priced seat at the substantially government-subsidized Opera was four francs, and at the subsidized Comédie-Française one paid at the least two and a half francs for an uncomfortable place in the pit. On national holidays, however, those elitist bastions were opened up to humbler people free of charge, another democratic gesture by the government.[10]

In plebeian places of amusement, social mixing occurred when the well-to-do and socially prominent dropped in to sample lowlife. "It is well known that the height of refinement for *mondains* is to come mix themselves in

these popular amusements," journalist "Jacques Lux" observed of street fairs in 1907.[11] At the end of the Old Regime the nobility had enjoyed rubbing shoulders with the rabble at fairs and Italian comedies; similar excursions downward became fashionable again in the 1880s. At the Folies-Bergère or the Cirque Fernando, middle- and upper-class spectators could relax and indulge in unpretentious common tastes. In the cafés-concerts, Georges Montorgueil testified, there reigned a "kind of freedom and openness in the American manner": men kept their hats on, dressed as casually as they liked, and smoked cigars. "It's the ideal of 'no bother' and it is the only [ideal] that people in these places of distraction want in reality."[12] To join the rabble (s'encanailler) from time to time was apparently a refreshing flight from the predictable rituals of a restricted upper class.

On a more regular basis, people of different classes increasingly shared a common consciousness of amusements in Paris as a result of the new ubiquity of newspapers and posters. Whereas conservative papers such as *Le Gaulois* maintained traditional exclusivity by reporting on private fêtes held in noble

This poster for a Boulevard Sebastopol music hall solicits business by featuring, alongside the inviting young woman, a list of drink prices, showing how inexpensive an evening's entertainment and a few beers (or even a glass of champagne) were toward the end of the nineteenth century. (Anonymous, Collection du Musée de la Publicité, Paris) châteaux around the capital, the popular, large-circulation *Petit Journal* told of festivities open to all in the Paris region; on a summer Sunday in 1898, any reader learned, one could find games and prizes at a fair lighted with three thousand electric lamps in Neuilly, or watch the ascension of a manned balloon in Savigny sur Orge or *vélocipède* races at Villejuif, or take in a fête foraine and popular ball at Arronville. Big national fêtes such as Bastille Day were reported on for days before and after. Through the popular press, people scattered over great distances could vicariously experience festivals. Never before had such a large public shared in what could be called secondhand festivity. In addition, advertising spread new images of enjoyment that have remained identifying emblems of the period: Chéret's vivacious young women, Lautrec's dramatic red-scarved Bruant, the jovial Michelin tire-creature drinking a cup of rocks and iron scraps like a regular café bon vivant (1903). Souvenir books of the world's fairs, books on the circus (there was an outpouring of them at the end of the century), essays and memoirs on cafés-concerts, newspaper cartoons and posters showing such places as the Moulin Rouge and the Jardin de Paris further contributed to a new culture of entertainment shared by more people than ever before.

By 1900, too, the culture of the music halls had spread from Paris to most provincial centers. One could go to a music hall named the Eldorado in Nice, Lyon, Poitiers, Albi, and Belfort, and the same hit songs, published in Paris, could be heard at any of them. There was a Folies-Bergère in Brest, Lyon, Le Havre, and Rouen—and by World War I also in Tunis, New York, and Buenos Aires. Angers, Périgueux, Carcassonne, Marseille, Bordeaux, Béziers, Toulouse, and Saint-Etienne—each had its own Alcazar. Famous singers periodically toured these provincial halls, and talent scouts from Paris took local stars back to the capital. Toward the end of the century cafés-concerts began to appear even in small country towns, and even among peasants city songs became commonplace while traditional local tunes faded away.[13]

LOWLIFE AND HIGH LIFE

Though music halls drew much larger and more socially diverse audiences than the cabarets or classic theaters, they were not yet forums of mass culture.

The reason is not simply that the majority of people—still in the country-side—was not so fully partaking of music hall culture as city people, but also that within the urban population itself, social barriers and privilege remained strong and poverty widespread. An unskilled laborer in Paris in the late 1890s, typically earning little more than three francs a day, could hardly afford to frequent places that charged more than the price of a beer. Even skilled workers like masons earning seven francs a day in 1896 would find nights out at Paris's leading music halls expensive, though they certainly indulged in holiday splurges. The chic Olympia, which Oller opened in 1893, effectively shut out workers by charging an exceptionally high admission of five francs for men and two francs for women. The unemployed and the poor could never enter the likes of the Folies-Bergère.

For workers and small employees, splurges at the more celebrated places became harder after the turn of the century. The Folies-Bergère changed its pricing policy after 1900, making it no longer open to the many on an egalitarian basis. By 1903 the price for a standing place was up to three francs, while a seat cost four to six francs; by the eve of the First World War the best seats were up to ten francs. The Scala also went for the better-off customers; by 1913 its prices ranged from three francs eighty-five centimes to seven francs seventy centimes, while its old rival across the street, the Eldorado, kept admission down to two and a half to three and a half francs. The establishment that most dramatically changed its character was the Moulin Rouge. After renovations, the dance hall reopened in 1903 as a music hall and charged four to nine francs for a *fauteuil*. These higher priced music halls were now mounting costly lavish revues featuring "les girls" with brilliant decors and lighting and huge salaries paid to stars. Romi, historian of the music halls, dates the new style from a Scala revue entitled *Paris fin de sexe* in 1905, but one can easily find precursors in the 1890s.[14] Once the cafés-concerts and music halls had been inexpensive compared to theaters, and that was a primary reason for their popularity; after 1900 the leading music halls were becoming luxury-category entertainments, increasingly dependent on foreign and provincial tourists.

The workers and poor had their own cafés-concerts that attracted few others, not just out in the proletarian zone around Paris, but also in the center of the city. In a special issue on cafés-concerts, the *Paris illustré* noted in 1886 that workers made up the regular audience at the Ba-Ta-Clan and the Epoque, halls on the Boulevard Voltaire and the Boulevard Beaumarchais, respectively. At the Pépinière, Rue de la Pépinière, one found soldiers from nearby camps and domestic servants of the neighborhood. "These domestics come to the concert every evening: the *valet de chambre* correct, freshly shaved; the coachman, giving his arm to Madame's chambermaid." At the Concert-Cluny, butcher boys and other workers predominated; their singing drowned out the voices of the performers. Working-class clients also filled the Grand Concert de la Presse on the Rue Montmartre. At the Folies-Rambuteau, "a sort of barn," one found "a poor public, coming from everywhere, and the little Jewish France of the Faubourg du Temple." The Concert de la Gaité Montparnasse also served its immediate neighborhood, especially the local shopkeepers, tradesmen, workers, and their families.[15] Like most theaters, most music halls served primarily a neighborhood and a quite limited range of social classes.

For the poor there were also squalid dance halls and cafés where the sign "No consumption below 15 centimes" bespoke both the desperate hope of the destitute and the firm business sense of the people serving them. If one entered the cabaret Père Lunette in the narrow Rue des Anglais near the quays in the 1880s, one would find ragged men and women drinking and talking in two smoky, narrow rooms, while "baleful alcoholic young girls" sang with raucous voices. Along the wall opposite the bar, "crashed drinkers" slept, their heads pressed against an iron rod. In the café Le Drapeau, Rue Galande, gatherers of cigar butts sought a bit of warmth and sociability. In the Château Rouge, behind a tin-covered bar, the owner dispensed eau-de-vie to poor laborers, prowlers, and *filles hasardeuses* drinking or, face down on wooden tables, sleeping. At the Bal des Familles, Rue du Fouarre, people rarely danced, though three "lugubrious" musicians often ground on. The usual imperious signs on the wall insisted on order and profit without a hint of good humor: "Women only have the right to sit on the benches"; "Every dance begun is to be paid for as if it were finished." Such places were as devoid of a socially mixed clientele as of a festive spirit, most of the time. However, well-dressed men like Jules Claretie, who described these spots for his readers in *Le Temps*, could safely enter the Père Lunette or the Château Rouge, for these were not the worst or the roughest. In fact, they became common stops for tourists wishing to sample Paris lowlife, but such visitors, of course, came to look with self-distancing caution that precluded real participation. By 1900 the dives that Claretie described in the 1880s were gone. The mondains then dropped into night restaurants around Les Halles. Or if they wanted a full excursion to the lower depths, they went out to the faubourgs—to La Villette around the abbatoirs and the canal, toward Saint Ouen, or to the quartier of the Gobelins near the Place d'Italie.[16]

In the faubourgs were many worker cafés that drew few nonworkers. Habitués played checkers, dominoes, cards, and backgammon, smoked and talked, drank black coffee and beer, red wine and absinthe. Wives and children often came, too, partaking not just of the sociability but also of the heat and light that were luxuries in the working-class household. Clients joined in singing, especially the refrains, but festive abandon was rarely in evidence. Drinks were nursed along for hours, the small sums available for entertainment being carefully calculated. Most people left by ten or eleven at night.[17] These were neighborhood centers in workers' suburbs, serving customers who were almost exclusively working people.

A "night out" for the poor, waiting for a charitable shelter to open. Though the *Courrier français* was devoted primarily to the subject of pleasure, it also showed some of the same humanitarian sympathy and critical spirit that flourished in Montmartre cabaret songs. (Drawing by Heidbrinck, *Le Courrier français*, May 27, 1888)

Only a few weeks after Heidbrinck's drawing of the homeless men was published, this belle-époque male fantasy appeared in the same journal. It captures well the pleasure dream of editor Jules Roques and other men of the period who ostensibly sought to make such rollicking and erotic scenes happen from time to time.

ŒUVRE de L'HOSPITALITE de NUIT
59
ŒUVRE de L'HOSPITALITE de NUIT
RECONNU COMME ETABLISSEMENT D'UTILITE PUBLIQUE

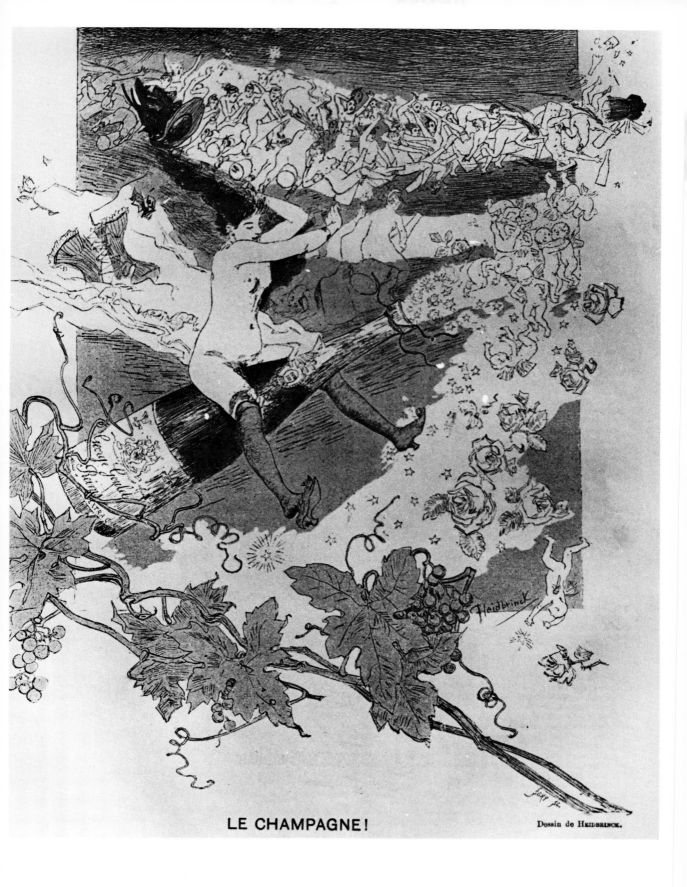

LE CHAMPAGNE!

Dessin de HEIDBRINCK.

The social elite were just as segregated at the Grand Café, the Théâtre Gymnase, the Comédie-Française, and the Opera. If they wanted to be quite safely correct, they went only on certain nights: Tuesday to the Comédie-Française, Friday to the Nouveau Cirque, other nights to the Ambassadeurs, according to one schedule for the fashionable. "One is not [correct] going Sunday to these 'dens of pleasure,' " warned boulevardiers Edmond Benjamin and Paul Desachy in 1893.[18] The elite alone attended such prestigious events as the Opera Ball where admission was a steep twenty francs for men and ten francs for women, and where black formal attire was required for men and fancy dress for women. At the racetrack, while the common people swarmed over the pelouse where anyone could stand for only a franc, the closest-to-center stands were limited to the well-to-do by an admission charge of twenty francs for men and ten francs for women; other stands—the pav-illons—were priced at five and ten francs, also too expensive for most com-moners. At the chic new Palais de Glace (skating rink) that opened in 1893, the basic admission was low, but once inside, people not actually ice-skating confronted seating choices that separated them socially; a special precinct was maintained for the gratin: the Prince de Sagan and other nobles quickly rented boxes for the season, just as they did for the Opera. When they went to the Olympia music hall, too, it was to sit conspicuously in boxes where their presence could receive this kind of notice: "All the boxes were adorned with the most richly attired, elegant personalities. So during the first part of the program the spectacle was as much in the hall as on the stage."[19]

As artist Jean-Louis Forain showed in his many scenes of the tuxedoed bourgeois backstage dallying with Opera dancers, the moneyed bought them-selves privileged access to enjoyments. In athletic clubs that sprang up in the last decades of the nineteenth century, democratic access was denied not only by the requirements of leisure and money needed to buy, say, a bicycle, which was a luxury until the late 1890s; the upper-class students of the Racing Club de France expressly forbade membership to workers, and the Union des Sociétés Françaises de Sports Athlétiques explicitly opposed mixing workers and members of "the ruling classes."[20]

The rich and the titled could duplicate the world of public entertainments for themselves in private exclusiveness. They put on masked balls and con-certs, ballets and witty revues in their mansions and country homes. Using his American wife's $15 million fortune, "Boni" de Castellane had 250 people in for sumptuous dinners and music weekly. To launch the newspaper *Le Journal* in 1892, Emile Charles Lucas gave a party at which six large glass plaques descended set up with dinner and lighted by electric footlights that turned the crystal and muslin tablecloths alternating shades of blue, rose, and green.[21]

In 1880 Ernest Molier set up his own private circus in his riding stable on the Rue Benouville where such illustrious scions as the Comte de Sainte-Aldegonde clowned in a pantomime, the Comte Hubert de La Rochefoucauld performed on the trapeze and horizontal bars, and others played as equestrian stars and acrobats for an equally well-pedigreed audience. There the leisured found challenge and excitement and, as distinguished amateurs, displayed an aristocratic prowess rivaling that of the professionals. Molier proudly noted in his memoirs that "the elite of the magistrature, medicine, finance and the nobility" took part for more than forty years. In 1880 Molier could not seat the unexpectedly large crowd of three hundred who showed up; for decades the socially prominent vied for the distinction of being invited and performing there. In the new age of democracy the Cirque Molier allowed the elites to have their circus and their distance from the *canaille* too.[22]

Despite the vogue of occasional slumming, suspicion and hostility toward newer popular entertainments festered in the middle and upper levels of society. Minister of Fine Arts Jules Simon fulminated in 1872 against "these base shows [of the cafés-concerts] which spread and sell poison around us"; from that moral point of view the situation continued only to deteriorate through la belle époque. In 1886 in a special issue devoted to cafés-concerts, a *Paris illustré* article blasted them as "the wonderland of the ugly, the obscene, and the grotesque. . . . it's degradation [*abrutissement*]." "Nothing is more grievous for the sincere friends of art than the growing success of those establishments which at this century's close threaten the downfall of good taste and the lowering of the intellectual and moral level of the masses," wrote a historian of Marseilles in 1891, as he noted the spread of "splendid cafés-concerts in the style of the Parisian Folies-Bergère, . . . pernicious products of the unlimited liberty of theaters." "In sum, the inquietude of the belly and the-below-the-belly composes almost all the repertory of the café-concert," lamented writer Gustave Coquiot in a book on the subject in 1896.

Even music hall star Paulus railed against "the invading march of filthy licentiousness" in café-concert songs.[23]

The subjects of songs and jokes that drew the biggest and surest laughs, Montorgueil reported, were diarrhea and constipation, beans, and breasts—their smallness or ampleness. In the early 1890s the enormously popular Pétomane threw Moulin Rouge audiences into hilarity by playing "Au clair de la lune" on a flute attached by a hose to his anus, not to mention his farting both like cannon fire and like a bride on her wedding night and then the day after. The hefty singer Dufay amused by cracking nuts on her robust chest, which she explained was "made of iron"; her rival Demay broke them by sitting on them. She also sang such ditties as:

> I am married to a man
> Who has the sweet name of Victor,
> But what annoys and wears me out,
> Is that he has the fault of snoring loudly.
> Sleeping he makes so much noise
> That he frightens the people of the neighborhood
> And to calm their alarm
> I am obliged to repeat to them:
> It's Victor who is snoring, the precious thing,
> It's Victor who is sleeping,
> It's from his nose that it comes out.[24]

Jeanne Bloch (1858–1916), one of the most popular of many *excentrique* singers, was both a singer and a natural comic. She often wore a colonel's cap for songs about the army, but her essential standby for comedy was her formidable girth. In a revue at the Cigale music hall, her partner tried but could not fully embrace her. A spectator cried out, "Make two trips," and Bloch as well as the audience broke into hearty laughter. (Collection du Musée de la Publicité, Paris)

Female singers also won favor with a startling frankness about money and sex, expressed in such remarks as "to love equals to pay, give and take / cash down [*donnant donnant*]" and "I find men perfect if they are generous."

Alongside love songs—tragic or happy, and an occasional artsy classic chanson for which Yvette Guilbert became so famous—went the chauvinist swagger of a Paulus, the drunken gestures of Bourgès, the nonsensical rhymes of comic soldier Polin, and the inane saws of Dranem (for example, "Les P'tits pois").* Mixed throughout was violent slapstick; "always delighting," noted Montorgueil, was the liberal distribution of blows and cuffs to the ear and mouth, breaking teeth and noisily knocking them out. The chahut, or cancan, also delighted many, but to some, including even a music hall insider like André Chadourne, the dances of La Goulue (Glutton) and Grille d'Egout (Sewer Grating) were "appalling exhibitions of women snatched from the lowest gutters." From 1894 on, Victorian-style striptease acts, involving more display of petticoat and chemise than nudity, became part of the music hall repertory, bringing new outcries of disgust and condemnation. Dancers like Violette entered the stage to calls of "Take your pants off" and "higher, show it." A lascivious taint derived also from reports that some

---

* "Les p'tits pois" (small peas), subtitled "Chanson patriotique," was an outstanding example of what the French lightheartedly call "chansons idiotes." In the first verse the singer announces: "Since our world has been world [*monde*, also meaning "clean"], people have made up dirty [*immondes*] songs whose subjects are idiotic. Me, I've just made up a new song. It's witty and full of life. Moreover, here's the refrain: Ah! Les p'tits pois, les p'tits pois, les p'tits pois / It's a very tender vegetable / Ah! les p'tits pois, les p'tits pois, les p'tits pois / *That* you don't eat with your fingers." The second verse is about a young man asking to be exempted from military service; he states as his reason the fact that he is a peasant and then breaks into the refrain: "Ah! Les p'tits pois, les p'tits pois, les p'tits pois / It's a very tender vegetable / Ah! Les p'tits pois, les p'tits pois, les p'tits pois / *That* you don't eat with your fingers."

Another verse is about the singer's experience of dancing with a fat dowager at a ministry ball and how he was jostled in the nose by her breasts; "there's one woman who has made me sweat," he exclaims, before breaking into the refrain, "Ah! les p'tits pois," etc. Another verse is delivered by a politician in the Charente who is campaigning and stating as his profession of republican faith the refrain, "Ah! les p'tits pois, les p'tits pois," etc. Still another is about a bride on the day after her marriage saying to her mother: "Marriage is very nice . . . Ah! les p'tits pois," etc. A final verse is a defiant warning to the enemy that if they invade France again, this time the French will succeed and the enemy will skedaddle, crying, "Ah! les p'tits pois," etc.

The satirical journal *Assiette au beurre* devoted its December 7, 1901, issue to censorship and songs in the cafés-concerts. The caricaturist Ibels had fun with the ambiguity involved in marking these questionable acts "approved by the censor."

Eccentric Genre: A Bloch-like
woman sings a song "They Are Golden."
On his wedding night
A lieutenant as waggish as they come,
Unbuttoning his bride,
Caught sight of two pretty boobs.
At first he paused in ecstasy
Like a rat before an elephant.
Then, gracefully drawing back,
He cried out like a child:
How nice they are!
How cute they are!
You could call them two little macaroons.

Peasant Genre: "The Kidney Bean of Nicaise."
Nicais, do you want, for only a second,
To lend me your flageolet? [bean; also a flute-
like instrument]
No, no, miss, for all the world
I don't lend my fla, my geo, my let,
I don't lend my flageolet.

Socialist Genre: "Long Live the Strike!"
When I see these poor sawers of boards,
I say to myself: there's a lousy job.
During the week, holidays and Sundays,
They always have to be busy sawing,
Me, if I were in the game
Instead of sawing bark and trunks
In their place, in the sawmill,
I would send through, for sawing up, all the bosses.

Bacchic Genre: "I Have My Panache."
My mother-in-law who had slurped up
Not a little sweet wine
Passed out after the gruyère.
To make her come to, my buddies
Tapped on her hands.
Me, I thumped her on her percolator [head].
The Big Drummer struck her on the belly,
So lit up was he that he believed
That on the head of his drum
He was beating.

Ils sont en or

Dans la nuit de son hyménée
Un lieut'nant des plus folichons,
En dégratant la mariée,
Aperçut deux jolis nichons.
Il resta d'abord en extase
Comme un rat d'vant un éléphant;
Puis, se reculant avec grâce,
Il s'écria comme un enfant :
Qu'ils sont gentils ! Qu'ils sont mignons
On dirait deux p'tits macarons.

VISÉ
PAR
LA CENSURE

Eccentric Genre

Peasant Genre

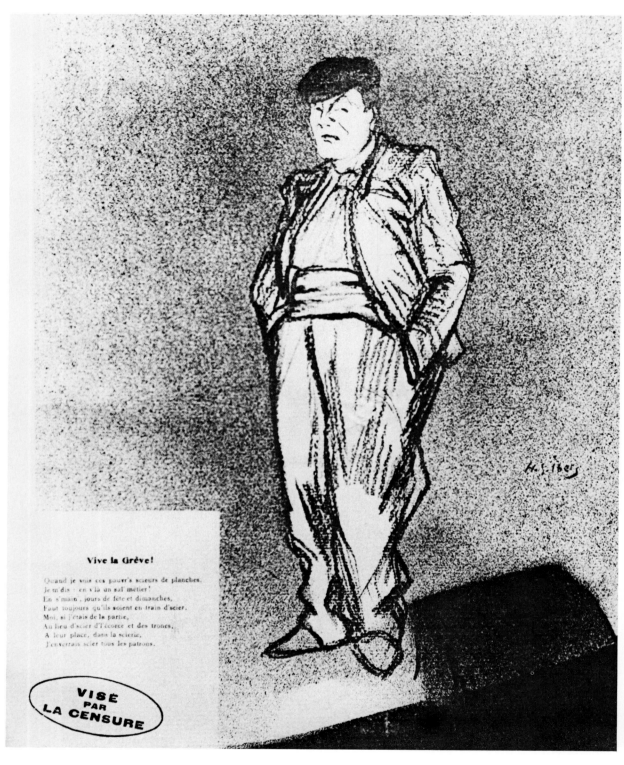

Socialist Genre

J'ai mon panache.

Ma belle mèr' qu'avait liché,
Pas mal de petit vin sucré,
Se trouva mal après l'gruyère.
Pour la fair' revnir, les copains,
Lui tapotaient tous dans les mains,
Moi, j'lui cognais sur la caf'tière,
Sur l'ventr' la grosse caiss' lui frappait,
Tell'ment éméché qu'il croyait
Qu'sur la peau d'sa caiss' il tapait.

VISÉ PAR LA CENSURE

Bacchic Genre

directors forced women performers to make themselves available after the show—for the directors themselves or for select clients. Spectacles such as women's wrestling (borrowed from the fairs) and sometimes fatal daredevil stunts brought further reproach—and eager crowds—to the flourishing establishments.[25]

Such places were also notorious for their excesses of smoke and noise. "People came there to make a row [du potin]," recalled Yvette Guilbert. "People came there to make some chahut"—that is, uproar, rowdiness. So "loud-mouthed singers were hired to cover the everyday noise with their voices."[26] The slang term for the roughest cafés-concerts—*beuglants*, or "bellowing"—captures the objection well. Even in their more deluxe forms, the music halls could arouse a gamut of complex and troubling feelings:

> At first, in places of pleasure [wrote a journalist who knew such places well (1897)] one's sensibilities, softened in the evening after the day's browbeatings, . . . must brusquely receive the brilliance of lights, the fracas or the tickling of musical numbers, the nervous irritation of laughs, the brushing of more or less easy women, violently decked out, musk-scented and there with the intention of pleasing. If one adds to these decorative elements the manner-affecting influence of alcohols drunk and cigarettes burnt, one will easily conceive how sensations are exaggerated and how even the chance visitor can experience the intoxication of contrasts in "places of pleasure," at the price of some weariness. . . . As soon as he enters, he will find himself penetrated with a peculiar and a little painful lucidity. . . . little by little, from this showy tinsel, he will feel a vague and desperate optimism emerging, all enveloped by a delicate and tired ennui, pressing the temples gently like a caress.[27]

Abrasive stimulation, "a vague and desperate optimism," weariness and ennui—a stream of feelings like these, quite unlike those promised by the posters outside, suggests the variety of reactions that even one individual spectator, novice or veteran, could experience.

Clearly, responses and enjoyment could also vary considerably from one spectator to another. In some cases, audience responses seemed to reflect differences in social, economic, and educational backgrounds. At the Folies-

Bergère, Huysmans related, most of the audience laughed at a pantomime in which Pierrots entered a cemetery, noticed a tomb marked "Here lies a person killed in a duel," took fright, and fell over together; most took it to be just "a burlesque skit of funambulists" in the silly, lighthearted tradition of French fairs. But for "more reflective and active minds," it was "a new and charming incarnation of the lugubrious farce, the sinister bouffonnerie" deriving from a special English caricatural aesthetic of "cold madness" and spleen.[28]

In other music halls and the circus, clowns Footit and Chocolat did numerous routines in which the English-accented bully Footit got laughs at the expense of his naive, would-be dandy black partner. One famous skit showed a first-class passenger being helped aboard a train with fulsome courtesy by porter Footit; then a second-class passenger was put aboard curtly; finally Chocolat and his bag were thrown and kicked into the third-class car. Another of their routines had Chocolat playing a game of guessing whether Footit's hand was open or closed behind his back; after several practice games, they play for a hundred sous and Chocolat, of course, loses; when the victim asks to switch roles for a game, Footit refuses, saying: "The good sportsman is the one who always wins." That sort of comedy understandably got fewer laughs with plebeian audiences. The duo had their longest engagement at the high-priced Nouveau Cirque. Meanwhile the Pépinière with its clientele of domestic servants favored Labiche-style vaudeville showing flunkies opening the master's mail, ignoring the ringing service call, spitting on the dishes while drying them, and scrounging cigars from the back of the secretary; to middle-class observers, such "entertainment" amounted to corrupting lessons later put into practice in real life.[29]

Economist Frédéric Passy spoke for the sober middle class in deploring the economic waste, the immorality, and the drunkenness nurtured by the cafés-concerts. D'Avenel, too, expressed objections in economic terms: the food and drink sold for one franc fifty centimes, he complained, was worth only fifteen centimes, and the song lyrics were worth nothing. Differences of taste and status made it difficult, if not impossible, for the classes to unite in leisure or for them to forge a completely shared leisure culture. Political differences played a role, too, though less often mentioned; in worker cabarets, songs about the Paris Commune and May Day, for example, were

CHAMPS-ÉLYSÉES
Jardin de Paris
DIRECTEUR CH. ZIDLER
Spectacle Concert
FETE DE NUIT BAL
Les MARDIS, MERCREDIS, VENDREDIS & SAMEDIS
Imp. CHAIX. (Ateliers Chéret) 20, Rue Bergère Paris

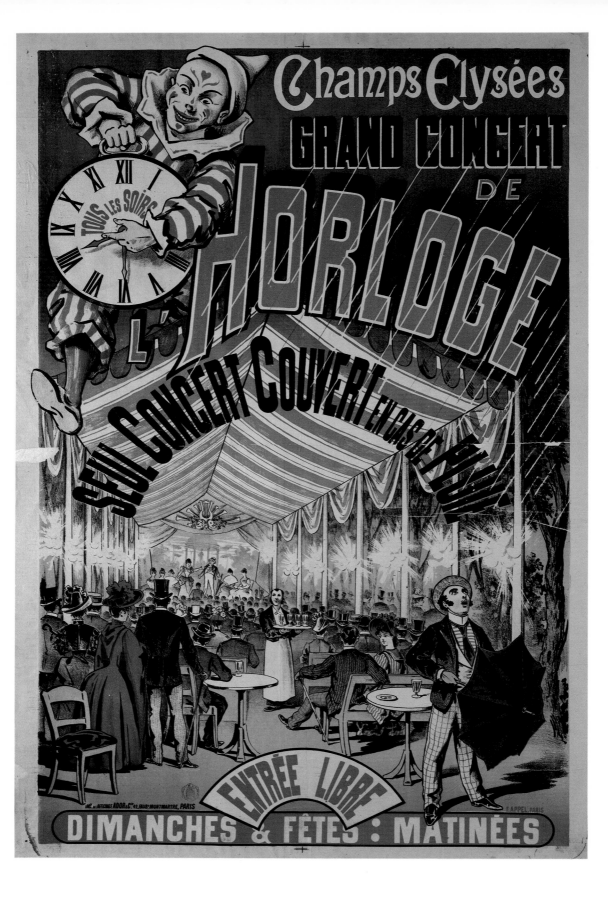

often favorites, but they were hardly amusement to the large part of French society wanting order above all.[30]

THE ROLE OF GOVERNMENT

The government gave force to bourgeois sensibilities by censoring songs and plays that were too politically threatening or too racy. In the early 1880s authorities stepped in to prohibit billiard playing in cafés—ostensibly to keep youth away from places of prostitution. They also tried to stamp out illegal gambling, whether on lotto or bookmaker betting. After prominent bourgeois residents and politicians denounced the uncleanliness and noise of fêtes foraines in Paris, governmental repression went into effect there, too. In 1893, for example, the mayor of Neuilly announced ordinances prohibiting the "throwing and selling of confetti and spirals, . . . exhibits having an immoral or repugnant character, games of chance, . . . pigeon shoots, the use of percussion caps or firecrackers placed under the wheels of bicycle

In contrast to the usual poster full of glad and glamorous people, Toulouse-Lautrec shows us an unamused woman spectator watching a comic singer who appears to be Polin. (Courtesy of the Boston Public Library, Print Department, Wiggin Collection)

Jardin de Paris—a poster by Chéret. In its most successful period—the late 1880s and 1890s—the Jardin de Paris was a summer branch of the Moulin Rouge, the two establishments having the same owners. As Chéret's poster promised, the place offered a wide variety of entertainments: sketches, dance acts, songs, night festivities, and a ball. (Collection du Musée de la Publicité, Paris)

In the 1880s and early 1890s, the Horloge boasted of being "the only café-concert covered in case of rain" in its competition with other summertime outdoor spots near the Champs-Élysées. But its tentlike covering offered protection that was primitive compared to the new movable roof at the Ambassadeurs (1893). (Collection du Musée de la Publicité, Paris) merry-go-rounds, the sale of all objects that are indecent or of a nature to disturb public order." At the same time an attack on nudity and stripteases was led by Senator Bérenger, with much less success. The government did succeed in banning bullfights in Paris after 1890, but in the provinces the "sport" and the battle went on. As late as 1934 as far north as Brest, bull runs drew large crowds for two days in spite of the opposition of the clergy, the League for the Protection of Horses, the Society for the Protection of Animals, and the International Antivivisectionist League.[31]

All in all, government efforts to bridge the gap between elites and common people were small and ineffective. The republican leaders' strongest desire was to uplift the people morally—that is, to inculcate bourgeois morality in them—and to secure them ideologically to republicanism. The leaders' primary faith was in education—from above. Apart from July 14 observances, they showed no interest in encouraging popular recreations created by the people themselves. They made no effort to learn from the common people and to adopt proven popular forms. They placed their greatest hope in the leisure sphere on fêtes, which were somehow to erase class antagonisms and, as though by magic, to carry a happy unity over into daily life.

On close examination, even government efforts to broaden access to festivities appear half-hearted and ineffectual, as critics from the Left tirelessly charged. For the 1889 world's fair, the leaders at last responded to criticism by offering one day with no admission charge, but only at the very end of the season,[32] and the saving of admission was not enough to make it worthwhile for a worker to pass up a day's pay. Republican leaders liked to contrast themselves with monarchists and Bonapartists who were afraid of contact with the masses, but republicans persisted in putting on ceremonies and fêtes restricted to the leading few. Though these few may have been democratically elected, they were nonetheless an elite treated as privileged.

In France before the First World War, government was still the only overarching power that could bring together the deeply estranged classes. Commercial enterprises such as cafés-concerts were still too localized and, like newspapers, tended to serve fragmented clienteles of different social niches and geographic areas. The early cinema had similar limitations. Although the state did make great strides toward providing a unifying national culture through the public schools, in the domain of amusements the state's failings compounded its other great failure to improve the work life of the French laboring classes. Workers probably suffered in their "free time" much more than most people knew. It was in leisure and in consumption, sociologist Maurice Halbwachs pointed out in 1912, that workers most keenly had the sense that their life was "painful and abnormal" by comparison with surrounding social life.[33] Rather than amusements drugging them into forgetfulness of pain and inequalities, a night out exposed them to the abrasive view of the better-off so conspicuously living it up as they could not.

Through the period a chorus of critics repeated the refrain that a truly democratic culture with good entertainments and fêtes was still to be achieved. At the time of the Dreyfus crisis, new efforts to unite the people and the cultural elite—through a new popular theater, "popular universities," and new democratic fêtes—briefly seemed promising, but none grew to national proportions. Unfortunately, the initiators of those efforts failed to address squarely the problem of how to encourage democratic control and popular creativity. It was an important step to give more people access to entertainments, which then became "popular," but the truly thorny problem was how to ensure that the people created or shared in creating their collective leisure activities. The new big-business forms of entertainment were certainly not making the problem easier to resolve; on the contrary, music halls, circuses, and fêtes foraines were growing larger and more expensive to produce—and more and more in the control of a few. In music hall songs and the new cinema as well, the dominance of Paris grew unchecked, with the same result.

It was easier to overlook the second problem than to grapple with it. The officials of the Third Republic were middle-class men who engineered what they conceived to be festivities for the good of the people, just as bourgeois populists such as Michelet had sought to provide popular literature for the people. In moments of truth Michelet admitted to being less than fully in touch with the people and to creating less than popular writing. Officials of the government, never so self-critical publicly, preferred, like d'Avenel, to hold to the official rhetoric—maintaining that a flourishing democracy was bearing fruits for all.

5
The World's Fairs
and Other Extravaganzas

[See page 123 for full photograph.]

At eleven-year intervals through 1900, Paris, mecca of pleasures, multiplied its attractions a hundredfold by hosting "universal expositions" and inviting the world to enjoy them. What English-speaking peoples called world's fairs the French found it natural to call fêtes, connoting a fuller emotional experience of joy and celebration. Official rhetoric dubbed them festivals of work, peace, and progress. Officially they were educational rites, encyclopedically instructive and morally improving. Since the first one in 1798, their purpose was to serve industry and commerce through serious displays of products and national accomplishments in official pavilions from scores of countries and firms. But the two expositions at the end of the nineteenth century were also fun fairs; journalists, guidebook writers, memorialists, and the observable behavior of crowds made that clear. Vying with the official pavilions were commercial entertainments such as panoramas and cafés-concerts inside and around the fairgrounds. There were also periodic fêtes and concerts organized by the fairs' officials to attract larger crowds and to keep them coming back. In the face of such variety, visitors had to choose, and their choices and reactions can help us clarify what amused and attracted and what did not.

DE PLUS EN PLUS FORT!—Nicolet, eighteenth-century impresario

In size and attendance, no festivals of the nineteenth century came close to rivaling the world's fairs. No entertainment district in any city offered so much. No other tourist attraction drew so many tourists. Even the Third Republic's first fair, held in 1878 before the regime was firmly established, outdid the exhibits of the Second Empire in size, entertainments (though limited compared to later efforts), and number of visitors. But of the next fair, the *Bulletin officiel* could justly exclaim, "The characteristic of the current Exposition is 'the colossal.' " More objective witnesses, like memoir writer Lucien Biart, could report in 1889, "There is only one cry: this is the most grandiose, the most dazzling, the most marvelous spectacle ever seen"—superlatives that were commonplace in reporting on the late nineteenth-century fairs. To the sounds of Gypsy orchestras and Spanish mandolins, military bands and Arab tambourines, visitors could delight in a kind of world tour, moving from a Swedish chalet to an Indian palace, feasting their eyes on marble nymphs and satyrs or a Japanese garden. Wandering amid blue cupolas, golden domes and minarets, pagodas and towers of every style, cartoonist and writer Fernand Bac felt himself "reborn to a new world," one filled with the "magic of the new times" by "ingenious sorcerers."[1]

The bigger than ever Exposition of 1889 covered 958,752 square meters, or some 237 acres; that was about 53 acres more than the one in 1878. The official exhibits alone numbered over sixty thousand. Guidebooks allowed that visitors could "see" the exposition in ten or twenty days, a length of time available only to the privileged few. Commercial attractions not emphasized by the guidebooks could take up many additional days.[2]

A reconstructed Bastille at the 1889 fair, for example, was an exposition within the exposition, a cornucopia of amusements piled on in the most eclectic mass-market manner. Customers could not only look at a huge reproduction of the gloomy fortress and the adjacent Rue Saint Antoine, but they could also go inside for banquets in the Hall of Festivities, ride on the montagnes russes or American horses, see "enchanted fountains with colored-light projections," take in music hall acts in a Théâtre des Variétés, watch a pantomime entitled "the escape of a prisoner of the Bastille" (a suspenseful adventure ending with the recapture of the prisoner), look at a panorama of the Church Sainte Marie in 1789, and stroll and shop in old-looking cabarets, restaurants, and boutiques with merchants in historic costume. In addition, the public was periodically lured there by special events such as a balloon ascension and a Bacchus festival with a parade of a hundred peasants in costume, trumpeting dragoons, a knights' carousel, martial bands, and street singers and acrobats. This amusement-park Bastille turned the historic symbol of bitter conflict into fun and considerable profit; it amassed receipts of 538,748 francs in 1888 and 529,023 francs in 1889—twice the amount reported by the Cirque Fernando and the Ambassadeurs.[3]

On the opposite side of the fair, outside the gates on the Avenue Rapp, the *Pays des Fées* (fairyland) appealed to childhood fantasies with sets out of "Little Red Riding Hood," "Sleeping Beauty," and other tales. Here, too, the entrepreneurial imagination cast its net broadly. Inside the giant belly of the Blue Elephant from "The One Thousand and One Nights," grown up children watched the exotic dancing of "la belle Féridjé." Or they could ride the inevitable montagnes russes, laugh at themselves in the Hall of Mirrors, shudder at the exhibit of Bluebeard's victims, watch trained dogs and bicycle stunt riding, or hear singers in the café-concert. This storybook amusement park, well advertised by an eye-catching Chéret poster, received favorable press notice and drew good crowds of adults and children. One of many attempts to profit from the extraordinary crowds drawn to the fairgrounds, it lived the same half-year life that the Exposition did, but its Blue Elephant continued to receive visitors after being moved to the garden of the Moulin Rouge, another establishment created to profit indirectly from the Exposition.[4]

These attractions and the pavilions generally attempted to be grandiose and spectacular, but as such they hardly rivaled two structures that dominated the entire festival set. One was the tallest structure in the world, promptly nicknamed "the colossal": the thousand-foot Eiffel Tower. The other was the largest iron-framed building ever constructed: the Galerie des Machines, a sweeping 377 feet wide and 1,378 feet long, covering nearly fifteen acres. Such sights may well have made for "the most grandiose" spectacle, but were they also entertaining?

Undoubtedly immensity could be impressive to sightseers. The Galerie des Machines was a stupendous curiosity to the crowds of 1889, though the sight of the sixteen thousand machines inside disquieted some. "The word *gigantesque* besieges, obsesses you, in the face of the exuberant grandeur of this vessel [that is] so light and clear, in spite of the enormity of its columns and its arches," observed Huysmans; "people go out stupefied and ravished."[5] But no one spoke of the Galerie des Machines as an amusement; it was too closely associated with work and production.

The Esplanade des Invalides became an exotic wonderland during the 1889 world's fair. At left: the Algerian bazaar and the Palais de Tunisie (tallest tower). Just to the right of center: the Pagoda d'Angkir. On the right: the castle tower, the Ministry of War's entry. (Bibliothèque Historique de la Ville de Paris)

In crowds averaging 174,816 a day, people came to the world's fair of 1889 to see and to discover. "Obviously with its picturesque qualities, [the exposition] is extremely attractive to the eyes," remarked journalist Paul Bourde (*La Lecture* 9 [1889], p.337). In the center background is the Central Dome on the Palace of Diverse Industries with the Luminous Fountains in front. The men on the right are looking up at "the colossal": the Eiffel Tower. (Bibliothèque Historique de la Ville de Paris)

People of modest means brought their food and drink with them to the world's fair of 1889 and spent the whole day there for less than the cost of an evening at a theater or music hall. (Bibliothèque Historique de la Ville de Paris)

The Eiffel Tower, however, was a different matter. Unlike so much in the official displays, it was not simply to be looked at but also to be played on. It delighted visitors with a 120–kilometer view from its upper reaches. It gave the pleasure of mountain climbing, but more quickly and decisively and without interfering obstacles. It gave people unusual physical sensations on the rapid elevators, as the montagnes russes were doing on a smaller scale. In the 1878 and earlier fairs, "captive balloons" had provided similar views and thrills. But the big balloon of 1878—le Grand Captif—could hold only fifty people and permitted little activity aboard; the Eiffel Tower could take on ten thousand at once and give them a wide choice of activities. The tower was an unusual new place for drinking and dining with its many bars and restaurants. It gave rise to new play such as dropping little balloons containing notes asking the finder to return them to a given address—play promising surprises and new human encounter. As a popular attraction, the tower was an unquestionable success. Although it was never officially class-ified as an amusement, visitors flocked to it as to no official showpiece. By

1889: a reconstructed Bastille—as an amuse-ment park, a panorama (right), and visitors on a fun ride. (Bibliothèque Historique de la Ville de Paris)

Just outside the reconstructed Bastille in 1889, well-dressed riders of wooden horses turned their back on the powerful political symbol and blithely whizzed down a roller-coaster track, at the same time providing a spectacle for others. (Bibliothèque Historique de la Ville de Paris)

the end of the 1889 Exposition more than 3.5 million people had paid about 6 million francs to ascend it.[6]

The fair's official festivities also reached prodigious proportions. To commemorate the centennial of Bastille Day, 2,000 musicians went to the Champ de Mars with banners of corporations and districts of 1790 to give a "concert gigantesque." On August 4, after the splendid flourish of releasing thirty thousand pigeons in the Tuileries Garden, 1,200 musicians played for an audience of twenty thousand.[7] Colossal ensembles of choirs and bands became the norm in state festivals at the end of the century. Playing in the open air without loudspeakers, the amassed legions boomed out the Marseillaise with ground-shaking fortissimos. In the centennial banquet of mayors, too, as we have seen, the 1889 fair attained the gigantic. Driven by an optimistic competitiveness, the impresarios of the fin-de-siècle fairs pushed for the ever more impressive, convinced that the past must be continually outdone.

The Universal Exposition of 1900, of course, was still larger than its predecessor. Extending over 277 acres, not even counting the Vincennes annex, it offered about 40 more acres of sights. Visitors could still play on

The 1889 world's fair exhibit of E. Mercier Champagne of Epernay, which boasted of having the largest *caves* of the Champagne region. The firm displayed its objects of pleasure and commerce—"the nectar of the Marne"—on a typically spectacular scale. One of some fifty thousand exhibits at the fair, "the largest cask in the world" held wine enough to fill 200,000 bottles and weighed 20,000 kilograms, the firm announced. (Bibliothèque Historique de la Ville de Paris)

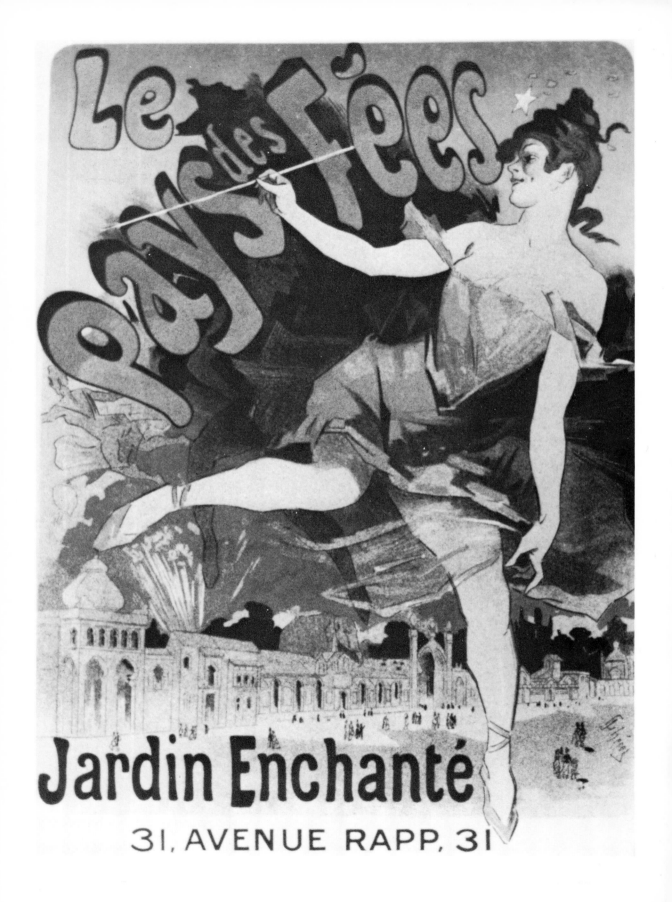

the giant iron tower, and about a million did. Though the 1900 fair did not outdo that crowning fixture, it did add a new purely commercial toy of a novel gigantism: a 106–meter-high Ferris wheel that could carry 1,600 passengers at once; the Grande Roue of Paris was "the most gigantic ever built," boasted the advertising. The other colossal structure of 1889, the Galerie des Machines, this time had its interior dominated by a giant screen twenty-one meters by sixteen meters, on which a projector with a 150-amp lighthouse beacon showed *moving* pictures to audiences of up to 25,000. And this time, when a nation's mayors sat down together for a "pantagruelic feast," it was shared by a record-setting 20,777. The festivities and entertainments not only were bigger but seemed proportionately a greater part of the fair's attractions.[8] More than ever before, the whole fair was a vast feast of amusements.

ATTRACTIONS OF ABUNDANCE AND LIGHT

A number of leading commercial entertainments were taking the same course toward gigantism as the fairs. At the Hippodrome de l'Avenue de

The Enchanted Garden, an ancestor of Disney's fantasylands, was an attraction near the 1889 world's fair. Chéret, typically, directed his advertising imagery to adult males, though most of the amusement park centered on childhood stories. (Musée Carnavalet, Paris)

l'Alma, a show larger than any circus of its time, crowds favored such grand spectacles as thundering deer hunts, chivalric tournaments, races with hundreds of stampeding horses, epic battles of Russians against Cossacks or Vercingetorix against Romans, and Nero at the burning of Rome—with a cast of six hundred in action at once. The 1900 Exposition catered to this taste by presenting a mock naval war with thirty battleships bombarding and burning a maritime city.

American entertainments were showing the French new possibilities. In 1889, heralded by "gigantic" posters covering the city's walls, Buffalo Bill brought his Wild West show to Neuilly, where he succeeded in competing with the Exposition and other Paris attractions. His 200 cowboys, cowgirls, and Indians, 150 horses, and 20 buffaloes staged exciting chases and fights of "the Far West," a French fascination that movies would feed after 1900. In the world of the circus, a new magnitude was inaugurated by the American Barnum and Bailey circus on its five-year European tour at the turn of the century. In its Paris stint from November 1901 to late March 1902, "the greatest show on earth" introduced the French to the three-ring, jumbo circus. In fact, it introduced three rings, two platforms, and an encompassing track, all offering simultaneous spectacles. Barnumesque advertisements blared out the details of the new scale: "100 different circus and hippodrome numbers, all grandiose and sensational over 3 arenas, stages, 1 horse stadium and in the air—1,000 men, women, children, horses, wagons, etc. . . . 3 elephant troupes, 2 camel troupes, 500 horses, etc. 350 artists appear at the same time." A few days later another newspaper notice enumerated the total differently but no less impressively: "2 menageries, 3 circuses, one hippodrome, 1 museum of living phenomena, an aerial gymnasium, 2 Olympic stages, 1 horse stadium." Without any numbers given and without even a dream-evoking "etc.," the company of clowns was billed simply as "the international Congress of the kings of craziness—the most colossal assembly of jokers and amusers ever seen."[9]

French journalists did not question the figures and in many cases testified to the success of the grandeur. A reporter for *Le Temps* observed that

> people were particularly fond of the Queen of Sheba's procession, the
> 18 elephants, the monkey and pig fights, the 70 trained horses. . . . But

people are especially struck by the enormity of all the human and animal personnel: 900 artists, 450 horses, 750 diverse wild animals, etc. It's truly, as the posters say, "the greatest show on earth" [quoted in English]—la plus grande exhibition du monde.[10]

Gate receipts show that the American formula did work well with Paris audiences: the Barnum circus even during only a brief engagement took in more than twice the amount garnered by any other circus in 1902 (1,642,566 francs 50 centimes).

Although French circuses did not take up the American challenge by adopting three rings in the years before the First World War, they did increase the number of wild animals and the variety of the acts. Whereas in 1900 it was customary to see twenty or thirty animals in a circus in France, a decade later sixty was commonplace.[11] It may be true, as circus historian Roland Auguet has argued, that fifty lions performing in an arena are no better than thirty—if one is primarily considering the skill of the trained animals. But the larger number no doubt was more impressive; the sight alone of such numbers of exotic animals was more unusual and the danger to the human performers was multiplied—both adding to audience excitement.

To lift people out of the commonplace, to give them a taste of the extraordinary was fundamentally what the circus promised and generally delivered. Like the world's fairs, the circus did it by flaunting an excess betokening wealth and power, an excess that could be intoxicatingly attractive to people accustomed to humble surroundings. It was altogether a wondrous overflowing of human skill and daring, the poetry and eroticism of lithe strong bodies in movement, animal cleverness and grace—a feast of color, sounds, and smells. Breaking with normal constraints of the economical and moderate was one characteristic of every festive time and place, and in that sense the circus was an almost permanent fête, remarkable even in a period when rival entertainments were regularly and flamboyantly surpassing traditional limits. Like the world's fairs, the circus brought ordinary people close to a dream world of abundance and miracle.

So did another form of extravaganza pioneered in the belle époque: the new technology of brilliant multicolored electric lights, supplement to that older crowd pleaser, fireworks. The Eiffel Tower was at no time so entrancing as when it was *embrasé*—suddenly set ablaze with lights all the way to the top where a tricolor beacon launched a bright beam over half the city. Electrical magic also made possible a new dazzler combining color and water: the "luminous fountains" that made their triumphant debut in 1889 along with the Tower. One such fountain built on the popular theme of "France Lighting the World" consisted of allegorical figures transformed at night by three hundred sprays of lighted water showering over them first like golden rain and then like a stream of rubies and emeralds.[12]

At the 1900 fair the favorite light show came from the sparkling Palace of Electricity whose ornate white facade served at night as a starry backdrop for a rainbow-brilliant thirty-foot-wide sheet of water cascading ninety-five feet in a Château d'Eau. Other wonderland sights were Venetian fêtes with illuminated boats on the Seine and the fête of flower-covered automobiles carrying Japanese lanterns. In the music halls of the end of the century, revues were spectacularly lighted stagefuls of color and movement with lavish costumes frequently changed in the course of the shows. At the Folies-Bergère, spotlights played on the radiantly swirling robes of American-born dancer Loïe Fuller with an entrancing effect that made her a star of the era. From 1898 on, the Salon de l'Automobile, a trade fair showing off the newest cars with similar light magic, drew awestruck praise and crowds up to forty thousand a day.[13] *Féerique* was the way French observers described such sights—dreamlike, fairyland brilliant, like an enchanting world of "The One Thousand and One Nights."

The public's fascination with lights is readily understandable when one recalls how much a rarity they still were, a novelty, indeed a luxury in everyday life at the turn of the century. But a more general explanation for the appeal of spectacular lighting and gigantism might be that the French suffered from an ennui that was particularly acute in the late nineteenth century. This was an interpretation of the times favored by contemporaries, who commonly attributed the malaise to skepticism that eroded away a sense of cosmic purposefulness and sapped dedication to worthwhile pursuits like work as well as traditional pastimes.[14] The prominence of so much pleasure seeking in Paris may also have contributed to the problem. The deluge of publicity and greater awareness of entertainments perhaps only increased the ennui of people who did not partake of much of what they now knew was going on—or who found the ballyhooed amusements disappointing. In any case, to explain turn-of-the-century sensationalism by invoking the ennui factor does not take into account centuries of the same popular preferences, having in common a deeply rooted fascination for the unusual and the spectacular. Long before the fin de siècle, well before Barnum and his famous "freak" shows, fairs drew crowds with exhibits of five-footed sheep and fat women called *colosses*, and civic festivals had entranced crowds with fireworks. Grandeur had long amused, just as trained fleas and dwarfs did—as unusual curiosities. Battles and disasters also fascinated the fin-de-siècle public. But if they were the entertainment choice of bored people, it must be added that they too had long been favorites. As a *Courrier français* poet wrote sardonically:

> It is well known that the Parisian
> Loves the Ugly, the Prussian,
> The Abominable,
> All Monstrosities.
> That his taste for obscenities
> Is impeccable.
> So in the panoramas
> Or in the diaramas
> For ten centimes
> You can buy yourself horrors,
> Assassins, emperors,
> Heaps of Crimes.

In the country and small towns, it took even less for an event to attract attention as extraordinary. Commercial entertainment came each year in the form of a visiting circus with only a few horses and a thirty-meter "umbrella" tent. In rural France, watching a train go by was popular entertainment.[15] So was almost anything that was unusual and not costly to see. What was new at the end of the century was that a rising level of prosperity and new technology made possible a new magnitude of spectacles, new forms of the extraordinary and sensational, traditionally the stock-in-trade of popular entertainment.

LA FOLIE DES GRANDEURS

Already at the 1878 Exposition the visitor confronted an *embarras de richesses*: 190-odd acres of "steam hammers, carding mills, sewing machines, pictures, marble statues, big guns, dolls, colossal looking glasses, pickle bottles, carved bedsteads, embroidered petticoats, China vases, iron safes, anchors of toothpick"—to mention only some of the displays recalled by an English visitor. The effect could be numbing or worse. "I have descried on some thousands of faces, not only French but foreign, among the visitors to the Exhibition, a listless, fagged and bewildered expression," recounted the Englishman. "Three hours of contemplation [of clocks, paintings, statues, tapestries, etc.] . . . to say nothing of the flying glances which we have cast while hurrying through the cases full of boots and shoes, riding-habits, combs and brushes, and ladies and gentlemen's underclothing, are apt to induce a state of mind far exceeding dejection and trenching on downright exasperation."[16]

As if 52,835 exhibitors were not enough, the Exposition of 1889 increased the number by almost 9,000. "At bottom, it's too big, too immense, there are too many things and one's attention, diffused, attaches itself to nothing," complained crusty Edmond de Goncourt, who also complained about the crowds' noise and silly busy-ness. "I have just seen so many plows, so many rollers, so many reaping machines, that my brain, I admit with a little shame, is weakened," confessed a French journalist. "It seems to me that they are reaping under my left eyebrow, shelling corn under my right eyebrow, and driving a harrow in my stomach." The journalist Lucien Biart also conveyed a sense of the overwhelming scale in quantitative terms: a visitor who walked all the aisles of the Galerie des Machines, including the periphery of the second floor, would have covered six kilometers, he calculated. Even the semiofficial report of Emile Monod admitted that the "admirable exhibitions" of motors, surgical tools, and other specialized objects "remained dead letters for many visitors."[17]

The problem of "wearisome proportions" that the Englishman identified in 1878 only grew worse in 1900 with twenty thousand more exhibitors and forty acres more than in 1889. The fair's organizers had added an electric moving sidewalk to the transportation facilities that had proved inadequate before, but in the end people had to walk a great deal to see the sights. "At 3 o'clock in the afternoon," observed André Hallays, "all the walkers of the Exposition already looked dead-tired." With a torpid pace, people lumbered through gallery after gallery without giving a minute's attention to anything in particular—a "dismal promenade," concluded Hallays. They "passed abruptly from Scandinavia to the Far East, crossed the Retrospective of Heating to come upon fourgons of artillery, discovered the bathtub of Marat in the Public Assistance exhibit . . . and baby rattles in the Retrospective of Metallurgy." The unexpected was amusing, Hallays found, but the overall effect was incoherent and tiring.[18]

While officials of the fairs tried to stress themes such as work and peace, critics lambasted the efforts as ever bigger Towers of Babel. The 1900 fair was most heavily criticized for having no theme, focus, or ideal. The chief administrator, Alfred Picard, called it "the balance-sheet of the century," but it offered no neat or clear tallying; it was a bewildering hodgepodge, a colossus of Victorian bric-a-brac and runaway eclecticism. Great size had become a substitute for creative changes. In the 1900 fair, contributors resorted to the hackneyed monumental style and rococo structures of staff and stucco, profuse with garlands, flowers, and allegorical statuary.[19] The decor on which so much effort was spent could not produce festivity or even gaiety; yet more than ever these were what millions of visitors sought at the fair.

Bigger spectacles did not necessarily provide audiences with fuller effects. The shadow theaters that enjoyed a renaissance at the end of the century charmed by evoking grand scenes with minimal means. At mammoth concerts, pantomimes, and pageants, the view from the more remote seats or standing places was less than satisfactory. At the 1900 Exposition ten thousand people were herded into the Salle des Fêtes to see some twenty Opera dancers who were "lost in this immensity," observed Hallays.[20] Grandeur also reduced the audience's interaction with performers. In the cabaret and music hall, audiences joined in singing familiar choruses and cried out to performers, who responded directly and spontaneously. In the circus, a close rapport between audience and performers was made possible by the seating around an open ring without barriers of footlights or railings; other spectators forming a backdrop to the show became a part of the spectacle. At the fêtes

The ceramics exhibit hall at the 1889 fair in its
vast dull stillness is a reminder of how unenter-
taining much of the Universal Exposition was.
(Bibliothèque Historique de la Ville de Paris)

1889: obvious fatigue amidst the "most grandiose" spectacle of the period. (Bibliothèque Historique de la Ville de Paris)

foraines, members of the audience participated in the act as the magician's volunteer, as a target for balls thrown by others, or as one having his fortune told. The give-and-take of banter and cries along the sideshow platforms formed part of the festive atmosphere in which customers played.

In the best of fêtes, it was long noted, participants and actors became one and the same, together forming the spectacle and sharing strong emotions. That sort of involvement could happen in huge amphitheaters or fields, as it did during the 1789 revolution, but not if the emphasis on decor and staged spectacle dispersed people over hundreds of acres and reduced their part to passive attendance. In their stress on immensity and technological novelty, the fairs were exercises in a quixotic quest for the old festive alchemy, which was never produced by strictly external stimulations. The "progress" celebrated there was too disparate, scattered, and remote from everyday life to unify and to stir the ungrouped visitors as fêtes could for a crowd. The fairs were, as historians have often noted, successful distractions, politically beneficial to the beleaguered Third Republic, but they fell far short of being successful festivals.

THE ALLURE OF EXOTICA AND HISTORY

If gigantism had its limits as a crowd pleaser and could not assure festivity, the fairs nonetheless succeeded as giant variety shows—at least for those willing to sample without dutifully trying to see everything. Among the most consistent big-crowd draws from the 1878 Exposition on were the displays of exotic people, costumes, dwellings, and dances. Around tropical huts of the Okandas and the Alfurs, the Loango village and the Kabyle tents, curious Westerners never stopped gathering. From Tunisian markets and Moorish cafés, they streamed by the tents of Algerian desert tribes, Tonkin huts, and Angkor pagodas. This colonial and extra-European part of the Exposition was considered the less serious part to officials, as though the Empire and the non-European world were playthings, remote and curious, and little more. Historians have often cited the popularity of such exhibits as evidence of French nationalist pride in the new Empire being created in Africa and Southeast Asia. But it is clear that exotica coming from other places were just as popular; the *danse du ventre* from Egypt and the *corridas*, or bullfights from Spain were so popular in 1889 that they spread through Paris and outlasted the Exposition as commercial entertainment.[21]

In 1889 no entertainment produced more of a sensation than the Rue du Caire—with its Arab cafés, authentic old houses, *souks* (markets), and especially its *danse du ventre*. People of all social levels flocked there. Edmond de Goncourt, who scoffed at the luminous fountains as "childish trifles" and disdainfully remarked on the "coarse bestial joy" of the crowds, went to the fair more than a dozen times and wrote in his journal about nothing more than the belly dances. He would have preferred to see the dance performed by a nude woman, he admitted, so that he could see the moving of the woman's organs and the changes in the belly area, but he found enough interest in the semiclothed woman to keep him watching. What he found most extraordinary was one dancer who "when people applauded her, with her body completely immobile, seemed to make little salutations with her navel." The dancer, however, was not the sole spectacle. Goncourt also found amusement in noticing how a clergyman looked aside when the movements became too suggestive. Some found the *almeys* monotonous, mechanical, and coarse, as writer Paul Marguerite did, but clearly many were fascinated, responding variously to the dance's sensuality, exoticism, or graceful movement. The dance became a rage—introduced not only into Paris music halls but into private homes as well. After hearing about a woman practicing the dance in her bedroom, Goncourt admitted to being "persuaded that three-fourths of the women in Paris were secretly working on the dance."[22]

At the 1900 fair the three entertainments that earned the most in admissions were the Swiss Village, which brought in 2,169,000 francs; the Palais du Costume, 1,320,000 francs; and "Old Paris," 1,036,000 francs. The Swiss Village, also the largest of the fair's attractions, was a twenty-one-thousand-square-meter land of artificial mountains, fir forests, Alpine torrents, chalets, pastures with herds of cows and sheep, an auberge on a little lake, and a chapel of William Tell. It offered not only the illusion of faraway natural beauty but also the performances of folk dancers, shepherds wrestling, and weavers, lacemakers, wood sculptors, and other artisans in traditional costume demonstrating their crafts. Three hundred men and women peasants played their roles in a mountain village. The Palais du Costume capitalized on interest in feminine beauty and historic fashions; on

display there were lace, velours, and silk dresses of centuries past modeled by wax figures representing personages of the Empire, Directory, Louis XV, and other periods. "Old Paris" took customers even further back into the past. In the reconstructed city designed by caricaturist and author Albert Robida, visitors wandered in narrow medieval streets ("chatnoir-esque," Hallays called them) full of picturesque cabarets and shops and churches with belfreys and ogives galore. A cast of musket-carrying soldiers, heralds of arms, mystery players, and merchants and craftsmen in historic costume completed the set.[23] None of these leading attractions depended on overwhelming grandeur or amazing new technology. None gave glimpses of the future, as star attractions of later world's fairs would. Rather, all appealed to a nostalgic interest in traditional, distant settings and ways of life.

Cinema, the most important technological innovation in entertainment, was another means of satisfying that interest. By 1900 it had already outgrown its initial appeal as pure novelty; it could no longer amuse the many simply by showing banal scenes of workers leaving a factory, or a train entering a station, or a gardener watering with a hose (in the first version only his

The serious and thorough report by Emile Monod acknowledged that the rue du Caire "certainly constituted one of the most powerful attractions and one of the greatest successes of the Exposition" of 1889. Exotic dancing was one new entertainment introduced at the Paris universal expositions. Pictured is the Almeh Aïousché in the Café Egyptien. (Musée Carnavalet, Paris)

"Old Paris" at the 1900 fair was designed by former Chat Noir artist Robida. Here it is viewed from the Pont de l'Alma. (Bibliothèque Historique de la Ville de Paris)

[Illustrations between pages 144 and 145]

Jules Chéret's poster of 1889 for the Moulin Rouge. As the poster announces, the new dance hall was open every evening and during the day on Sunday, but it reserved its *grandes fêtes* for Wednesday and Saturday, when the greatest number of people were free for a night out. (Collection du Musée de la Publicité, Paris)

Poster for Peugeot bicycles by E. Vulliemin. On the eve of the First World War, the bicycle, already well established as exciting sport, was being promoted for its potential in modern war. The Peugeot company presented its latest sleek product here in favorable association with the most prestigious of military traditions, the noble warrior on horseback. (Collection du Musée de la Publicité, Paris)

At the 1900 Exposition, no attraction took in more money in admissions than the huge theme park called "The Swiss Village," featuring pastoral scenery and village life transported right into Paris. (Bibliothèque Historique de la Ville de Paris) garden, not himself). Cinema was so well established in Paris outside the Exposition that its presence in national pavilions and numerous attractions was in itself unremarkable. It drew crowds above all by showing remote places just as the Swiss Village, the panoramas, and the colonial exhibits did. At the Cinéorama, for example, spectators stood in a balloon nacelle and took a soaring movie tour of the world—an Italian carnival, a Spanish bullfight, an open sea, and a vast desert, all projected on ten screens around a polygonal hall.

Even though people could now see moving pictures, panoramas were still big business in 1900: the amount paid in concessions for them represented a figure (201,485.80 francs) five times that paid for theater concessions at the fair. Most of those panoramas appealed to the public's keen taste for travel. Customers paid one- and two-franc admissions to see "Living Pompeii," "Rome," "Vesuvius in Paris," and "Le Tour de Monde"—painted on huge canvases in lifelike detail. Some panoramas even featured canvases that unrolled to give viewers a sense of the trip itself—a train trip from Moscow to Peking, for example, at the Transsiberian attraction. In the Maréorama, viewers stood on a rocking steamboat deck, felt wind blow, and smelled salt air as distant Mediterranean ports became larger and clearer. In brief and concentrated experiences, the panoramas and cinemas alike offered what the Exposition itself did: a tourist's view of distant and immense scenes, full of variety and activity strikingly different from everyday life in Paris 1900. They attested to an "extreme change" in French taste, wrote Louis de Fourcaud in 1889: "finally emancipated from classical influences," people were "seeking the picturesque at all costs."[24]

FEARS OF SURFEIT

Like the cinema, expositions could not appeal as novelties indefinitely. Already at the time of the 1889 fair, organizers had realized that the format was becoming stale and worn-out and the efforts too similar and repetitious. The 1900 fair left most reviewers feeling that the Exposition closing the century was also closing the era of great expositions. As one journalist put it, the 1900 fair "seems to have wanted, by its colossal proportions and by

BAL
du MOULIN ROUGE
PLACE BLANCHE
Tous les Soirs
& DIMANCHE JOUR
GRANDE FÊTE LES MERCREDIS & SAMEDIS
92.13.208 IMP. CHAIX (Ateliers Chéret) 20, Rue Bergère, PARIS.

E. VULLIEMIN.

CYCLES PEUGEOT
VALENTIGNEY - Doubs
REPRÉSENTANT :

IMP.ies LEMERCIER, PARIS.

the immensity of its accumulated efforts, to render vain all similar effort."
Trying like earlier fairs to outdo its predecessors, it had "perhaps too much
inordinate ambition [*trop démesurée*]."[25] The 1900 extravaganza did turn out
to be the last one in the established pattern of eleven-year intervals and the
last before what used to be called the Great War. Afterward the Third
Republic never did succeed in matching its size and drawing power.

Was the amusement-seeking public losing interest in the fairs? Were the
every-eleven-year events suffering from the same over-familiarity and rep-
etitiousness that plagued July 14 festivities in the city? Critics thought so,
but it is more likely that the disheartening postmortems primarily expressed
the doubts of middle-class taxpayers and organizers about the political and
economic profitability of the expositions. The record-setting attendance figures for 1900 certainly suggest continuing public interest; the real question
was whether the interest was in anything more than amusement. After 1900
it was hard to make the case that fairs could be significant teachers of the
masses; it was difficult to argue that a bigger fair would have a more gal-
vanizing effect as a salutary fête, uniting and inspiring the people. What was
clear was that the fairs were becoming mostly colossal fun fairs.

The conservative elites and middle-class republican leaders of France had
always had reservations about that kind of fair. The government that decorated the Salle des Fêtes with scenes of workers working was not one to
continue to buy ever bigger games for the plebs. Not only were the expositions
expensive, wastefully so to some, but they also threatened to be corrupting.
When Jules Claretie reflected on "the colossal American-style exhibitions
and spectacles which leap to the eyes" in 1900—naval battles, immense
processions, giant amphitheaters—he sensed a decadence that bode ill for
the future of the arts, if not for France as a civilization. He was far from
alone. Would the workers go back to work after such fun? What would take
the place of "the enchantments of each evening [at the fair]?" worried the
Vicomte de Vogüé in 1889. "How would a crowd intoxicated by those
Neronian sensations be rehabituated to normal ennui?" In the privacy of his
personal journal, Edmond de Goncourt expressed the same worry that de
Vogüé shared with the readers of the *Revue des deux mondes*. Goncourt even
went on to make explicit a final fear that de Vogüé had left unmentioned:

While looking at the Exposition and on everyone's face the coarse bestial joy which twists up even the gray moustaches of old women, I think of the ennui of next year for these people who have taken the habit of partying, and I fear that from this ennui there will emerge a revolution.[26]

Après la fête, on gratte tête, warned the old folk saying, summing up age-old experience. At the end of the century, elites had more specific historical reasons for fearing too much of a national good time. Those who remembered, as de Vogüé did, how similar intoxication at the Exposition of 1867 had been followed by the "great sorrow" of 1870–71 watched later revels of Paris-Babylon with dread. "Clamour about pleasure" could be a sign of catastrophe to come. The apprehension even touched foreigners such as Belgian writer Eugène Demolder, who described the 1889 Exposition as a *"branle-bas de joie* [a joyous commotion or hoedown] . . . above the black and unsoundable gulf where our times seem to descend—a dizziness, a drunkenness before the probable cataclysm of wars and revolutions."[27] The people's "joyous hoe-down" could elicit not only reactions of contempt and alarms about deca-dence but also presaging fears of twentieth-century cataclysms. In the light of such anxieties, it appears that the expositions, as entertainments, were *too* successful.

6

The Rhythms of Modern Life

Footit, an English bully with a strong English accent, and Chocolat, a Cuban-born dandy and inveterate victim, were star clowns at the Nouveau Cirque in the late nineteenth century. In their pantomime of 1888 pictured here, the laughs as usual came at Chocolat's expense, this time as he attempted to take part in his own wedding. The clowns never missed an opportunity to fall into the pool in the middle of the circus arena or to push others in.

When the Barnum and Bailey circus burst onto the Paris scene in the winter of 1901–02, it introduced the French not just to brassy American advertising and unprecedented enormity but also to a new-style pacing. In three rings and two platforms, the acts pressed on nonstop. "Attention is never relaxed or stopped on a detail," complained a reviewer for the *Revue bleue*. For two and one-half hours, "unrelenting, merciless, the band continues with its noisy and sad refrain." The circus of the New World was "a vast machination, an American, gargantuan, indigestible distraction," summed up the critic.[1] Appropriately, that "vast machination" played in the Galerie des Machines, left over from the 1889 fair.

A parody presented at the Cirque Molier expressed a similar judgment. In the pantomime "Barnum Express," the American impresario arrives in Paris to find that he has to wait some time for the next express train. Heralded by an *auguste* and a blaring band of twenty-five bizarrely costumed musicians, he goes to his confrere Molier and asks him to present the attractions of the French circus—rapidly, of course. Molier agrees and blows his whistle to begin. The show proceeds frenetically, the amateurs going through their routines at comically high speed. Impressed, Barnum proffers a large sum to buy the entire circus and merrily leads away the parade of about eighty French circus stars.[2]

Certainly no one in France could mistake Barnum's show for anything seen in Paris's three permanent circuses or in the small traveling circuses in the provinces. Traditional French circuses were paced leisurely to allow concentration on the central attraction: highly trained horses mounted by attractive young women. The horses showed off an intricate choreography and served as dashing platforms for the acrobatics of their glamorous riders. As the Joanne guide to Paris made clear, circuses were above all *spectacles équestres*. With the equine emphasis the traditional French circus enjoyed a social prestige and dignity rooted in the ancient association of horsemanship and nobility. In the second half of the century, however, that supremacy of the horse was fading in big-city circuses, which played to socially diverse audiences no longer enthralled by the prestige of *haute école* and dressage. Clowns came to play a larger role, filling time between animal acts and in some cases becoming main attractions in their own right. Acrobats and trapeze artists and lion acts also took on increased importance.[3] But the result still did not approach the continuous and multiple razzle-dazzle of the American circus.

In work, too, the Americans were bringing a new rhythm to the Old World. In the decade after the Barnum and Bailey circus tour, the "scientific management" techniques of engineer Frederick Winslow Taylor began to gain some French acceptance. Industrial magnates Louis Renault and Marius Berliet led the way in importing Taylor's methods for steadier, mechanical pacing of workers' movements. In 1912 Taylor's *Principles of Scientific Management* was translated into French and seven thousand copies were printed. Taylorism did not change the work life of many Frenchmen before the First

Seurat, *The Circus*, 1890–91. In his last and unfinished painting, Seurat featured the leading attractions of the traditional, almost intimate, one-ring circus (here Montmartre's Cirque Fernando) and depicted spectators of various social ranks and moods—with ennui and distraction as evident as delight. (Cliché des Musées Nationaux, Paris)

World War, but as an apparently successful and "scientific" American system, it was important because it promised to carry forward processes already under way, stirring employers' hopes and labor leaders' anger. Through the nineteenth century, French industrialists had been imposing tighter, more extensive regulations on workers, and since the 1880s French engineers had been anticipating Taylor with their own techniques for increasing efficiency and worker discipline. As workers responded with strikes and other resistance, French industrial relations entered a period of crisis.[4] In work as in leisure, a new regularity was challenging the traditional rhythms of irregular, individually set movement.

Already several decades earlier, the new rhythm was triumphing in one of the fastest growing entertainments—the music hall. Whereas in the theater intermissions sometimes took up more time than the play, in the music hall the acts followed one another almost without interruption. A preference for more continuous entertainment was one of the reasons an important part of the public was shifting from theaters to music halls.[5] In fashionable restaurants, too, managers began having violins and singers perform continuously, producing the "ready-made commodity, like endless pasta, music, music, music," Colette remarked in her newspaper column in 1913. "Between two tangos, between a slow waltz and a ragtime dance there is no longer even the normal interval . . . the moment of silence and moral darkness during which the brain and the stomach can collect themselves again." She wanted to shake the managers and make them understand that "there is no such thing as cheerful music, if it is not interrupted, varied and assisted by considerable silences.!"

> Understand that for the most trivial mind gay music which is gay for two, three hours and more is a funereal ordeal! After the first bracing whiplash of bows, after the thousand stinging mandolins, see faces become set, mouths become silent, see anxiety and musical fatalism on people's faces! You are encouraging not appetite but at the very most melancholy drinking, the nocturnal and gloomy habit of drinking champagne on an empty stomach, taken like absinthe without food.[6]

Whether the purpose was to promote steady consumption or, in a manic and misplaced desire to please, to give the customers maximum pleasure, the new entertainment machines were geared to produce "the ready-made commodity" unremittingly.

A number of technological changes also made for more evenness in urban leisure. The construction of movable roofs over the Paris Hippodrome (1878) and the Café des Ambassadeurs (1893) permitted a regularity of performances and audience comfort no matter what the weather. Oller's Piscine Roche-chouart (1885)—Paris's first heated indoor swimming pool—eliminated the dead season for that sport. By the end of the century, further, urban night spots were on any night of the week regularly lighted by electricity and easily accessible by new mass transport—horse-drawn trams and then electric street-cars and by 1900 a subway. Electric lights in store windows extended the pleasures of window shopping into the night. Department store owners sought to extend shopping time into Sunday as well at the turn of the century. In 1880 the Republic had abolished legal sanctions making the seventh day a time of rest; in the anticlerical Third Republic it was to be a business day like any other. Did such changes lead to a more "mechanical" rhythm in leisure life generally?

Viewed from our present perspective, the changes appear far from complete. In the music hall, the continuity of the spectacle in fact allowed a great deal of irregular attention on the part of the audience. Instead of being tied to a precise curtain time, spectators could arrive at any hour they chose. They could watch an act or ignore it and think about business or a love affair, or read a newspaper, as Georges Montorgueil noted. At any time they were free to talk and to walk around; one of the great innovations of the Folies-Bergère was its addition of a large *promenoir* that permitted customers to stroll around the hall and to mingle freely from any seat in the house. Everywhere and at any time, they could smoke, eat, and drink; men could keep their hats on. Whenever they chose, they could leave.[7] As Roland Barthes has observed, discontinuity—or interruption—was built into the very program of the music hall; in contrast to the theater's "connected" time woven into a pattern of unfolding drama, time in the music hall was in itself immediate and interrupted, a series of discrete segments of varied gestures without unifying signification.[8] The music hall or café-concert allowed a freedom unknown in the conventional theater. At the circus, too, spectators were free to move about when they so desired. They could wander about the hall and explore "backstage" scenes, inspect the animals close up, smoke, eat, or talk without inhibition. Even the American circus made a concession to the leisurely approach by opening the menagerie to all ticket holders an hour and a half before the performance began.

Such preferences in leisure may have been due in part to conditions of work life in the period. As the pressures of new technology and tightened work discipline grew,[9] workers such as artisans and small shopkeepers were clinging to freer individual rhythms in work and tenaciously prolonging older, now endangered ways of life. For such workers, the *caf'-conc'* was a place of leisure suited to their customary life of considerable autonomy. For others whose work life was already more tightly regimented, the music hall offered a compensatory freedom and looseness permitting the play of individual moods and movement. Department store clerks required to stand all day, government clerks required to sit at a desk all day, industrial workers tied to a machine had reason to avoid any confining constraint after hours, and in the music hall's fluidity and negation of clockwork discipline, they found a welcome refuge.

The French circus after the Barnum tour illustrates well the more general resistance to the new American or modern style in France. No French circus producer adopted the three-ring format until after the First World War, and even then it was no runaway success. Circuses in France before 1914 became either a music hall kind of variety show or remained reassuringly classical. Oller's Nouveau Cirque was the most successful of the first sort; the classical version, represented by the Cirque d'Hiver and the Cirque Fernando (1874–98, then renamed the Cirque Médrano), satisfied by offering the more familiar routines, ordered by a traditional code that was easily grasped. By 1900 such circuses were already quaintly old-fashioned.[10] They were not only the places favored by Degas, Toulouse-Lautrec, and Seurat but also the kind of show that parents took children to see without uneasiness or surprises.

Part of the appeal of the traditional circus and the fêtes foraines seems to have been that they were disarmingly naive and honestly artificial—reminiscent of an earlier age. To the perceptive columnist "Jacques Lux," they charmed by recalling a freedom, a looser rhythm of life that in cities had succumbed to a modern urban order and regimented work:

In the large city, where for a long time everything is regulated and policed, where men are applied to laborious and subdivided [*hierarchisée*] tasks, [the encampment of carnival people] evokes the adventurous life, roving on the main roads, with long leisure at shady stops, and enchanted warm summer evenings: all a tradition, magnified by the Romantics, which appears to us now quite distant and as good as extinct.

Similarly, the street fairs still flourishing in Paris had "a wholly provincial savor."[11] For so many Parisians of recent provincial origin, traditional entertainments evoked a charming nostalgia, a reassuring reminder of the past amid so much change in Paris life generally.

The weekly calendar of amusements also proved resistant to any dramatically different modern rhythm. With long hours still the rule for workers, most time off was treated more as rest time than as opportunity for recreation. On week nights, including Friday, audiences were generally small in music halls, popular theaters, and dance halls. Thursday being a day off for students, the Cirque d'Hiver was able to do well with a matinee that day, and the Bullier dance hall in the Latin Quarter filled up on Thursday evenings. But for working people, Saturday was *the* night out. Saturday was payday for 85 percent of Paris workers,[12] and it was the one day that was not followed by another working day. Hence workers filled up cabarets and cafés only on Saturday nights and holiday evenings. The hit song "Viens poupoule!" recreated the archetypical scene:

> Saturday evening, after work [l'turbin]
> The Parisian worker
> Says to his woman: for dessert
> I'll treat you to the café-concert
> Arm in arm, we'll slip up
> To the twenty-sous balconies
> Put on a dress quickly, we must hurry
> To get a good seat
> For we must, my *coco* [pet or darling],
> Hear all the *cabots* [performers].
> Come, little chicken [repeat], come.[13]

Tous les Soirs

NOUVEAU CIRQUE

RUE St HONORÉ, 251

JEUDIS & DIMANCHES MATINÉES

Sunday remained the day of leisure in the cities as in the traditional countryside. It was a day when theaters and music halls and circuses offered matinees and lowered their prices competitively. Panoramas, the Musée Grévin, and dance halls commonly dropped their prices to half the weekday admission. Sunday was also a time for strolling on the boulevards and idling in squares and parks. While the affluent paraded and dined in the Bois de Boulogne, the workers of Belleville and Ménilmontant went to the Bois de Vincennes at the other end of the city and picnicked on garlic *saucisson* and wine while their children played on improvised swings. With transportation advances at the end of the century and slightly higher wages, Sunday became a day for outings in the countryside. Parisian workers took inexpensive trams and trains out to pastoral spots along the Seine—Billancourt, Bougival, and the Ile de la Grande Jatte. Couples lounged in the sun along the banks of the river, drinking *picolo* (light cheap wine), eating small fried fish, and relaxing in a heavy tranquility. In provincial industrial centers such as Fougère, workers spent Sundays and holidays out of town fishing, visiting relatives, dancing in village auberges, and taking trains to any nearby town

Poster for the Nouveau Cirque (anonymous). The fashionable, high-priced Nouveau Cirque (1886–1926) on the rue Saint Honoré was the most innovative and modern circus in France. Notably, it offered aquatic acts, water ballet, and clowning in the swimming pool under the main arena. (Collection du Musée de la Publicité, Paris) offering a fête. At Roanne, workers played *boules* by cafés along the Loire and strolled on the bank with friends and family. The town fell silent as early as 9 o'clock, except for an occasional accordion and handful of youthful dancers.[14]

SOCIAL VARIETIES OF FREE TIME

For the better off, the leisure calendar was less weighted toward Sundays and holidays. Within the week, bourgeois and upper-class amusement seekers established a round of different in-spots for different nights. "The Tuesdays of the Elysée-Montmartre are as sought after, and as well attended, as the Fridays of the Hippodrome, the Saturdays of the Circus, and the Sundays of the montagnes russes," explained Jules Roques in 1888 for the benefit of the Parisian uninitiated. Guidebooks informed the out-of-towners of when to be where. According to a guidebook of 1900, Monday and Friday were the chic days for the Opera, Tuesday for the Théâtre Français, and Saturday for the Cirque d'Eté. At the Palais de Glace, patrons segregated socially not so much by the day as by the hour. Respectable and stylish people—especially women—showed up to skate and socialize in the afternoon; after 5 P.M. a racier crowd took over, starring celebrated demimondaines like Emilienne d'Alençon, Liane de Pougy, and Caroline Otéro.[15] The Parisian penchant for fashion and deference toward the socially prestigious accounts for much of the rhythm of leisure time in the more expensive places.

The smartest of Paris's social elite compressed a busy season of high life between the opening of the Hippodrome in the fall and the Grand Prix horse race in the late spring. Returning from fall hunts in country châteaux, the upper class plunged into a winter whirlwind of receptions, charity parties, balls, and salons. They also patronized entertainments such as the Opera and theater and the select music halls. Some interrupted their Paris rounds to go to Monte Carlo and Nice, Cannes or Antibes after New Year's or to the races at Pau in late January. After the Grand Prix, especially from the 1880s on, came a dead period in the capital, at least for the upper crust. Jules Claretie, director of the Comédie-Française, lamented in 1885 that with most theaters closing for the summer Paris no longer had a summer life: "Official life, artistic life are concentrated in the winter season; . . . the

Parisian year ends with the month of May and begins with the month of October." Writing just before the First World War, Gustave Coquiot observed that June was a feverish finale to the Paris season; in June "all the apotheoses burst out"—large art sales, masked balls, great horse races, and great comedies in outdoor theaters like the one in a park at Maison-Laffitte.[16]

In the summer "Tout Paris" gathered at places like Trouville, gambling in the casino and attending races. They played on their yachts in the Argenteuil basin, or they went to the thermal stations Biarritz, Evian-les-Bains, Vichy, Le Mont-Dore, and Châtelguyon. For those of high social standing, staying in Paris in the summer could be sheer misery, as Edmond de Goncourt testified about July:

> The boring vexations of life take on a particular intensity in summer, at this moment when the Parisian remaining in Paris is given over to solitude and is no longer taken away from himself by dinners, parties, visits, the contact at every movement with bustling and distracting humanity.[17]

The leisure of the rich and chic often ended up being a hectic race from one social event to another, one shopping expedition to another. Affluent women went to their couturier and bootmaker, the candy shop and the flower shop, and then to the golf course, tennis courts, Bois de Boulogne, expositions at the Bagatelle, garden parties and open-air balls, teas at the Carlton or Ritz, concerts, opening days at art exhibits, illustrious lectures and sermons, charity sales and charitable societies for teaching and feeding the poor, and plays by Jules Lemaitre, Maurice Donnay, and Jean Richepin. Much time also went into large family dinners and ritual social visits—six to eight visits in an afternoon, according to a recent study of ladies of the North.[18]

Their male counterparts filled afternoons with polo, pigeon shooting, or fencing, followed by a shower and *le cercle* (club recreation), teas for flirting, dinner, and evening entertainments on the town. Their lives were a "frantic rush," Coquiot concluded, with never a minute free, a constant effort of dividing some few minutes available among a thousand things to do.[19] In a letter to his mother in the late 1880s, journalist Jean Lorrain made it clear how full an evening of leisure could be for a dapper boulevardier. About six o'clock he dressed handsomely in his drugget suit, white vest, cravat of white embroidered quilting, and small black bowler, and then took a fiacre to the Bois de Boulogne to see the people returning from the races. Leaving his carriage at the gate, he walked around the forest and then dined alone at the Porte Maillot "in a restaurant full of jockeys and bookmakers. Afterwards, I had my coffee at the Pavillon d'Armenonville, in the Bois, for there is gypsy music there, and came home by way of the . . . Moulin Rouge and the Jardin de Paris, where I have free admission."[20]

At least some of these people were no doubt what Paris observers Benjamin and Desachy called "prisoners of pleasure," drudges slaving away at their leisure. In the duller provincial towns particularly, many of the country's half million *rentiers* who admitted having no occupation doubtless lived considerably slower-paced lives, whiling away hours in fewer places—in a favorite café or a courtroom, for example—but the reference to prisoners may well be just as applicable. Though the social elite believed themselves to be free spirits acting on impulse (*prime-sautiers*), observed another reporter of Paris social life, in fact they were locked into routines dictated by habit and social custom: "Without being aware of it we pass our life turning a little in the same circle, like a circus horse under the whip of Monsieur Loyal."[21]

Many industrial workers, in contrast, led lives that were far from routine and predictable or uniform. Miners often did not show up for work on Monday, observing the old customary pseudoholiday "Saint Monday," in the years up to the First World War. Many factory workers' lives were irregularly interrupted by seasons of unemployment. Fougère shoemakers labored sixty-hour weeks from October to February on the manufacture of summer shoes, but from mid-July to September they were only partially employed making winter shoes, and the rest of the time they were thrown into total unemployment, the duration of which varied from year to year according to the state of the economy and the factory. In Paris most domestic women flower makers endured some unemployment between March and September after a hard season when work might go long into the night; out of season, they scraped by with meager welfare aid or family resources or found other jobs such as feather making. Many domestic servants found themselves laid off in the summer months when their master left Paris for the mountains or beach.[22]

The patterns of work and leisure varied not just by class and occupation but also by sex and marital state. Working-class women caring for children and household while also earning money by sewing or flower making continued the traditional mixture of varying work and leisure time. Meanwhile, their men were experiencing more regimentation of work and the imposition of time discipline, making work cleanly distinct from leisure. Occupied with incessant tasks and no clean-cut time boundaries, married working-class women were least involved in entertainments outside the home, though some joined their men in nearby cafés on occasion. The large group of women employed as domestic servants (in 1901 nearly 45 percent of all working women in Paris) had such long hours—fifteen to eighteen a day—and such close supervision that their participation in public entertainments was for most limited to a part of Sunday, according to historian Theresa McBride's findings.[23]

Middle-class women with servants to do much of the household work could live more flexible and variable lives than their working husbands, though they were subject to the dictates of fashion already noted. These women were important patrons of the theaters and skating rinks, but overall they seem to have altered their traditional leisure less than their English counterparts. In particular, they do not seem to have played such a large role in the expansion of commercial entertainments as did women in the more industrialized and in some ways less traditional English society.[24]

The growing number of women working outside the home—in department stores, clerical jobs, and factories (but only a very small minority in the latter)—experienced the same modern alternation of long stints of work and shreds of free time that men did. Married working women, then as now, had less free time than men because they were burdened with more of the household tasks in addition to their paid employment. Single employees, male and female, had the most disposable time for frequenting cafés, restaurants, and music halls and for bicycling and strolling on the boulevards. These bachelors with free time and money appear to have been central to the growth of the entertainment business in belle-époque Paris.[25]

For all kinds of people, of course, the weather and seasons made for some variety in amusements. Outdoor sports, embraced by the upper levels of society, regularly changed by season. The fashionable skated on the lakes in the Bois de Boulogne only briefly during the coldest months. With the coming of good spring weather, they turned to cycling, boating, and swimming. The Bois de Boulogne then filled withs strollers, horseback riders, and automobilists—the latter considered sportsmen in the period. And workers as well as bourgeois then went rowing and dancing at Bougival and Asnières on the Seine.

Commercial establishments such as music halls and circuses also followed a seasonal cycle. Like the theaters, the Folies-Bergère closed for the summer, forgoing much foreign tourist trade. Outdoor cafés opened in the gardens of the dance halls Elysée-Montmartre and the Bullier. Each summer when the Moulin Rouge closed, as it did through most of the period, its branch the Jardin de Paris opened under the chestnut trees along the Champs-Elysées. There too the Pavillon de l'Horloge and the Ambassadeurs opened for the summer as open-air cafés-concerts. In the same way the Alcazar d'Eté took over for the Alcazar d'Hiver in the rue Faubourg-Poissonnière, the Printania

At the end of the nineteenth century, the Jardin de Paris was one of the most prestigious summertime open-air cafés-concerts. Roedel's drawing in the *Courrier français* depicts it as a kind of arboreal Moulin Rouge: a natural meeting place of the beautiful and well-to-do.

took the place of the Parisiana, and the Cirque d'Eté each April relieved the Cirque d'Hiver. The summer was also the time for the Jardin d'Acclimatation—a zoo—to open in the Bois de Boulogne, for regular races to be held at Longchamp and Auteuil, and for concerts to be given by the Garde Républicaine in the Tuileries, the Palais Royal, and the Luxembourg gardens. Fall brought annual reopenings of the music halls, theaters, and the Palais de Glace—occasions for showing off renovations, inevitably ballyhooed as resplendent.

The rhythm of leisure life also remained variable because workers and some bourgeois were actively resisting moves toward a more uniform week of work and business as usual. "The hairdressers began [it], and then the employees in the shoe business, and those of the grocery shops, jewelry, perfumery [joined in]; in sum, no one wants to work Sundays any more," noted a journalist in 1902.[26] The resistance took concerted form as an organized labor effort to fight for one day off each week, preferably Sunday. Employees were fighting chiefly against small retailers trying to keep them on the job to profit from Sunday shopping. Finally, in 1906, after years of demonstrations and militant politicking, department store clerks and other employees secured by law the right to one day off, normally Sunday. They gained that victory not with the force of Sabbatarian religious zeal as in England but with labor and progressive political allies joining together with the owners of large department stores opposing Sunday business for their own economic reasons. Similar resistance resulted in the closing of the Universal Exposition galleries in the evenings in 1900, dashing the fair organizers' hopes for extended days with the extensive use of electric lighting. After the 1900 fair, worker resistance and employers' desires to economize brought about the general closing of Paris stores in the evenings.[27]

ILLUSION AND REALITY OF FLUX AND NOVELTY

Traditional time patterns persisted in the modern city with remarkable tenacity. Outside Montmartre and Les Halles, all-night cafés were extremely rare. As in a traditional agricultural society, summer activities were markedly different from winter ones, with the busy season and the slow season simply the reverse of what they were in the country. Yet just as the regular stream of strollers on the boulevards gave the illusion of a whole population at leisure, so Paris places of pleasure with their limited hours and seasons were enough to feed foreigners' fantasies about the city's round-the-clock orgies of fun. Early in this century, an English *Pleasure Guide to Paris*, for example, exulted about the "delightful experience of being suddenly transported from the dull commonplace surroundings of a silent and monotonous life in England or elsewhere to the exuberant joy of a gay city which laughs, sings, dances and shouts, eats and drinks from twilight to dawn." French guides to pleasure nourished the same myth. "Here [in Paris] pleasure is a cult which has its bell-ringing fêtes, but whose altars are never left idle by devotees or even fanatics," wrote Camille Debans in his book *Les Plaisirs et les curiosités de Paris*.[28]

Certainly the city did offer variety and novelty in a profusion hard to find elsewhere. Compared to provincial towns and villages where a small and seedy circus came through once a year, where a pathetic *saltimbanque* performed on his ragged rug at an annual fair, and where a Bruant or Paulus only rarely came to relieve audiences from derivative and vocally unaccomplished amateurs, Paris was an unending feast. There music halls and circuses changed acts frequently, just as cabarets and cafés-concerts changed songs. There even one of the oldest forms of entertainment, the street fair, was rapidly changing and adopting the very latest, especially mechanical rides like the roller coaster and, in the late 1890s, the newest motion pictures. The "sensation of being current"—being up to the minute—was "one of the clearest characteristics of our civilization," declared sociologist Gabriel Tarde at the turn of the century.[29]

By way of explanation, he called attention to the effects of the swiftly changing technological bases of civilization: the press, telegraph, telephone, and railroads were accelerating the movement of people and ideas and, it seemed, conditioning the public to demand change in entertainments as well. Within the entertainment world itself, competing businessmen were vying for more customers by offering something for every taste, something for every moment, and something different as often as possible.

For their part, the seekers of new amusement seem to have been in flight from routine and constraint. In their accelerating world, "joy commanded by the calendar" became just one of many constraints that were no longer acceptable. The new entertainments that flourished were ones that imposed no obligation on partakers, did not require long concentration, and did not depend on rigid scheduling. The work of the people who chose such diversions was hardly more draining physically than that of their predecessors, but the growing number of jobs entailing specialized and regimented tasks was perhaps a source of the belle-époque repugnance for sustained attention after hours. Popular entertainment choices seem to corroborate what social observers commonly pointed out about their contemporaries: their "immense fatigue," restlessness, lack of fulfillment—their ennui, in a word. The old work culture and its accompanying leisure traditions were being undermined and disrupted or destroyed; freed also from the thrall of Church and throne, belle-époque seekers of pleasure went out sampling and exploring—in search of distraction and too often elusive delight. What the more critical and jaded of them increasingly found was the mechanical production of commercial entertainment that was wrapped in glittering novelty but was essentially more of the familiar "unending pasta."

7

The Spectacles
of Modern Life

[See page 171.]

STREET ENTERTAINMENT

No public pleasure of the belle époque is more easily underestimated than the simple one of seeing the sights of the city while strolling in the streets. Tourists following a Baedeker guidebook began at the Place de la Concorde; there they admired the famed beauty of Paris's vistas and parks and then went on to see the harmonious architecture of the Louvre and Notre Dame and the works of art inside. But Parisians of the period evidently delighted more in seeing movement and human action than monuments. To spectators in the street, Paris was an ever-changing spectacle, if not always a fête. Before their eyes, a motley cast made daily appearances: glamorous *courtisanes* in sumptuous fiacres, flashy pimps, top-hatted clubmen, ragged beggars, workers in blue roughcloth, flower sellers amid mounds of color, "hommes-sandwich" and shouting newsboys, eccentrics and madmen. Several thousand provincials and foreigners arriving each day added their costumes to the scene; during the universal expositions, their number swelled by tens of thousands.

Paris had never before offered so full and animated a spectacle. As the population of her twenty arrondissements grew from about 2 million at the beginning of the Third Republic to almost 3 million in 1914, with the population of the *banlieue* growing even faster, the traffic in the streets multiplied at a still greater rate, even after the addition of the underground metro in 1900. Between 1891 and 1910 vehicle traffic increased tenfold.[1] Bicycles, electric tramways, automobiles, and motorized buses all made their debuts in the period, drawing attention as novelties before becoming fixtures of street life.

Despite the danger that street-crossing pedestrians faced from carriages and cars, despite congestion and noise and horse manure and pickpockets, Parisians of all classes took promenades in their *quartiers* and beyond. For workers in their Sunday best and rentiers making their daily rounds, the walks were enjoyments or diversions cleanly divorced from work. For the housewife going to market, the home-working seamstress and flower maker stepping out for supplies, or the lawyer's clerk running an errand, the walks were moments of liberty and refreshment commingled with work and business time. Whether in the drabbest neighborhood of tenements or amid the most elegant mirror-bejeweled cafés, promenades were perhaps the most common and accessible amusement in Paris.

"The first thing to see for any newly-arrived is obviously the boulevard," advised a guidebook of 1878. The author meant not Haussmann's recently created straight and broad thoroughfares but the older tree-lined *grands boulevards*, which stretched for five kilometers from Madeleine to the Place de la Bastille.[2] Out of the capital's three-thousand public ways, they were the busy golden way of a half dozen theaters, some twenty notable restaurants, thirty cafés, and hundreds of handsome stores and boutiques. There a host of peddlers, acrobats, jugglers, and hurdy-gurdies performed amid kiosks, booths, benches, and light poles. There shop windows, as Atget's photographs show us, took on the mysterious beauty of still lifes and immobile pantomimes; there walls and Morris columns were the fullest galleries of bright posters. And by 1911, some places along the way began to glow with lighted signs that were "like permanent and regular fireworks"—neon gaily "triumphing."[3]

On the boulevards the crowds to be seen were the biggest and the most varied; in the late afternoon and evening they piled up in pedestrian bottlenecks; with a careless turn a stroller would be poked in the eye by a cane or hit in the chest by someone's elbow. Sidewalk cafés there enjoyed such good patronage that they continually expanded outward, making pedestrian passage difficult. At 5 o'clock the pulse of the boulevards quickened as strollers flocked to favorite places to take absinthe and apératifs. At night the boulevards blazed with lights, and the cast changed. Dusk brought out what an English guide to Paris delicately called "nymphs of the pavé," promising additional pleasures off the street. When they began to disappear and the boulevards quieted after midnight, tireless spectators moved to Les Halles to take in the nightly show of fifteen thousand vehicles bringing butter and cheese, petits pois and apples, hogs and beef to the bellies of Paris. In

Raffaëlli, *Paris, Boulevard des Italiens* (1911). A large cast of strollers and horse-drawn vehicles fills the stage of one of the grandest of Paris's grands boulevards. (Phot. Bibliothèque Nationale, Paris)

its ordinary activities Paris itself was a permanent universal exposition, a "city of 365 Sundays," remarked Emile Bergerat in an aside while reporting on the 1889 fair.[4]

Funeral processions, dog fights, collisions of wagons and omnibuses, a fallen horse being beaten by a furious master were special dramas that invariably drew audiences. Public executions by the guillotine attracted crowds to the main entry of the Dépôt des Condamnés at the Prison de la Roquette; the Joanne guide to Paris told tourists where to find this *grand guignol* theater. There were also seasonal attractions. In the days before New Year's, the boulevards filled with booths full of toys and eye-catching gift novelties. In the week before Easter, the Boulevard Richard Lenoir became a savory open-air *charcuterie* for eating where onlooking crowds were drawn to "ham fair" (*foire aux jambons*). Just after Easter, Parisians flocked to the *foire du Trône* where they bought gingerbread (*pain d'épices*), rode on wooden merry-go-round horses, played cheap *mirlitons* (reed pipes), and watched the feats of strongmen and magicians. In the summer, they went to the other side of the city for the fête de Neuilly, where at night an especially chic crowd showed up to mingle with people who sold their fleas to the showmen—one franc for a dozen ("but no fleas from animals," the buyers insisted). Beyond a belt of hundreds of waiting fiacres, a mixture of nobles, prostitutes, and clerks milled around lotteries and booths of jugglers, lion tamers, acrobats, wrestlers, snake charmers, ventriloquists, three-pawed dogs, and trained fleas—trained, for example, to sit around a minuscule table and take coffee in genteel leisure. Posters and billboards, barkers and their performers—dwarfs, giants, clowns, and conjurors—entertained passing crowds of people who did not pay even a sou or enter a single tent amid that bounty of wonders, the fête foraine.[5]

Nothing better demonstrated the high status of the everyday boulevard as spectacle than a new panorama that opened at the 1889 Exposition. In the circular building holding the canvas entitled *Le Tout Paris*, customers paid to see not a historic battle scene or a sweeping view of a city or port but the sights of contemporary boulevards around the Opera. The glittering new Opera (finished in 1875), the Avenue de l'Opéra (opened in 1877), and the adjacent Boulevards des Capucines and Italiens had become the new prestigious hub of Paris; there the fashionable gathered at establishments like the Grand Café, "the most chic" in the city according to the daily *Fin de siècle*. The panorama *Tout Paris*, like the cinema born six years later, made sight-seeing easy; it selected and focused on the choicest images and presented them in concentrated form. All the customers had to do was to look, and before their eyes appeared some eight hundred portraits of the rich, the famous, and the beautiful of Paris: the Prince de Sagan, La Goulue, Sarah Bernhardt, Pasteur and Paulus, "Mlle. C." and "Madame de R."[6] Like other panoramas, this one catered to a taste for skillfully wrought realism in illusion and a burgeoning touristic desire to see the most touted sights easily and quickly.

Distinctively, this one presented the sight of celebrities, set off against the most urbane backdrop of the new Paris; the entertainment here was not to enjoy someone's acts or works but just to *see* the celebrities themselves. In the modernized huge city of so many anonymous faces (then a population of almost 2.5 million), to recognize some that many people could recognize was somehow appealing. Were people paying to see the prestigious so as to feel themselves close to or a part of the in-crowd? Were they paying to gain importance by having been the privileged viewer, able to share the experience later with friends (picture souvenir books were sold)? Evidently. Despite its fashionable attractions, this panorama was probably less effective than the usual distant scene since its all-important human subjects were frozen in a stillness and in groupings as unnatural as the viewer's encountering them all together at one time. The soon-to-be-invented movies would do much better. The painted *Tout Paris* turned out to be no runaway success and did not outlive the Exposition; it reported 310,076 entries—not a large number for a panorama though considerably more than what the *Exposition des Aquarellistes* drew—53,514.[7] Nonetheless, the panorama of celebrities was a harbinger and perhaps a symptom—a symptom of a deficiency in people's lives, of an impoverished public life in the modern urban world. In 1889 many were ready to pay to have a visual pseudoencounter with public figures set in an embellished reproduction of Paris public space—all made familiar and prestigious by far-reaching media, the press and posters.

In *The Banquet Years*, Roger Shattuck has written beautifully of Paris as a stage on which belle-époque Parisians acted out their lives with fine theatrical flair. We have just seen how Paris life could be viewed as entertainment of many sorts: a continuous street fair, a pantomime, a variety show, a universal exposition. And it must be added that these are not just metaphors and interpretations imposed by latter-day historians; more important, they were ways in which everyday urban life came to be viewed in the period.

A special issue of the *Figaro illustré* (March 1888), for example, was devoted to "the spectacle of the street"—with the boulevard presented as the "true *Théâtre des variétés.*" Tourist guides and their consumers also approached Paris life as a series of spectacles and scenes. From the Exposition of 1889 on, picture postcards of Paris became commonplace as new means of preserving the spectacle and of sharing it with acquaintances back home. In newspaper columns and books, writers such as Jules Claretie, Jean Lorrain, Georges Montorgueil, and Emile Goudeau regularly depicted everyday urban life as pageantry and human comedy. In the 1890s the now thoroughly Parisian Goudeau, for example, took his readers on vicarious strolls through the city and its seasonal rites in such books as *Paysages parisiens, heures et saisons* (1892), *Tableau de Paris* (1893), and *Paris Almanac* (1895). News-

France's Parliament was caricatured as a circus by E. Cadel in *Le Sourire* (28 October 1891). The deputies, who earned twenty-five francs a day, performed in a great variety of amusing ways; the playbill announces a "grandiose presentation of equilibrist budgets, . . . animal cries, great parliamentary boxing by all the troupe." (Collection Jacques Gournay)

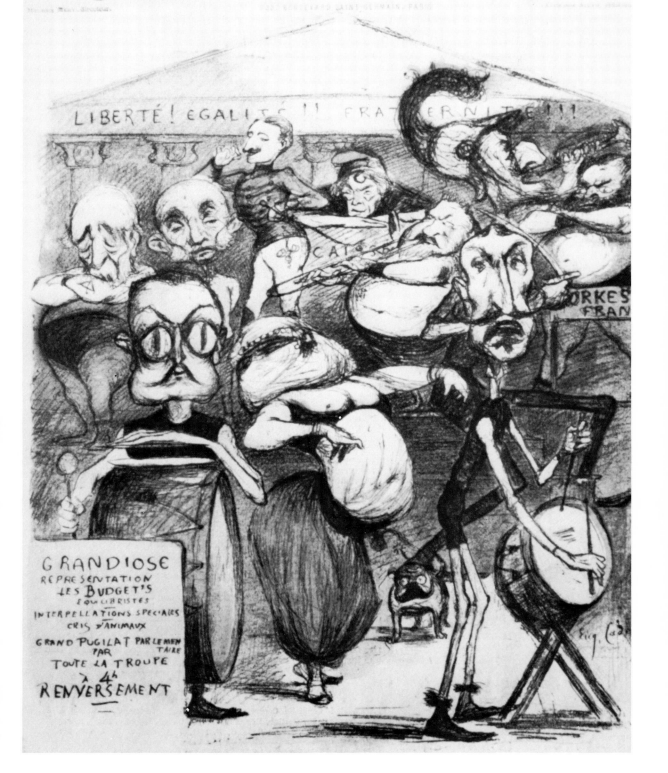

papers such as the *Fin de Siècle* and the *Courrier français* specialized in relating the more rakish boulevardier's view of Paris to readers who may rarely have seen the boulevards. At the same time, artists such as Raffaëlli, Bonnard, Caillebotte, Pissarro, and Vallotton created an unprecedented wealth of paintings and prints of the modern thoroughfares, while Degas, Seurat, and Toulouse-Lautrec painted scenes of the boulevardiers' café, music hall, circus, and racetrack life. In the humor journals, caricaturists used the forms of boulevard amusements to ridicule the nation's powerful, picturing politicians and generals as clowns and carnival hucksters.[8]

Entrepreneurs, artists, and writers absorbed in the world of spectacles were making entertainment a pervasive way of understanding and living. They were nurturing a new need in people hitherto less able to see or taste such fruits, a need that social critics deemed artificial and pernicious. Optimistically viewed, it was what permitted Camille Debans to boast in 1889 that "Paris is the only corner of the world where pleasure is a social necessity, a normal state."[9]

FLANEURS AND BADAUDS

The writers and artists who creatively focused on city sights perpetuated a tradition of what the French called the *flâneur*. In fin-de-siècle Paris, the flâneur was not so much the dandy out to make himself seen, not so much the flamboyant individualist that Baudelaire presented, as the connoisseur of the city's finer mundane delights: the sight of a millionaire rubbing elbows with a ninety-franc-a-month clerk on the boulevard, the comedy of a smart monocled monsieur pursuing a beautiful woman, the titillating view of a working girl lifting her skirts to cross a rain-filled street—to mention only a few singled out by De Lannoy's *Plaisirs et la vie de Paris*.[10] Like a noble or a dilettante, the flâneur enjoyed freedom from work or any utilitarian activity; he was free to enjoy experiences for their own sake, finding amusement and beauty in the unexpected as well as in everyday sights. The flâneurs that we know best were journalists, playwrights, and essayists such as Aurélien Scholl, Georges Courteline, and Maurice Donnay. They made their living in a world of entertainment and art, and when they went out on the boulevard, they mixed work and leisure, savoring the latest witticisms and news and taking what they could back to their writing and theater. In their art as in their enjoyment of the boulevards, they celebrated modern life.

Another sort of stroller was the gawker, or *badaud*, less artistically discriminating than the *flâneur*. Centuries before, Rabelais had scornfully observed how silly and empty-headed Parisians would gather around to watch any mountebank or mule with cymbals. A *Physiologie* of 1841 identified those badauds as simple triflers born in backwater places like Carpentras and Quimper or tourists from London running around holding maps and looking at monuments.[11] Some, however, were true Parisians, a guidebook of 1878 assures us, Parisians who might spend the day watching the Seine flow by or following the movements of a fisherman on the river bank. "There's one who really has patience," exclaimed one such spectator as he pointed to a fisherman. "He has been there for more than six hours, and I haven't yet seen him catch a thing." The "busiest idlers" in Paris were those who regularly watched construction projects in the streets, declared one guide.[12] Invariably, a crowd of onlookers also gathered to watch the sidewalk "puller of teeth" at work, the *arracheur de dents* who often peddled hair-growing lotion too (see illus.   ), and the worker posting the latest poster. Or they simply watched people passing by, visually so diverse and artful in adorning and presenting themselves. Such spectators found their paradise at universal expositions where sights were much more exotic and crowds more varied than the usual Parisian ones, captivating as the usual were.

To badauds, even the most meaning-laden festival or ceremony was just another spectacle. In 1889, the centennial of the Revolution, most world's fairgoers saw the sights without interesting themselves in the history being commemorated. No doubt the same was true of many at just about any July 14 celebration. The common people simply loved "fireworks, torchlight retreats, all public rejoicings" as good times, without caring about the political event giving rise to the festivity, observed Henry Leyret. People went "out of simple pleasure, out of curiosity, as they go to great burials, the most often without the slightest feeling of regret for the person being buried." Perhaps skepticism played as great a role as indifference in the detachment of such people. So it seemed to essayist Paul Pottier, who argued in 1899 that people had experienced so much false advertising (*puffisme*) and political deception that they became uncommitted badauds.[13] In public places, they

Badauds gathered on a street corner in 1889 to
see—just about anything. We will never know
exactly what in this instance. But is not the intent group enough to make one want to go
closer and find out what was there? (Bibliothèque Historique de la Ville de Paris)

A street dentist at work attracts the inevitable
crowd of badauds on a Paris boulevard, ca.
1900. (Musée Carnavalet)

[OVERLEAF] A street performer and his audience
in Marseille, ca. 1900. (Photo Séeberger.
© Arch. Phot. S.P.A.D.E.M., Paris/V.A.G.A.
New York, 1985)

sought visual amusement, believing nothing and only looking—without cost or effort or risk.

As spectators, they were at their best when they had no social ties to those being observed. The true flâneur went out alone, noted authorities on the subject. The *Physiologie* of 1841, for example, warned the novice that if you took someone along, it would be only a simple walk at best or a series of frustrations, as your companion—understood to be a woman—held you up in front of a hat shop window when you wanted to see Polichinelle or to follow a *grisette*. The flâneur strolled without purpose or goal, but he had to be free to follow any whim and to savor the unexpected. The badaud was so absorbed in the sights around him that he too confined himself to solitary looking. In a mid-century book on Paris streets, Victor Fournel distinguished the badaud as one who lost his individuality, his nature as a distinct human being, so lost was he in the spectacle and the crowd.[14] He was not part of any celebrating community; his pleasure was devoid of the emotional transport and collective uplift that idealistic contemporaries sought in fêtes. His activity entailed no human bonds, and it brought no fraternal ties. The badaud escaped the isolation of his room and found contact with a larger social world than workplace or neighborhood, but he remained uninvolved, alone, even among other badauds.

SPECTATORS AND STRANGERS

Belle-époque Paris was filled with a growing number of people lacking strong social ties to the society they viewed in leisure. In addition to large numbers of foreign and provincial tourists, there were the unemployed and the rentiers, who lacked the social life that went with having occupations. There were also employees in the expanding bureaucracy and workers in the new chemical and food industries growing up in suburbs like Ivry—all without established rites bringing them together in leisure. The decline of social bonds that Durkheim and others were decrying was perhaps most noticeable among once large groups of artisans such as tailors, shoemakers, tanners, and dyers in the center of the city. In crafts being undermined by technological change, workers who had already lost touch with the Church and its fêtes were falling away from the social customs of their predecessors at work.

In the faubourgs, Henry Leyret observed toward the end of the century that entire crews of workers no longer gathered around a bistro table for drinks and a *gibelotte* (fricassee of rabbit) to welcome a newly hired worker. What he interpreted as "indifference," "egotism," and a desire to economize had reduced the welcoming group to a remnant who at most simply shared some liters of wine in the shop or in an *estaminet*.[15]

In the early twentieth century, as workers gained new free time, many fished, gardened, rode bicycles, watched boxing matches, and went to the movies. Many still drank together in cafés; in the South they continued to join in *boules* tournaments, and miners in the North still gathered to watch cockfights. But never before had so many workers filled so much after-work time independently of a communal association. Socialists and labor union activities brought only a small minority of workers together in new rites and festivals, and there the solidarity rested more on individual choice than on the influence of ingrained shared tradition. Never before had people been so free to choose their leisure as individuals, Michael Marrus has emphasized, and never before were they so separated from community causes and commitments to celebrate together.[16]

Yet for the most part the French before 1914 were not the isolated beings that alarmed social observers like Paul Leroy Beaulieu had foreseen in the 1860s; they were not a "mass of individuals, living side by side in the most unequal destinies, remaining strangers one to the other and nourishing toward their neighbor only sentiments of indifference, contempt, or envy."[17] In the city of millions at the turn of the century, many lived as strangers to their neighbors and as such were readily spectators of one another, but they still grouped as families and in private associations to celebrate special events. As Henri Baudrillart noted at the beginning of the Third Republic, those private celebrations were taking on the importance that parish and work group fêtes once had had. Families—worker families—also took Sunday promenades together on the boulevards, and they went together to cabarets to talk, to sing, and to drink. The more prosperous middle-class men were forming and joining English-style clubs, or *cercles*, where they sat in large leather armchairs, smoked cigars, and exchanged stories in the expansive language of male libertinism.[18] Young men, especially of the middle and upper classes, formed football and cycling clubs, which engendered new rituals and celebrations modeled on older ones. In Brest, for example, beginning in 1895 the Véloce Club Brestois celebrated the festival of the patron saint of cyclists, Saint Germain the Scot.[19] It was public and community socializing that was most in decline, as the case of dancing makes clear.

At the end of the century, dancing flourished at family gatherings such as wedding parties held in restaurants and rented halls, where a piano or small orchestra played polkas and waltzes. People also danced at special charity parties, at a once-a-year dressmakers' ball, at school and Masonic and veterans' balls in a café basement or a wineshop *entresol*. In similar places the natives of Brittany or the Auvergne gathered periodically to dance and make merry. Out well beyond the boulevards, workers and *apaches* danced in neighborhood *bals de barrière*. These were not in places where outsiders could safely join in; the slang term for such dances—*casse-gueule* (a dangerous joint, literally a bash in the mug)—made that clear. On Saturday or Sunday evening there were an estimated two hundred small *bastringues* where *bals musettes* (popular balls, originally bagpipe dances) were held on the exterior boulevards or in the "zone" beyond; there, *en famille*, lower-class people paired off to "sweat one" on the dance floor and to "strangle a parrot" (drink a glass of absinthe) afterward. Students and grisettes danced at the old Bullier Hall in the Latin Quarter, while less fortunate local youth in Montmartre still gathered to dance in neighborhood places such as the Moulin de la Galette.[20]

But on the boulevards and streets of the center of Paris, fewer people went to public places to dance as the century closed. By 1885, journalist Emmanuel Patrick observed, public balls were dying or were almost dead. The great Château Rouge and the Mabille had closed in 1882; the Reine Blanche closed in 1884. When Georges Montorgueil surveyed the situation in his book *Paris dansant* (1898), most of the famed dance halls of the century had disappeared. The Bal Rivoli had become a lecture hall, and the Frascati on the rue Vivienne had turned into a furniture show room. Cafés-concerts had drawn customers away and in several notable cases had taken over the very sites of venerable dance halls; the Élysée-Montmartre, demolished in 1893, had given way to the Trianon Concert, the Boule Noir had become the Cigale, and the Grand Turc, the Fourmi.[21]

Participation gave way to spectacle first in places frequented by better-off

Workers drinking and dancing to the music of a
musette (bagpipe, at right) at the Barrière de la
Villette in 1881, or perhaps earlier. (Musée
Carnavalet)

Another spectacle in a popular dance hall: this "sketch by Couturier was made on the night of March 22, 1889, during the women's wrestling" at the Elysée-Montmartre.

clients, readiest to spend money and buy entertainment. The higher one went in society, the less one danced, Montorgueil observed. By the turn of the century, the most fashionable balls were places where people no longer danced. At the former Mabille, transformed into the Jardin de Paris, foreigners, the rich, demi-mondaines, and cocottes watched variety show acts, drank, and chatted. The Moulin Rouge was to take the same route; dancing there was already declining in the 1890s; in the early twentieth century the dance hall became a music hall with customers watching lavish revues. The famous chahut, or cancan, was partly responsible; such skilled professionals as Grille d'Egout, La Goulue, and Nini Patte en l'Air had put on such a show and had received such star fame that customers were embarrassed to dance in their presence, noted Montorgueil. The popularity of the belly dance contributed to the same result. In the early nineties, ballroom managers resorted to hiring people to dance to keep up the appearance of public participation; circles of spectators formed around the few decoys, *employés au plaisir*. "We expect [joy] of places where our ennui seeks its cure and is not cured at all, precisely because we have brought our ennui there," Montorgueil observed. "There is joy only where we bring it. . . . gaiety," he concluded, "has its springs in ourselves."[22]

In good weather the urban leisured flocked to riverside spots near Paris almost as ritually as they had once congregated in city dance halls. At Bougival and Joinville-le-Pont couples and small parties of friends laughed and danced and drank together in rustic *guinguettes*, but rarely did a larger community of merriment emerge. On a Sunday afternoon on the Isle de la Grande Jatte, as Seurat painted it in 1884–86 (see illus.), people rested on the bank, languorously wooden and detached, staring at sailboats or lost in reverie.[23] On the grass a stiffly seated gentleman with top hat and cane, a reclining worker in cap and jersey, some bustled ladies and silent couples appear oblivious to others, even to a trumpet player facing the scattered idlers. Perhaps they were communing with nature and contemplating restoratively, but they seem too crowded and subject to interruption to be seeking real solitude. Most of them appear to be watching the spectacle of others and of boating without being more engaged than the badauds of the bustling boulevard. In their passivity and detachment, they inhabited dis-

A summer outing along the Seine: drinking, eating fried fish, amorous play. "For all it's a fête," wrote Charles Monselet in a poem that this drawing illustrated (*Paris illustré*, July 1885, p. 141).

continuous worlds, linked only by chance proximity one afternoon. In the circus or music hall, they might have come together as consumers just as separately as they came together on the Grande Jatte. That afternoon leisure public was not the same as the morning parish or the Monday work crew or the people of a neighborhood, and the leisure group itself was unintegrated. In modern urban leisure the individual's social world was fragmented.

It was the era of various publics, sociologist Gabriel Tarde noted in the 1890s. The unity of the publics was "incomplete and variable," indistinct, always in process, being renewed and then disjoined. The unity came not from shared custom but from the passing and partial common experience that the press provided its readers and the railroad its passengers. The telegraph and telephone also brought together transitory publics.[24] To Tarde's examples one can add the new music halls and cinemas, the most important new shapers of leisure publics. More than ever before, commercial entertainment was the fount of shared images and mentalities.

In November 1888 at the presidential mansion, President Grévy invited guests to enjoy France's first entertainment transmitted by the *théâtrophone*. Now an audience hearing the same opera could be physically scattered about the city, listening to the music over amplified telephones.[25] They missed not only the visual performance but also the experience of sharing it in an assembled group, subject to contagious applause or laughter. The théâtrophone spread and became a common boulevard entertainment by the early twentieth century; one could go to the Théâtre des Nouveautés on the Boulevard des Italiens, for example, and for a small price hear plays or operas "live" through the electrical device. Phonographs provided a similar experience of dispersed individuals far from the performers listening in their residences or, after 1900, in one of the several *salons des phonographes* in Paris. Well before the heyday of radio and television, new forms of technology were emerging that served both to eliminate interaction between audience and performers and to fragment audiences.

Something similar was happening in the age-old street fairs. At the end of the nineteenth century, fair showmen were quick to adapt the modern technology of steam engines and electric organs, sirens and loudspeakers. Those noises added to the traditional din of cries, singing, and firing of pistols and rifles in target shoots. Verbal exchanges among the leisured became almost as difficult as communication of customers to performers. The old intimacy between popular crowds and forains was further strained as the street-show entrepreneurs became bourgeois, big businessmen with considerable capital investment and a genteel manner of speaking and living.[26] The individual fairgoer was left to a more strictly visual experience when strolling by the booths. At the same time proliferating mechanical rides absorbed customers in their own sensations and turned them into moving objects in orbits apart from the milling crowd.

A NEW SPECTACLE INDUSTRY

The most thoroughgoing transformation of life into captivating spectacle took place through the new magic of the movies. Though they separated audience from performers definitively, they also created transitory new publics sharing the same view of the same scenes and sometimes sharing reactions of laughter, hisses, and applause. But critics of the cinema observed that in the darkened halls (darker than other spectacle halls) where the new vivid images held sway, there was strangely little audience reaction. Were the moving images so entrancing that they turned people into gaping badauds?

Cinema was born and nurtured in the badauds' stamping ground, the Paris boulevards. On that cold night of December 28, 1895, when Louis Lumière gave the first commercial show in the basement of the Grand Café at 14 Boulevard des Capucines, only the most inveterate boulevardiers turned out. Thirty-five customers paid a franc each to see the new spectacle. Though the press virtually ignored the debut, word did spread quickly; audiences grew rapidly and competing entrepreneurs scrambled to get into the new business. Within weeks the music halls were incorporating the novelty into their catchall programs. The Folies-Bergère showed "American Biograph" movies between song and dance and acrobatic numbers. By April 1896 the Eldorado and the Olympia were competing with their own movies, and the Théâtre Isola was screening a color film of Loïe Fuller doing her serpentine dance. Also as early as April 1896 magic-show impresario Georges Méliès had introduced kinetograph-animated photography into his Robert Houdin Theater on the Boulevard des Italiens, and soon he began to make and show his own creations. In a large department store on the Boulevard Barbès,

Dufayel featured movies near his furniture gallery. The street fairs were also quick to adopt the new entertainment. Pétomane, the enterprising Pujol, ran a movie booth in Paris fairs for three years beginning in 1899, and by then the fair showmen were major providers of the new entertainment. By the turn of the century another forain named Charles Pathé had turned from playing popular novels on a phonograph to the movie business, establishing a dozen fairground theaters, some of which held as many as a thousand seats, in the foire du Trône and the fairs of Neuilly, Clichy, and Batignolles.[27]

Like the spectacle of the boulevard, film fascinated with external appearances, visual sensations, available for little cost and with little formality. As in any successful boulevard and street-fair entertainment, prices were low—from fifty centimes to one franc usually; some small *baraques* charged as little as twenty centimes. And customers did not have to bother with dressing up or observing any particular etiquette modeled by their social superiors. In short, it was entertainment for the common people, and they responded to it unhampered by any precedent making for stuffiness or pretensions.

At first moviegoers, like ordinary badauds, watched not only the most banal scenes of public life—a train pulling into a station (Louis Lumière, 1896) and Lumière workers leaving the factory in Lyon—but also the exceptional sights that always drew crowds: a parade, the Czar's visit to Paris in October 1896, President Faure in Russia in August 1897, and the Festival of Flowers at the 1900 Exposition. Like the badauds of the boulevards, moviegoers gave their attention to moving subjects not requiring long concentration. The first films lasted only about a minute or two each; the entire program of ten different films lasted about twenty minutes.[28] Such visual experiences were unusual only in that the scenes were being mechanically reproduced with movement in a way never seen before. With unprecedented visual verisimilitude, life was recreated by machine as spectacle. The spectators ready to appreciate it—practiced badauds, if you will—were numerous and primed for cinema well before its invention.

On the early screen they found all the traditional fare of boulevard entertainment. Magician Georges Méliès, richly experienced in illusion making, gave audiences the most astounding new sensations on film. After building France's first movie studio at a cost of twenty thousand francs in

Like the music halls, fairground entertainers quickly added the brand new cinema to their traditional offerings. The forains here present their customary *parade* (stiffly posed for the photographer) to tempt a crowd to enter for the full and varied show inside. (Photo Séeberger. © Arch. Phot. S.P.A.D.E.M., Paris/ V.A.G.A., New York, 1985)

1896–97, he used his genius for special effects to make magic films—*L'Escamotage d'une dame chez Robert Houdin*, for example—and went on to specialize in such fantasies as the *Fée des fleurs* and *Le Voyage dans la lune*. Continuing a tradition of metamorphic popular imagery, former Incoherent artist Emile Cohl produced new cinema magic by drawing right on individual film frames, thus creating one of the world's first animated films in 1908. As early as the turn of the century, Louis Lumière had adapted movie equipment to the taste for panoramas; with a camera on a gondola or a tram, he showed large scenes of faraway charm and beauty, bringing to Paris the sights of Venice and Moscow, Saigon and Cairo.[29]

Movies not only offered the encompassing views of panoramas, mystifying marvels, and the banalities and pageantry of public life. They were also used to serve up the fare of the theaters, especially drama. As early as 1897 the Lumières made little historical dramas such as the *Assassination of the Duke de Guise*. The music hall gag or sketch, the prototype of which was Lumière's *Arroseur arrosé*, dated from early 1896. As longer music hall farces also passed over into film, master comics Max Linder and Charlie Chaplin moved into the new medium and developed there an economy of motion and timing that perhaps even improved on precinema acts. Melodrama, too popular to be overlooked by filmmakers, was successful in the 1906 production *Histoire d'un crime*; romances and horror serials (*feuilletons*) also found their way into early film and attracted audiences as they had in the older forms of theater and print.[30] The movies turned out to be the ultimate protean entertainment.

By 1906 longer films were being made, which singly were now considered sufficient major attractions. About the same time new halls were built specifically for movies, still centering on the boulevards. In 1908 a serious and successful effort was made to draw a higher class of people to the movies with a production drawing on the prestige of literature and the theater. Press magnate Pierre Laffitte hired renowned actors, including Charles La Bargy of the Comédie-Française, and had academician Henry Lavedon write a text and Camille Saint-Saëns compose music for the first "art film." But the effort was not followed by other successful ones. Cinema long continued to suffer the disdain of the moneyed and classically cultured.[31]

The largely popular audiences before 1914 were sufficient to make movies a big business. The Lumière brothers had scarcely dreamed that within weeks of that inauspicious debut in 1895 their *cinématographe* would be earning from 2,000 to 2,500 francs a day. Other entrepreneurs better sensed the financial possibilities and moved in aggressively. As early as 1896 Léon Gaumont, a manufacturer of photographic equipment, and Charles Pathé, a shrewd street-show businessman, had acquired movie equipment and began building empires of film production, distribution, and screening, and financing theaters. Pathé was first to develop special cinema halls in cities throughout France and in 1907 pioneered the business of film rentals, which grew faster than outright sales of films, Méliès's method. Since filmmaking required so much capital for production and screening, control of the new business was to be much more concentrated than in most of the older entertainments, and the economic rewards were concentrated accordingly. The captains of the new industry cautiously fed the public what it seemed to want while also skillfully luring it through posters and the press. They held production costs and salaries down and enjoyed high returns. Just before the war, in 1913, receipts for movies in Paris were about 9 million francs and for all of France, 16 million francs.[32]

By the eve of the First World War, movies seemed to be a conquering force that threatened to supplant most other entertainments. Panoramas, circuses, and theaters, already losing a popular following around 1900, declined further. It is not so surprising, then, that the old Cirque d'Hiver on the Boulevard du Temple became a Cinéma Pathé (1907) and the Hippodrome in the Rue Caulincourt became the Gaumont Palace (1911). The success of the new entertainment was more dramatically signaled when music halls began to be turned into movies palaces, as the Parisiana was in 1911.[33] After the war, the Ba-Ta-Clan, the Cigale, the Gaîté-Rochechouart, the once great Eldorado, and the Scala went the same way. By 1914 there were already 1,200 movie theaters in France, about 260 of them in the capital. Already by 1914 cinema was taking in more money than music halls and more than cafés-concerts in Paris, though not yet more than all theaters combined. And in 1914 for the first time, a cinema—the Hippodrome—by earning 1,282,024.60 francs surpassed the perennial leader of the nonsubsidized entertainments, the Folies-Bergère.

Contemporary observers recognized the invention's extraordinary power well before that milestone. They noted that movies dealt in primitive gestures and simple images, a universal language that even the simplest, most un-educated, and fatigued spectator could follow. And the "living pictures" brought actors close up, producing an impact that players on a stage could not, especially for spectators in the poorer, distant seats. Further, movies required little reflection and little imagination—only looking, looking, look-ing, as one particularly unsympathetic critic remarked of the silent films.[34] Their special power over audiences aroused significant worries and objections from a variety of critics. Movies could be propaganda, it was noted, powerful influencers of behavior. Like a drug, movies dulled and warped spectators' sense of reality, reducing human dramas to a primitive simplicity. Movies were moving some young people to go out and imitate the action just seen on film—most alarmingly, to commit violent crimes, it was widely reported. Socialist leaders complained that movies were pacifying "circuses," and too many films portrayed workers as alcoholic and villainous. Early stag films shown in the back of wineshops and in fairground booths provoked the condemnation of police and moralists. The cinema seemed to be fostering habits and needs that threatened old ways of living, Max Nordau summed up in a French journal in 1914.[35]

Some commentators pointed out that cinema had great potential benefits. It could be a new art, the seventh art, delighting the reflective flâneur, creatively communicating human experience and not just distracting or hyp-notizing passive gawkers. It could be a new form of document, not only preserving the past, but resurrecting the dead and mechanically continuing life on the screen, an early reviewer noted. Movies could be educational, and they could be an added attraction in festivals.[36] They could serve to unify people—the hope of promoters of fêtes since the French Revolution.

Little came of such hopes before the First World War. The most important role of movies remained one of serving as cheap, undemanding entertain-ment. Whether their content was comedy, melodrama, or fantasy, movies provided, above all, striking visual display—a show of movement and energy requiring little sustained attention. So did the revues favored by the modern music halls, but cinema evidently had special advantages. The new magic of moving images in darkened halls perhaps better countered the isolation and ennui of spectators; apparently it allowed them to escape more easily their everyday constraints and to identify with heroes and a piquant variety of experiences beyond their usual ken—more effectively than did panoramas, the illustrated press, vaudeville sketches, or theater melodramas. Powerfully captivating through the primary visual sense, movies could "enlarge the horizon of spectators in a surprising way," providing vicarious adventure and revealing the interiors of palaces, distant lands, or tumultuous wars, wrote Max Nordau just before the outbreak of the war.[37]

If movies were liberating, they were also controlling. More than any other entertainment, they subjected people to mechanical, industrial, highly centralized power. They were standardized, mass-produced spectacles, each unvarying and unresponsive to audiences, each easily repeated anywhere and everywhere in uniform fashion. They were "image factories," as one contemporary critic wrote. Perhaps they created new habits and needs (the habit and need of going to the movies, at the least), but they also reinforced behavior already entrenched in industrial, urban work life. Treating spectators as inert and uniform parts of a grand machine—or system of production and consumption—the "image factories" extended modern work life into leisure, as Theodor Adorno has observed.[38] In taking people beyond old horizons, the movies took them farther from the festive community of the past.

8
Dancing on a Volcano

"At the montagnes russes"—a drawing by Heidbrinck published in *Le Courrier français*, April 22, 1888. The montagnes russes were favorite thrill-producing rides in the late nineteenth century. This one, new in 1888, was patronized by well-to-do adults on a fashionable central boulevard. It was razed in 1892 because its wooden structure was judged hazardous by authorities. The Olympia music hall was built on the same site and opened in 1893.

What the French call la belle époque existed, if not just in selective memory, sometime in a period between two disastrous wars. Whether one identifies that fortunate epoch with the 1880s or the years after the Dreyfus affair or the entire period of 1880 to 1914, it is clear that there was no lengthy time of calm or beautiful harmony. As a number of contemporaries put it, the French were "dancing on a volcano," which often stirred menacingly.[1] The era's tensions and conflicts showed up not only in political forums and street demonstrations but also in entertainments—in Montmartre chansons, in cartoons and dozens of satirical periodicals, in circus clown acts like those of Footit and Chocolat, in music hall revues charged with jingoism, and in the street-fair *jeu du massacre* in which customers threw balls at dolls representing the jaundiced Jesuit, the officious gendarme, and the red-whiskered Englishman.

If in such ways they danced on a volcano, it was hardly out of joy, an emotion commonly identified with liberating festivals. It was rather in a spirit of gaiety, which was loved as "a remedy for melancholy," acknowledged poet Hyren Nilhoc in the *Courrier français*.[2] That view of gaiety describes well the way such characteristic belle-époque figures as Chéret and Feydeau chased after lightheartedness and laughs. Knowing spleen and ennui all too well, they made resolute efforts to make merry. Amusements were feints at an enveloping somberness—willed temporary achievements, exertions after which one passed easily back to the usual dreariness. Similarly, festive moments were but instants of a delicious liberation, instants stolen from a heavy fate. In peasants' folklore and in the columns of urbane journalists alike, such moments were viewed as relieving counterpoint, bright but intermittent and ephemeral at best. Distractions and recreations, not leisure, prevailed in belle-époque thinking and living. The French of the time strongly appreciated the need for laughs and respite. They understood an important human need for escapism, *oubli,* "drunkenness," but seemed to overlook how difficult and incomplete such evasions usually were. Few commented on how much the world of work and cares colored and infiltrated people's after-work activities.

Going to the Grande Jatte or getting drunk in a cabaret appear to have been clear flights from conflict and anxiety, but most entertainments were not cleanly escapist. Many played directly with conflict and risk. Such play was possible because life was still heavily governed by rules and institutions providing reliable order. Just as the security of the institution of marriage allowed the play of mistresses and lovers, a basically stable political and economic order allowed people to indulge regularly in nonutilitarian amuse-ments and to ridicule authority and the underlying order itself. Cabaret singers and circus performers alike mocked leading politicians and censoring puritans with the confidence that their audiences would enjoy the momen-tarily liberating disrespect. In February 1893 at the Cirque Fernando, for example, a claque of "ridiculous Tartuffes" was "invaded" by an "army of chahut" (meaning both the dance and an uproarious row) composed of beautiful young women and Montmartre Bohemians who danced and strutted "to the applause of all." That circus revue, along with a host of cartoons and music hall revues, was parodying the ineffectually harrying League against License in the Streets with Senator Bérenger as chief laughingstock.[3] Neither the threatening volcano nor the authorities and rules were repressive and intimidating enough to kill play or to stifle humor. On the contrary, they unwittingly stimulated it.

In reality, the "army of chahut" was a quite small part of the pre-1914 French population of about 40 million, of which three-fifths was still rural. Most of the French, a people reputed to be frivolous and pleasure-indulgent, curiously undervalued what we would call leisure and fun. Peasants, the largest single class, had the lowest expectations; scarcely conceiving of lei-sure, they were far from considering it something to which they had a right, nor was it yet a social duty for them to partake of the new amusements (winegrowers perhaps being an exception). In the cities, where bons vivants and growing crowds of entertainment consumers were so conspicuous, a variety of economic and cultural inhibitors still weighed on the majority of the population. The better off commonly feared free time and fun when it was the *populo* that was gaining either and making their own choices of activity. A prominent part of the middle classes also had reservations about their own participation in public amusements. They embraced such activities often only after dressing them with respectability in the guise of civic devotion or charity. Their ambivalence showed up regularly in debates about the universal expositions as educational rites or simply fun fairs. Although this group was not as powerful and effectively repressive as their counterparts in the United States and England, they did not have to be for a similar result to obtain. Workers in more slowly industrializing France did not gain enough money and free time, nor did most liberate themselves enough from traditional mores, to come anywhere near Lafargue's utopia.[4]

Potential leisure ended up being exploited by influential rivals for their own ends. Many merchants used it for selling products, and others sought to transform it into so many hours of merchandised distractions. Political and religious leaders, like the Lille Catholics offering *foires aux plaisirs* in the 1880s, tried to outdo their opponents' similar efforts, which they condemned. All overburdened and corrupted what might have been leisure. Indeed, most amusement seekers and providers alike appear to have been working too hard to force fun into existence. Was it because they were driven by what E. P. Thompson has called a sense of time thrift (the modern attitude that "time is money")? Was it because people were being urged on by media images of others' high times or impelled by dissatisfactions to grasp for compensation?[5] Surely any of those prevalent mental states made leisure difficult, if not impossible.

Little in the period and little about the new entertainments encouraged people to cease their exertions, to soar above daily worries and cares, and to feel and affirm, restfully or exuberantly, how good life can be. Few adopted the old wisdom reiterated in a turn-of-the-century history book: "The true fêtes are those which improvise themselves."[6] Political leaders of the Republic ostensibly sought such a fête, spontaneous and joyous, yet they drew back from the risks of riotous transport and overturned order that might lead to a sense of collective rebirth; neither they nor Church and commercial leaders dared encourage or allow a breakthrough to a free dance of social life outside the established order and accountable clocktime existence.

THE ENJOYMENT OF DANGER AND DISASTER

The period called the belle époque is commonly interpreted as a last fling before a long anticipated cataclysm. According to this view, a sense of impending doom intensified the pursuit of pleasure. The French lived it up with a gnawing intuition that tomorrow they would die. Certainly there were forebodings expressed through the period. But in many popular entertainments people were not so much escaping dread as they were finding danger to be a part of their enjoyment. At fêtes foraines, Hughes Le Roux noted, the noises of cries, loud singing, the explosion of shooting-gallery guns and fireworks made people

> dream in spite of themselves of civil war and of barricades, [and it all] strikes into their bone marrow that thrill [*frisson*] that you get in front of the wild animals' cage, when you think that the gate could open and the lion, claws outstretched, could hurl himself on the spectators. . . . But this indefinable anguish itself is sweet, and certainly this apprehension is half the pleasure that many pretty women feel in coming to brush against the throng with rough elbowing from the common people.[7]

An exhilarating fear for entertainers' lives gripped audiences that watched women leaping and somersaulting on horseback, acrobats performing on flying trapezes and tightropes, and lion tamers working their wild charges. In the 1890s music halls began taking over such acts from the circus; in January 1901 the Folies-Bergère, for example, presented "Seeth the audacious lion-tamer and his twenty-one wild Abyssinian beasts." Seeth was popular enough to boost the establishment's receipts to nine thousand francs a night, several thousand over the ordinary level.[8]

The danger was real. And when the equilibrist Castaguet fell from the rope and died in 1888 or when lion tamers were mauled and killed the misfortune was apparently not a disappointment to many spectators. Le Roux maintained that people came hoping to see the *dompteur* eaten; he confessed that he himself did. In any event it is clear that a fatal act had final entertainment value for the illustrated press that unfailingly recounted and pictured the accidents on page one. Similarly, in traditional bullfights in the Midi, cockfights in the North, and the recently imported British form of

LES LIONS DE L'HIPPODROME.
MORT DU DOMPTEUR LUCAS.

IMAGERIE D'ÉPINAL. N° 71

A popular print (*image d'Epinal*) shows the lion tamer Lucas bleeding—brilliantly red blood—from more than twenty-five wounds after being attacked by five lions in 1869. A heroic worker (center) ran to the rescue and subdued the lions, but he was too late to save Lucas's life.

boxing (with slugging going on for as many as forty-nine rounds), the spectacle of blood and violence persistently entertained many.[9]

The thrill of danger took on the most up-to-date technological forms in leading music halls around 1900. Bicycle daredevils defied gravity in loop-the-loop tracks sensationally billed as "the circle of death"; next they began risking an open loop; in 1903 both the Olympia and the Casino de Paris were presenting acts of this sort. Next they cycled round a "deadly track" above an open cage of lions. Then in 1904 a young woman named Mauricia de Thiers "looped the loop" in an *automobile* right in the center of the Folies-Bergère.[10]

For a while around 1903 in Luna Park—Paris's Coney Island, created by an American—every man or woman could buy a ride on a loop-the-loop, otherwise known as "the buckle." The wild whirl proved to be too violent to stay in business long, but the amusement park filled in with other thrill trips, most of them imported from the United States. The old-fashioned merry-go-round, child's swing, and gravity-dependent montagnes russes were now replaced by fast electric motor cars racing down a track almost two

New music hall entertainment after the turn of the century: looping the loop in an automobile. From atop a fifteen-meter-high platform, the young woman's automobile plunged almost vertically, turned over and reversed itself in the air, and landed on a track near the floor. Applauding spectators were reportedly "breathless from excitement." Photo from *La Vie en grand air*, September 8, 1904. (Musée Carnavalet, Paris)

kilometers long, a water chute that added a bracing spray of cold water to the thrill of the car's plunge, and a "diabolic wheel" that shook and lifted its startled riders. Luna Park pleasurers could also descend into a "dark labyrinth" full of rude surprises—sections of floor that swung back and forth, suddenly dropped several inches, and shot up currents of air to blow off hats and lift skirts. These were nerve-racking games of dizziness and fear, to borrow Jean Cazeneuve's term—modern industrial forms of a "natural impulse" or play need that was once satisfied by dizzying dances. Through the elaborate new technology, as before through dance, people temporarily escaped from the normal tasks of coordinating and regulating their bodies, and they played with abnormal bodily sensations. The modern way of heightening their nervous tension (perhaps already greater than in premodern life) entailed subjecting themselves to frightening machines run for others' profit.[11]

A kind of playful danger was also chosen by the person on the brink of poverty who bet on horses. And at street fairs after 1900, the *Courrier français* reported, games of chance appeared in "astonishing numbers." At a New Year's fair on the Place de la République in 1902, for example, workers from Belleville and Ménilmontant no longer shot for macaroons by the dozen or shaggy plush monkeys; "today people gamble two-sou coins on the turning wheel." Roulette was reportedly the most frequented stand wherever the fair operators set up—in Paris as in the heart of Poitou and Brittany.[12] Chance and fear may also have been part of the fun of the elegant who visited lowlife dives or simply joined in rough-jostling fair crowds. The widely trumpeted desire for individual liberty or control of one's life did not preclude counterdesires for external determinism, abdication of control; within the limits of play it was apparently enjoyable on occasion to let go of the tasks of willing and reasoning, of being responsible, while anxiously indulging in wild hope and risk. In turning away from the too familiar and predictable, people may also have been fleeing all too predictable amusements, ones that cautiously stuck to hackneyed formulas and stale ingredients:

You believe that it's funny not to be able to walk into a music-hall without hearing a little woman say to you in a vinegary voice that she is a moving sidewalk and that people climb on her all day long?—which appears quite probable.

So complained a journalist writing in a paper that was anything but hostile to fun.[13] Entertainments laced with risk could serve as escapes from the safely familiar and routine in amusements as well as in work life. Anxiety and foreboding had their attractions.

Grisly popular tales and peddlers' news sheets (*canards*) picturing stories of a woman and children axed to death, of a traveling woman raped by twenty-nine men, of catastrophic fires and floods had for centuries fed a popular fascination with disaster, violence, and cruelty. At the 1889 world's fair, Debans noticed, people seemed to prefer attractions evoking "the most somber memories"—*la cité* under Henry IV with the little Châtelet prisons, tortures, and henchmen; the Tour de Nesle; the Bastille; the Tour du Temple with Louis XVI as prisoner. At the 1900 fair a "gallery of tortures" drew receipts of 14,813 francs, while a panorama showing Lourdes took in only 2,258 francs. It was not that torture shows were unusual; they were standard sideshow attractions. Paris's Grand Guignol Theater, which opened in 1896, also specialized in gore and death. The popular theaters of the *Boulevard du crime*—the Boulevard du Temple—had earlier served up enough similar fare to earn the district the description "a labyrinth of crimes and horrors." Around 1900, melodrama in the boulevard and faubourg theaters offered the same kind of chills with plays such as *The Mysteries of the Inquisition* and *Douglas the Vampire*. The enjoyment here, common enough today, seems to be in touching emotional extremes, in being moved to fear and horror by controlled artistic forms, which afford the privilege of experiencing the overwhelming feelings aroused by dreaded disaster without having to bear the real costs and pain.[14]

Some Parisians also took pleasure in greeting possible real disaster—global disaster—with macabre gaiety. In 1910 they found a pretext for partying in the approach of the "famous and dangerous Halley's comet." During the entire night of February 17–18, possibly the prelude to the fatal collision and the end of the world, many cafés in the capital remained open so that people might sing, dance, and dine to the end; some restaurants featured a

Réveillon de la Comète, a midnight feast like the traditional one on Christmas Eve. "People must make merry before dying," concluded Apollinaire in his reporting of the event.[15] In the years just after the comet's passing, as the murderous collision of armies threatened, was there similar enjoyment of the danger?

WAR AS ENTERTAINMENT AND FESTIVITY

Well back into the nineteenth century, amusement seekers found war to be entertaining. Battle scenes were favorites in panoramas and hippodrome spectaculars. In 1900 the panorama of Austerlitz, for example, took in 42,127 francs in contrast to the panorama of the Revolution's 16,385 francs and Golgotha's 5,139.75 francs. And no public celebration was complete without fireworks recalling battles with their thundering bombshells and flashes of fire. At the world's fair in 1900, the staged naval battle was a major attraction, we noted earlier, and at the Eldorado music hall early in 1900, the "*cinématographe parlé de M. Maire* made all the amusing or heroic episodes of military life parade before the spectators."[16]

As the little wars of the early twentieth century flared up around the globe, they provided fresh material for Paris entertainments. At the Cirque d'Hiver in 1901 audiences watched a military pantomime entitled "The Allies in China," and at the Nouveau Cirque in 1905 they watched a pantomime of the Russo-Japanese War. Though more lifelike than pantomimes and panoramas, the filmed views of war were less than fully truthful. All these forms of entertainment presented conventional images of war as noble pageantry, exciting spectacle, and all too human buffoonery. Manufactured for mass consumption for profit, they were facile and unchallenging variants of familiar formulas, sure not to shake and move people to fresh insights.

Danger and anxiety are probably enjoyable for most only so long as they are clearly controlled, limited, and artificial. Isn't play possible only when one is not trying to resolve grave problems and conflicts in real life? There is some evidence that after the turn of the century, war danger and general anxiety took a toll on the spirit of play. At Mardi Gras time in 1904, journalist Edouard Trogan observed that "popular joy is dead. . . . Apprehension of all sorts darkens people's spirit."[17] But one can doubt whether such an observation signaled something new, for that sort of requiem had been recurrent since the 1880s.

More important and convincing testimony about change came from observers of youth after the turn of the century. In 1902, for example, Louis Filliol reported, "The student of today has undergone the influence of external things and has become more 'serious,'. . . Today's [students] are more practical, more correct, colder. . . . It seems that the heart is drying up."[18] It would be more accurate to say that the heart was warming up and was throbbing to new causes and ideals: sacrifice, duty, and suffering. In an atmosphere darkened by bitter strife over the Dreyfus affair and the heightening tensions with Germany, the luxury of festive frolic faded, if it did not disappear. The emergence of a new rightist nationalism among Latin Quarter youth is well known and amply recorded.[19] Those who exalted military discipline, courage, and devotion to church and country were engaged in a new revolt, not just against the skeptical, rationalist, internationalist Left that triumphed in the Dreyfus affair, but also against the spirit of the belle époque and its libertine champions.

One can detect changes, too, in notable members of the older generation. One bellwether was Paul Adam, who before the turn of the century had crusaded for pleasure and liberty against the dogmas of obedience and suffering. By 1907, in an atmosphere darkened by growing threats of war, Adam was calling for checks on individualism, indolence, and the pursuit of pleasure. "In vain does one flee suffering," he observed in his now chastened and sober wisdom. Desire, "an imperious need," tortures us; appetites grow faster than our means of satisfying them, and attempts to satisfy them never fully live up to initial hope; the one who has discovered the insufficiencies of fulfilled desire is left with gnawing ennui. How then should one live? Part of his answer was to live more as a detached spectator. "The sole pleasure is to know one's pains well enough to enjoy the spectacle of them. . . . The secret of wisdom is to compose a purely spectator soul," watching one's existence instead of playing it passionately. The other part of his new ascetic strategy was to harden himself to woes by continually exercising himself with them. Rather than fleeing them or trying to defeat suffering, it is better to take them on continually, to train oneself to live with hardship, pains, anxiety, and disappointments.[20]

Toulouse-Lautrec's friend, Louis Bouglé,
adopted the name "L.B. Spoke" for his bicycle
shop for which Lautrec made this poster. Enthusiasm for bicycle racing spread rapidly in
France in the 1890s. In the mid-nineties, when
this poster was made, Lautrec frequently went
on Sundays to the Vélodrome de la Seine or
the Vélodrome Buffalo to watch the cyclists.
(Courtesy of the Boston Public Library, Print
Department, Wiggin Collection)

L'Automobile, 1896, by Toulouse-Lautrec. In
1896 sports enthusiast Toulouse-Lautrec made
this lithograph of his cousin, Dr. Tapié de Ce-
leyran, at the wheel. The driver, face black-
ened by exhaust, is so engrossed in the grim
heroic new "sport" of automobile driving that
he is oblivious to the attractive woman strolling
by with her dog. "The automobile is the sport
of the day, it's incontestable," declared a writer
for *Lectures pour tous* (no. 6, March 1902,
p. xx).

Like many members of the upper levels of society since the 1880s, Adam found the best training to be in sports. Now he wrote to cheer not the forward march of enjoyment but the rise of sports in France. For champions of sports the most encouraging developments of the era were the growth of bicycling and the good showing of French athletes in the Olympic Games, revived through the assiduous efforts of French aristocrat Pierre de Coubertin. "Already the practice of sports, so vigorously propagated since the invention of cycling, changes our lives," asserted Adam. "Gone are the indolence and softness in the large cities. Now each exerts himself to the utmost, competes," he maintained in a transport of missionary zeal for the new gospel of sports. That zeal readily combined with boisterous nationalist pride, another key ingredient in the new mood leading to the war. At the 1896 Olympic Games in Athens, Adam recalled,

> France revealed herself to be the most effectively sportive nation. Her athletes triumphed. Twenty-three first prizes, 8 second prizes and 13 third prizes assured her the laurels. Our people, formerly quite indifferent to the vigors of the body, in ten years has made itself an elite of happy champions.[21]

France especially excelled in the "warrior arts," Adams noted cheeringly: fencing, military shooting, and bicycle racing. Bicycles he believed would be particularly important for stealthy reconnaissance and for quick, quiet troop movements in the next war. Growing international tensions in the early twentieth century made sports, identified with martial skills since antiquity, all the more crucial to observers like Adam. Realizing that "there are always barbarians in the world," he urged his compatriots to bring about "the resurrection of . . . heroisms in the souls and bodies of Latin youth." Sports were the needed tonic to French energies; sports could increase the vigor of the nation, instill audacity, and foster a readiness to meet dangers. Sports brought out a "collective soul" in the participants: in their excitement they voluntarily put together their strength and shared the high emotions of hope (of winning), fear (of losing), and the dangers of the struggle. They learned cooperation and experienced solidarity to counter the excesses of individualism so prevalent with the French. Not only was sport a preparation for war, but war was a continuation of sport. "The one who points a battleship cannon will be only prolonging the gesture of the fist held out against the adversary." Quoting Nietzsche, Adam praised the taste for sports as a daily stimulant of "the will to power."[22]

To intellectuals like Adam and upper-class organizers like Pierre de Coubertin, sports were scarcely clean escapism. They were far from being play, done for their own sake. On the contrary, they were fundamentally utilitarian and serious, essential to national survival. It is doubtful that the growing number of youths who participated first in gymnastics and later in cycling and football fully embraced that ideological view. Middle-class and worker youths in gymnastic societies showed patriotic concern, but they also acted out of desires for male comradeship and cheap recreation offering opportunities for travel and social drinking. As participants, the less privileged classes overall were slow to join in the enthusiasm for sports, despite threats of war. Only a small minority of workers—chiefly male youths—joined bicycle and football clubs and played regularly. As spectators, however, urban masses followed football finals, boxing matches, and the Tour de France with passionate interest that was in part nationalistic.[23]

In other spectator entertainments, the common people even more clearly played out their war anxieties. In music hall revues, patriotic and bellicose themes became prominent several years before the war. In movie theaters, audiences of 1913 found a wave of new films catering to their preoccupation with war. The Cosmographe movie studio managed to make a rousing pageant of French military heroism out of the debacle of 1870–71. *Honneur au soldat* and *Ne touchez pas le drapeau* similarly reassured the apprehensive, playing on national pride and promoting patriotic unity with tableaux of the army's great maneuvers and apotheoses of the flag (in films like *Salute to the Sacred Emblem*). The giant Gaumont studio was not slow to meet the competition.[24] In contrast, Méliès's fantasy films were no longer well received, and after 1912 he made no more. But perhaps the most telling sign of the passing of an era was the demise of the *Courrier français* in 1913, the saucy voice of frivolity and pleasure since 1884. A new mood also showed up in Bastille Day crowds. The last two years before the war saw extraordinary, indeed spectacular, serious celebrations of July 14, sparked not by triumphant glee but by patriotic concern. Joan of Arc celebrations, the favorite of rightist nationalists, also evoked heightened enthusiasm just before the war.[25]

The outbreak of hostilities ended those spirited mass demonstrations. For four years Bastille Day became a somber solemnity without dancing, without games, and without battlelike fireworks. Only the rituals of remembrance and patriotic rededication remained. The outbreak of war also killed many commercial amusements. Horse racing stopped at the end of July 1914. With horses requisitioned for war duty, the Nouveau Cirque transformed its stable space into a bar. The Tour de France was not held for four years. The Jardin de Paris closed for the duration of the conflict. All Paris theaters closed on police order and remained closed for the first nine months of the war. The Bal Bullier, requisitioned by the government, was turned into a uniform factory. The cars of the giant Ferris wheel were removed and taken to the North where they became temporary housing for refugees. Six months after the war's beginning, the Moulin Rouge burned; it was not reopened until 1923. In August 1914 the City of Light fell dark. During the Great War, it was the places best suited to the dark, the movie theaters, that fared the best.

If Roger Caillois's argument is applied to that point in history, we would consider the war not so much an end to festivity as a continuation of fête in another form. Certainly war was the decisive break with the routine and cautious ways of normal life. It was the ultimate spree, a rejection of mundane limits, a breakaway to a primordial chaos. It was a fling into the normally forbidden, exalting spirits—at least initially—opening up the possibility of renewal or creation of another world.[26]

In the scholarly and popular understanding of fête in France, gaiety had not always been considered essential: people could throw themselves into voluptuous orgies of grief—as at Victor Hugo's funeral and President Carnot's funeral; the very phrase in French, *fêtes funèbres*, makes the point. Festivals of hatred and destruction were also understood in France long before Caillois's scholarly contributions.

War as fête lacked only what the belle-époque partisans had held to be essential: gaiety, if not joy. In the paroxysm of destruction, where was the merry uplifting of spirits? Granted, at the beginning, some combatants in-dulged in a taunting travesty of the culture of entertainments. In the trenches of 1914 German soldiers reportedly sang the music hall hit "Viens pou-poule"—in French—and the *poilus* opposite them took up the refrain:

Come little chicken
Come little chicken / Come!
When I hear songs
That makes me a turned on scamp / Ah![27]

But a grimmer mechanical carnage was to predominate. In a France still nursing along optimistic visions from the last century, war turned into a nightmare that could hardly be comprehended in concepts of festivity. War brought out the part of the French tradition that belle-époque champions had sought to conquer: the camp of suffering, sacrifice, and discipline. That camp had never been vanquished. It had been a functional part of the dynamics of the belle-époque psyche itself. In the war, it forcefully reasserted itself and indeed eclipsed the France of laughter and gaiety.

After the war it receded for a time, but took over once more just after the collapse of France in 1940. In July 1940 General Weygand, supreme commander of the defeated French armies, issued a manifesto indicting "the wave of materialism which has submerged France. . . . The spirit of enjoyment and ease," he charged, "are the profound cause of our weakness and our neglects."[28] It was an eerie echo of the indictment made by conservatives after the defeat of 1871.

So the Third Republic died branded with the stigma of enjoyment. Although it had been founded by stern moralists and devotees of work, it had acquired the identity fostered by the belle-époque militants of the 1880s. In the new order headed by another austere military commander, Marshal Pétain, now work, religion, and family were to supplant enjoyment and ease. Dances, identified with the pleasure-ridden Republic, were banned. In imitation of Nazi Germany, a program of Happiness through Work (*Le Bonheur par Travail*) was created; obligatory national work service for youth was established to suppress conflicts of classes, as fêtes had been expected to do earlier.[29] And sports were organized to promote discipline and unity.

Viewed in the moral light of statements like Weygand's and Paul Adam's long before, a light I find too illuminating to leave at the point they did, French history slips readily back into old myths, Manichaean and then Dionysian. Accordingly, it was "the Army of Suffering" that marched victoriously once more, this time under the Vichy leaders and Nazi masters.

But as before, the Army of Suffering met with rising resistance, and as before, a new Republic and new liberty again took flight—and restored exuberant celebrations of Bastille Day; new Gallic militants reasserted the right to enjoyment; and, on occasions such as the Liberation of Paris, French crowds once more rejoiced together in sudden and intoxicating freedom, risking public disorder and adding new scenes to a national legend of festive joy.

CONCLUSION

By the early twentieth century, most of what we know as the modern culture of entertainments was in place. The fin de siècle had been extraordinarily fertile. Its innovations quickly became institutions, ranging from a secular national holiday to the industrial marvel that is cinema, even cinema experimentally enriched with color and sound as early as 1900. Important later additions such as radio and television continued and strengthened changes that took shape back in the belle époque. The overall direction was toward more technologically based, commercial, private (even in public), and nationally uniform entertainments.

Viewed in the large with only the broadest strokes showing, France, as a kingdom of pleasures, may be said to have been undergoing the same decline of public pleasure that was common to the modern capitalist and industrializing West. As Johan Huizinga put it in his classic *Homo Ludens*, play has been on the wane since the eighteenth century. The French, like their neighbors, have assumed an overly serious, excessively utilitarian outlook—at the expense of a ludic balance of jest and earnestness. That spirit of play reasserted itelf only fitfully in the period treated here. Theodor Adorno's analysis may help clarify more of the big changes. Adorno points to the importance of a fantasy-crushing rationality and industrial technology that have become prevalent and have shaped the formation of a modern "culture industry." Under such conditions, entertainment has become standardized and homogeneous, mechanically evoking conventional responses. Mass producing for maximum profit, the entertainment industry has favored technique and facile formula over life-illuminating content. It has marketed its product to people as simply interchangeable consumers, and at every turn it assures them that there is no alternative to consuming. It has defrauded them of freedom after work and has impoverished their social and emotional experience of leisure. For those dependent on such entertainment, Adorno ob-

217

serves, free time has become an extension of work, both subject to a common system of production.

Closer historical studies of France, including this one, bring out more ambivalence in the changes. Historians note, for example, not only that magico-religious festivals waned along with traditional agricultural life generally, but also that new liberty and choice for individuals waxed. This book has emphasized mixed results from several major forces shaping the new leisure. The force of central government implanted national celebrations that were sometimes joyous, but it often withered them with its self-promoting control. Similarly, the growth of commercial "places of pleasure" made some kinds of amusement more common, but probably also aggravated boredom—for people not having access to them and even for some who did (habitués who tired of repetition, for example). A third and notoriously double-edged force, technology, made possible larger, more spectacular, and more easily reproduced amusements, but it also diminished people's participation, their sharing of responses, and their influencing of performances. The history of belle-époque leisure and fun is hardly a simple tale of decline and fall—any more than it is one of progress or of a golden age of gaiety and ease.

Attendance and admission statistics tell us that unprecedentedly large numbers of people went to the world's fairs, music halls, and cinemas—apparently in search of enjoyment. One who examines firsthand testimony finds that at the same world's fair or music hall, some individuals knew enjoyment, whereas others felt disappointment or had very mixed feelings. Although the subjective reactions cannot be measured or tallied, some relative dissatisfaction can be inferred from such statistical evidence as the diminishing numbers of customers for panoramas in the 1890s and later for music halls as cinema rose in popularity. We also find articulated criticisms, which I suspect represent the views of others who did not leave a verbal mark on the records. Those criticisms do more than give us a historical sense of audience reactions; they clarify and reinforce the more general critiques of theorists like Adorno; they help us understand the insufficiencies of modern entertainment too readily assumed to be entertaining.

The various criticisms in essence are familiar enough to us today; they suggest that what was offered was often inane, vulgar, meretricious, stereotypic, and simplistic, overdone and oversold. The pitfall here is that historically such critiques have often been a matter of the taste and traditions of one class condemning those of another. What is scorned as escapist or vulgar fluff may be to others artifice and play helping them cope with their everyday world or enriching a cramped and chafing existence in ways that the critic does not begin to consider. Further, in the period treated by this book, too many critiques simply deprecated apparent popular preferences without judging equally the entertainment producers who influenced their public and provided only certain choices. Debate on these questions will long continue; in closing, I am going to offer a contribution to it from a different avenue. To conclude, to understand what was missing, it seems to me most fruitful to look once more at some of the best moments in the period, to reflect on why they were so limited, and finally to conjure up visions of what might have been and might be (a judgment without which any written history becomes simply an apology for that which is or was).

Moments of obvious delight do sparkle through the drabness of most records that historians use. Some of those moments occurred in events called public fêtes. Others occurred in boisterous dance halls, in jovial boating parties along the Seine (as Renoir showed us), and, interspersed with work, in the *lavoirs*, where laundresses let loose with banter, laughter, and rough physical play. A kind of festivity also appeared in quiet places like the deluxe restaurants in the Bois de Boulogne, where—as one flowery writer related—after savoring delicate tastes and generous wines and conversing with companions cheered by fine champagnes, fortunate people listened to Gypsy waltzes, felt themselves caressed by breezes blowing through the cool of leafy arbors, walked through fragrant wooded *allées*, and knew with inward rejoicing that "life is perfectly good." Advertising and rising expectations impelled people to pursue such moments with more determination and to seek them more frequently than ever before. But those experiences could not be forced or willed into existence. They happened, and not always when and where people sought them. They happened to people at least momentarily fortunate enough, hopeful enough, and generous-spirited enough to rise above worries, suffering, and resentments. Whether in crowds or in couples, such times did not depend on elaborate arrangements or staging.

People experiencing festivity were those who managed to transcend the modern imperative to strive, to work, to seek the profitable and practical—at least momentarily. They were those who accepted themselves and others in feelings of restfulness, hope, and thankfulness, even thankfulness for something so general and basic as life. As Roger Caillois has pointed out, festivity is a breaking with mundane time and cares; it is a flight out of ordinary history. It has a timelessness about it, like an imagined paradise, like a dream that resists historical analysis as it often eludes efforts to produce it.

Yet the French of the belle époque conspicuously made strenuous efforts to buy and to do all that was possible to produce those festive moments. The economically advantaged regularly did all they could for themselves in privileged places like the restaurants of the Bois. Meanwhile public-minded figures such as politicians and publicists called for delight for the population as a whole and made efforts to create it. These people acted out of a concern about the country's deep divisions—religious, political, economic—and the growing specialization of labor. They insisted on the superior value of shared public pleasure, or "social joy" as sociologist Gabriel Tarde put it. Most commonly they proposed public fêtes as the fullest social joy.

This ideal of the fête was expressed not only in the eloquent writing and speeches of such notables as Jules Michelet, Léon Gambetta, and Romain Rolland, but also in popular newspapers and reports scrawled by half-literate village mayors. It was an ideal nurtured in a cultural tradition distinguished by bold thinkers—some revolutionary and utopian—who dared dream of a happier life and periodic joy for an entire people. At the same time it probably also owed much to a nostalgia for the fêtes of yesteryear, remembered or imagined. Elegantly or simply expressed, a vision of festivity seems to have been widespread—a vision of a gladdened people emotionally erasing their differences and together celebrating a common hope or a "gift" felt to be received. The ideal was shared public enjoyment that liberated from routine and restrictions, exhilarated and renewed, and suffused separate individuals with an enlarging sense of relatedness in a common cause.

We can find examples of such collective exaltation through the period from Bastille Day 1880 to the First World War, but not a clear increase of them or pattern of "progress" accompanying improvement in standards of living and reductions of working hours. There was no correlative "progress" not simply because the period's festivals and entertainments were often flawed and deficient. Nor was it simply that government and business failed to make proper clever arrangements for popular amusement. The problem, I think, was much larger and farther reaching. It arose as improving conditions eliminated the traditionally strong contrasts of hard work and hard play— of grinding material struggle relieved by periodic leaps into another order of life that was ordinarily relegated to myth, to dream, to the sacred. Under those improving conditions, modern people have ceased sharing the pressure of deprivation that from time to time bursts into an uproarious spree, suspending and reversing the normal order. Instead, the modern normal order has taken on many of the characteristics traditionally confined to festive times: indulgence, prodigality, waste, taboo breaking, destruction. And into its everyday texture have been woven entertainments that share in and reflect the normal conditions of our modern order: the more externally controlled and depersonalized work life, clock-bound and regular rhythms, the more predictable satisfaction of vital needs as well as commercially fostered "needs," the lessening of physical demands, the growing force of technology. For the many, these entertainments have tended to be as mildly and blandly amusing as work is mildly engaging. Both are tailored for people treated as objects.

The conclusion to this argument does not have to be that we must bring back the darkness in order to have better contrasts of brightness. Nor that we should create a homogenizing new world of commingled work and play without pain and disappointment. There is another possibility. It is that we can create social and work conditions that are much more satisfying to workers (all of us) as free and creative subjects. (On this ahistorical terrain, a resort to questions seems best—just two final questions). Would not better, more fulfilling mass entertainments be *demanded* if the majority were living and working with more creative freedom and hope? And would not such people be nearer the mysterious passage to the festive, readier for the delights of the "free flight of the spirit"?

NOTES

CHAPTER 1

1. *Le Temps*, July 15, 1880. p. 1. For the mayor's report on the festivities in La Boissière, see the Archives Départementales de l'Hérault (hereafter AD), 40 M 17; for Thiers, see AD Puy-de-Dôme, M 0132. The best general history is Rosemonde Sanson's *Les 14 juillet, 1789–1975: Fêtes et conscience nationale* (Paris: Flammarion, 1976).

2. Camille Pelletan, "Le 14 juillet," *La Justice*, May 24, 1880, p. 1; *Le Temps*, July 15, 1880, p. 7.

3. *Le Temps*, May 28, 1878, p. 1. Jules Michelet, *Nos fils* (Paris: Lacroix et Verboeckhoven, 1870), p. 422. See also the innovative proposals for new fêtes that scholar Henri Baudrillart presented in a major address to the five academies of the Institut de France on October 25, 1873—*Les Fêtes publiques* (Paris: Imprimerie de Firmin-Didot, 1873).

4. Eugen Weber, *Peasants into Frenchmen: The Modernization of Rural France, 1870–1914* (Stanford: Stanford University Press, 1976), chap. 21. I have also drawn on reports in the following departmental archives: Allier, Nièvre, Puy-de-Dôme, Cantal, Haute-Loire, Indre-et-Loire, Charente-Maritime, Haute-Garonne, Aude, Hérault, Gard, Gironde, Côtes-du-Nord, Ille-et-Vilaine, Finistère, Morbihan, and Loire-Atlantique.

5. On prices just before the festival, see Pierre Sorlin, *Waldeck Rousseau* (Paris: A. Colin, 1966), p. 248. On the first modern July 14, see Sanson, *Les 14 juillet*, and my article "Festivals in Modern France: The Experience of the Third Republic," *Journal of Contemporary History* 12 (July 1977):435–60.

6. Pelletan, "Le 14 juillet," *La Justice*, July 16, 1880, p. 1.

7. (Aramon) AD Gard, 6 M 1200 (July 1880). For Ars's report, see AD Charente-Maritime, 4 M 1/14 (July 15, 1881).

8. For Mareuil-sur-Lay, see AD Vendée, I M 497 (July 14, 1880).

9. On the republican rationale for fêtes, see Raspail's speech, reported in *La Justice*, June 12, 1880.

10. See, for example, Michelet's classic rhetoric about July 14 in *History of the French Revolution*, trans. Charles Cocks (Chicago: University of Chicago Press, 1967), p. 162; *Le Temps*, July 15, 1880, p. 1.

11. Aigues-Vives report in AD Hérault, M 17 (July 1880); Piré request, in AD Ille-et-Vilaine, M 374 (July 12, 1892).

12. On firecrackers as early as July 6, see the Archives de la Préfecture de la Police—Paris, BA 42702 357, July 1880; Thiers, AD Puy-de-Dôme, M 1032 (July 15, 1880). The story about the craftsman of the Rue Charlot comes from *La Lanterne*, July 8, 1880, p. 2.

13. Charles Moiset, "Les Usages, croyances, traditions, superstitions du département de l'Yonne," *Le Bulletin de la Société des sciences de l'Yonne* 42 (1888):104–05.

14. Murviel report in AD Hérault, 40 M 17 (July 1880); Thiers, in AD Puy-de-Dôme, M 1032; Chéméré report, in AD Loire-Atlantique, 1 M 677 (July 1881); Challans report, in AD Vendée, 1 M 497 (July 2, 1881).

15. Weber, *Peasants into Frenchmen*, esp. chap. 21; Morlaix, in AD Finistère, 1 M (July 15, 1880); Laroque, in AD Hérault, 40 M 17

(July 1880); Jarnac report, quoted in Yvette Renaud, "14 juillet 1880: Première fête nationale de la République," "*Aguiaire,*" *Revue de recherches ethnographiques* 4, no. 4 (July 1980):243; Gâvres, in AD Morbihan, M 2373 (July 1893).

16. On the fear of crowds, see Susanna Barrows, *Distorting Mirrors: Visions of the Crowd in Late Nineteenth-century France* (New Haven: Yale University Press, 1981).

17. Ernest Lavisse, "Jeunesse d'autrefois et d'aujourd'hui," in *A propos de nos écoles* (Paris: Colin, 1905), pp. 231–34.

18. *L'Eclair,* July 16, 1898, p. 2. For the "Jour de boire" ditty, see *Le Courrier français,* July 15, 1898, p. 3.

19. Saligny mayor's report, in AD Allier, M 708c (July 1880); Piré report, in AD Ille-et-Vilaine, M 374 (July 1892); Saint-André-du-Bois report, in AD Gironde, I M 711 (July 15, 1880).

20. Newspaper commentaries on the diminishing celebrations were commonplace; typical were those in *Le Petit Journal,* July 15, 1893; *Le Matin,* July 15, 1894; *Le Temps,* July 15, 1898. See the discussion in Rosemonde Sanson, "La Célébration de la fête nationale sous la IIIe République (1880–1914)," Thèse de 3e cycle, Sorbonne, 1971, pp. 271–78; an explanatory account that is drastically abridged appears in her book *Les 14 juillet,* p. 102; Alain Faure, *Paris carême-prenant: Du Carnaval à Paris au XIX siècle* (Paris: Hachette, 1978).

21. Eugen Weber, "Pierre de Coubertin and the Introduction of Sport in France," *Journal of Contemporary History* 5 (1970):3–26, and his "Gymnastics and Sports in Fin-de-Siècle France: Opium of the Classes?" *American Historical Review* 86 (February 1971):70–98. On proposals for a new popular theater, see David James Fisher, "The Origins of the French Popular Theater," *Journal of Contemporary History* 12 (1977):461–97.

CHAPTER 2

1. Jules Michelet, *La Montagne,* in *Oeuvres complètes,* vol. 3 (Paris: C. Lévy, 1901), p. 103.

2. August Montagu, *Manuel politique du citoyen français* (Paris: Les Libraires, 1881), p. 323.

3. André Siegfried, *Tableau des partis en France* (Paris: B. Grasset, 1930), p. 132.

4. Michael Marrus, "Social Drinking in the Belle Epoque," *Journal of Social History* 7, no. 2 (1974):115–41; Theodore Zeldin, *France, 1848–1945,* vol. 2 (Oxford: Oxford University Press, 1977), p. 699.

5. Statistics on spectacle receipts are taken from the *Annuaire statistique de la ville de Paris* (Paris: Imprimerie Nationale, each year from 1880 on).

6. Armand Wallon, *La Vie quotidienne dans les villes d'eaux, 1850–1914* (Paris: Hachette, 1981); James C. Haug, *Leisure and Urbanism in Nineteenth-century Nice* (Lawrence: Regents Press of Kansas, 1982); Maurice Agulhon, Tome 3, "Apogée et crise de la civilisation paysanne," in Georges Duby, ed., *Histoire de la France rurale* (Paris: Seuil, 1976), p. 352.

7. Le Docteur Francus, *Voyage dans le Midi de l'Ardèche* (Privas: "Le Patriote," 1885), p. 470; Jules Delvaille, "La Crise morale," *La Nouvelle Revue* (March 1905), p. 10.

8. Paul Lafargue, *Le Droit à la paresse* (Paris: Bureau d'Editions, 1935); Georges Chevrier, "La Liberté de la chair," *La Revue indépendante* (February 1885), p. 271; Peter Kropotkin, *The Conquest of Bread* (New York: New York University Press, 1972), p. 50.

9. Lafargue, *Droit,* pp. 14, 20, 29, 32–33 ff.

10. Alexandre Zévaès, *Sur l'écran politique: Ombres et silhouettes* (Paris: Les Editions Georges-Anquetil, 1928), pp. 186–88.

11. Steinlen, cartoon entitled "Fête nationale" in *Almanach de la question sociale* (1896), p. 45; Widhopff cartoon in *Le Courrier français,* January 21, 1900, p. 7.

12. Anatole France, "La Liberté par étude," *Cahiers de la Quinzaine,* no. 3 (1902):13.

13. Noël Richard, *A l'aube de symbolisme: Hydropathes, fumistes, et décadents* (Paris: Nizet, 1961) and *Le Mouvement décadent* (Paris: Nizet, 1968).

14. *L'Hydropathe*, February 19, 1879, p. 3.

15. On L'Abbaye, see the entire issue of *Le Courrier français* for May 23, 1886.

16. On Lévy and the Incoherents, see the entire issue of *Le Courrier français* for March 12, 1885; also F. Bac, *Intimités de la IIIe République*, vol. 1 (Paris: Hachette, 1935), pp. 508–11.

17. Jules Claretie, *La Vie à Paris, 1883* (Paris: Victor Havard, 1884), p. 401, article dated October 12, 1883; John Grand Carteret, *Les Moeurs et la caricature* (Paris: Librairie Illustrée, 1888), pp. 530–31; Anne de Bercy and Armand Ziwès, *A Montmartre le soir, cabarets et chansonniers d'hier* (Paris: Grasset, 1951), pp. 93–94.

18. Goudeau, "L'Incohérence," *Revue illustrée* 3 (1887):229; Lévy, "L'Incohérence," *Le Courrier français*, March 12, 1885, p. 4.

19. Claude Ruggieri, *Précis historique sur les fêtes, les spectacles et les réjouissances publiques* (Paris: L'Auteur, 1830), p. v; Mrs. Gore [Catherine Grace Frances], *Paris in 1841* (London: Longman, Brown, Green, & Longmans, 1842), p. 261.

20. Alfred Fouillée, "Psychologie de l'esprit français: Autrefois et aujourd'hui," *Revue des deux mondes* 138 (November 1, 1896):60; Henry Maret, *Pensées et opinions* (Paris: E. Flammarion, 1903), p. 261. See also J.-E.-M. Cénac-Moncaut, *Histoire du caractère et de l'esprit français*, vol. 1 (Paris: Didier, 1867), pp. 72–73.

21. The English guide is *The Pleasure Guide to Paris for Bachelors* (London: Nilsson, n.d. [ca. 1903]), p. vi; Alfred Delvau, *Les Plaisirs de Paris* (Paris: A. Faure, 1867); Camille Debans, *Les Plaisirs et les curiosités de Paris* (Paris: E. Kolb, 1889), p. 11; Richard H. Davis, *About Paris* (1895; reprint. Upper Saddle River, N.J.: Gregg Press, 1969), p. 47.

22. *Paris after Dark, Night Guide for Gentlemen*, 13th ed. (Boulogne: J. Boyer, n.d.); Albert Wolff, "Courrier de Paris," *Le Figaro*, February 24, 1882.

23. Maxime du Camp, *Paris, ses organes, ses fonctions et sa vie* (Paris: Hachette, 1872), 6:383.

24. Ibid., p. 384.

25. Auriol, "Les Dernières nouvelles de Paris," *Le Chat noir*, December 19, 1885, p. 614.

26. On Roques's defense of the forains, see *Le Courrier français*, December 2, 1888.

27. François Gauzi, *Lautrec et son temps* (Paris: David Perrat, 1954), pp. 71–76.

28. Jules Claretie, *La Vie à Paris—1884* (Paris: Victor Havard, 1885), pp. 219–20, and *La Vie à Paris—1885* (Paris: Victor Havard, 1886), pp. 496–99; George Auriol, "Rodolphe Salis et les deux 'Chat Noir,'" *Mercure de France* 9 (1926):315–32.

29. Francis Carco, *La Belle époque au temps de Bruant* (Paris: Gallimard, 1954), pp. 24–25, 48. Jules Bertaut, *Les Dessous de la "Troisième"* (Paris: Tallandier, 1959), p. 76.

30. Paul Adam, "Les Energies," *Revue blanche* 10, no. 71 (May 1896):435, 438, 441.

31. Georges Brandimbourg, *Le Courrier français*, February 23, 1890.

32. On Vendean dancing as rebellion: AD Vendée, 1 M 498, Prefect to Interior Minister, July 21, 1889.

33. Jacques Lethève, *La Caricature et la presse sous la IIIe République* (Paris: Armand Colin, 1961), p. 45.

34. Emile Goudeau, *Dix ans de Bohème* (Paris: Librairie Illustrée, 1888), pp. 95, 101, 139.

35. Ferran Canyameres, *L'Homme de la belle époque* (Paris: Les Editions Universelles, 1946); Pierre Andrieu, *Souvenirs des frères Isola: Cinquante ans de vie Parisienne* (Paris: Flammarion, 1943).

CHAPTER 3

1. Jules Lévy, *Les Hydropathes* (Paris: A. Delpeuch, 1928), pp. 5–15; *L'Hydropathe*, January 22, 1879, article on Goudeau, p. 2; Emile Goudeau, *Dix ans de Bohème* (Paris: Librairie

Illustrée, 1888), pp. 148, 162–66; Noël Richard, *A l'aube de symbolisme: Hydropathes, fumistes et décadents* (Paris: Nizet, 1961), pp. 20–23, 34.

2. Of the numerous accounts of the Chat Noir, some of the most useful are the following: George Auriol, "Rodolphe Salis et les deux 'Chat Noir,'" *Mercure de France* 9 (1926): 321ff; Edmond Deschaumes, "Le Cabaret du Chat Noir," *Revue encyclopédique*, January 16, 1897, pp. 43–45; Michel Herbert, *La Chanson à Montmartre* (Paris: La Table Ronde, 1967), pp. 153ff.

3. Yvette Guilbert, *Autres temps, autres chants* (Paris: Robert Lafont, 1926), pp. 45–53; Maurice Donnay, *Mes debuts à Paris* (Paris: Fayard, 1937), p. 239.

4. On the Incoherents' art, see Jules Lévy, *Catalogue de l'Exposition des arts incohérents à l'Eden Théâtre*, October 17–December 19, 1886 (Paris: Imprimé par G. Chamerot, 1886).

5. Gabriel Astruc, *Le Pavillon des fantômes* (Paris: B. Grasset, 1929), p. 140.

6. Louis Morin, *Carnavals parisiens* (Paris: Montgrédien, 1898), p. 7; *Le Courrier français*, March 12, 1885, p. 2.

7. Jules Claretie, *La Vie à Paris, 1884* (Paris: Victor Havard, 1885), p. 219.

8. Anne de Bercy and Armand Ziwès, *A Montmartre le soir: Cabarets et chansonniers d'hier* (Paris: Grasset, 1951); Jean Foucher and Georges-Michel Thomas, *La Vie à Brest, 1848–1948*, vol. 2, *La Vie quotidienne* (Brest: Editions de la Cité, 1976), p. 26; C. L. Amory, *Cinquante ans de vie parisienne* (Paris: Jean Renard, 1943), pp. 18–19.

9. Horace Valbel, *Les Chansonniers et les cabarets artistiques* (Paris: E. Dentu, 1895), p. 75.

10. *Le Courrier français*, March 13, 1887, p. 11.

11. *Le Courrier français*, October 26, 1890; Hermann Schardt, *Paris 1900: Masterworks of French Poster Art* (New York: Putnam, 1970), p. 88; Ernest Maindron, *Les Affiches illustrées* (Paris: Launette, 1896), pp. 196–97.

12. Adolphe Willette, *Feu Pierrot, 1857–19?* (Paris: H. Floury, 1919), pp. 121, 137; see also *Le Pierrot*, November 16, 1888, p. 2.

13. Herbert, *La Chanson à Montmartre*, pp. 395–96.

14. Paulus, *Trente ans de café-concert* (Paris: Société d'Edition de Publications, n.d.).

15. Léon de Bercy, *Montmartre et ses chansons* (Paris: H. Daragon, 1902), pp. 100–01; Jean Nohain and F. Caradec, *Le Pétomane, 1857–1945* (Paris: Jean Jacques Pauvert, 1967); *Le Courrier français*, October 19, 1890, p. 2.

16. Bercy, *Montmartre*, p. 63; Vincent Scotto, *Souvenirs de Paris* (Toulouse: S.T.A.E.L., 1947), p. 82; *L'Encyclopédie française*, ed. Lucien Febvre (Paris: Société de Gestion de l'Encyclopédie Française, 1935), vol. 8, sec. 52, p. 4.

17. Scotto, *Souvenirs*, pp. 46–47.

18. Aurélien Scholl, *L'Echo de Paris*, January 19, 1900; Koenraad Swart, *The Sense of Decadence in Nineteenth-century France* (The Hague: M. Nijhoff, 1964).

19. André Gide, *Nouvelles nourritures* (1935; reprint. Paris: Gallimard, 1964), pp. 228. Goudeau, *Dix ans*, p. 2.

20. Much biographical detail on Montmartre singers can be found in Léon de Bercy's *Montmartre*. Lemercier is quoted in André Billy, *L'Epoque 1900, 1885–1905* (Paris: J. Tallandier, 1951), p. 187. See also Bettina L. Knapp, "The Golden Age of the Chanson," *Yale French Studies* 32 (May 1964):82–98.

21. Louis Chevalier, *Montmartre du plaisir et du crime* (Paris: Robert Laffont, 1980), 2d and 3d parts.

22. Ibid.

23. *Le Siècle*, June 27, 1881—an article clipped and filed in the Paris Police Archives, BA 471, 40. On confetti, see *L'Illustration*, March 3, 1894, p. 171.

24. Nohain and Caradec, *Le Pétomane*, pp. 61–62.

25. *L'Encyclopédie française*, vol. 8, sec. 52, p. 4.

26. Jules Bois, "Petites décadences," *Le Courrier français*, September 20, 1891.

CHAPTER 4

1. Charles Dauzats, "Le Monde et les étoiles," *Le Figaro illustré*, June 1896, p. 106, a special issue on the cafés-concerts. Claretie is quoted in Paulus, *Trente ans de café-concert, souvenirs recueillis par Octave Pradels* (Paris: Société d'Edition et de Publications, n.d.), p. 149; André Chadourne, *Les Cafés-concerts* (Paris: E. Dentu, 1889), p. 368.

2. All the figures of reported receipts are taken from the *Statistique de la Ville de Paris* (Paris: Imprimerie Nationale), an annual volume from the 1870s on. For the observation on the Folies-Bergère's public, see "La Rampe s'allume" by Gabriel Mourey in *Le Courrier français*, September 21, 1890, p. 4; J.-K. Huysmans, "Les Folies-Bergère en 1879," *Croquis parisiens* (Paris: H. Vaton, 1880). See also the suggestive observations of Timothy J. Clark, "The Bar at the Folies-Bergère," in *The Wolf and the Lamb: Popular Culture in France*, ed. Jacques Beauroy, Marc Bertrand, and Edward T. Gargan (Saratoga, Calif.: Anma Libri, 1976), pp. 233–52.

3. Huysmans, *Croquis parisiens*, pp. 29–30; Georges d'Avenel, *Le Mécanisme de la vie moderne* (Paris: A. Colin, 1902), 4:392; Georges d'Avenel, *Le Nivellement des jouissances* (Paris: E. Flammarion, 1913).

4. Michelet's proposals for a democratic culture may be found in his *L'Etudiant* and his books *Le Banquet* and *Le Peuple*; see, for example, a concise statement of his hopes in *The People*, trans. John P. McKay (Urbana: University of Illinois Press, 1973), p. 208. For background going back to the 1789 Revolution, see Jacques Charpentreau and René Kaës, *La Culture populaire en France* (Paris: Editions Ouvrières, 1962), pp. 17–19 ff. See also Jules Simon, "La Fête et la foire," *La Lecture* 9 (1889):31.

5. Deputy Achard, *Rapporteur* for the bill to establish July 14 as the national holiday, *Annales de la Chambre des députés* 3 (1880):237—a debate of June 8, 1880.

6. Councilman Engelhard, *Procès verbaux, Con-seil municipal de Paris* 1 (1880):1026—a session of June 29, 1880.

7. d'Avenel, *Le Nivellement*, esp. pp. 316–17.

8. *Le Courrier français*, April 2, 1893. p. 3, and April 14, 1901, p. 2.

9. E. de Gramont, *Mémoires*, vol. 2, *Les Marronniers en fleurs* (Paris: Grasset, 1929), pp. 172–73. Comparing figures from the *Annuaire statistique* on 1892 and 1909, for example, one finds that the number of spectators on the pelouse increased almost 900,000, and sums wagered at Longchamp increased from about 19 million francs in 1892 to over 28 million in 1910. See also Henri Thétard, *Histoire et secrets du turf* (Paris: R. Laffont, 1947), pp. 54–59, 232, and Henry Lee, *Historique de chevaux de l'antiquité à ce jour* (Paris: E. Fasquelle, 1914), esp. pp. 525–30.

10. Prices are taken from guidebooks, advertisements, and articles of the period, esp. in *Le Tout Théâtre* and *Le Courrier français*.

11. Jacques Lux, "Divertissements parisiens," *Revue bleue* 7 (April 13, 1907):480.

12. Georges Montorgueil, *Le Café-concert* (Paris: "L'Estampe Originale," 1893), p. 1.

13. Léon Lacaze, *Le Théâtre concert* (Bordeaux: G. Delmas, n.d. [ca. 1900]), final section listing music halls in the provinces; François Caradec and Alain Weill, *Le Café-concert* (Paris: Hachette, 1980), p. 115; Eugen Weber, *Peasants into Frenchmen: The Modernization of Rural France, 1870–1914* (Stanford: Stanford University Press, 1976), pp. 444–45.

14. Romi, *Petite histoire des cafés-concerts parisiens* (Paris: Jean Chitry, 1950), p. 42.

15. *Paris illustré*, August 1, 1886; *Pleasure Guide to Paris for Bachelors* (London and Paris: Nilsson, n.d. [ca. 1903]), p. 77.

16. Jules Claretie, *La Vie à Paris, 1882* (Paris: Victor Havard, 1883), pp. 219–21 (column dated April 2, 1882); *Paris-Parisien 1900: Ce qu'il faut savoir, ce qu'il faut voir* (Paris: Paul Ollendorff, 1900), p. 344.

17. Henry Leyret, *En plein faubourg* (Paris: G.

Charpentier & E. Fasquelle, 1895), pp. 90–91, 97; Alvan F. Sanborn, "Paris Working-man's Cafes," *North American Review* 158 (1894):251–54.

18. Edmond Benjamin and Paul Desachy, *Le Boulevard, croquis parisiens* (Paris: E. Flammarion, 1893), p. 13.

19. *Le Courrier français*, December 17, 1893, p. 2, and September 15, 1901, p. 4.

20. Eugen Weber, "Gymnastics and Sports in Fin-de-siècle France: Opium of the Classes?" *American Historical Review* 81 (February 1971):83–94.

21. Paul Morand, *1900* (Paris: Editions de France, 1931), pp. 226 ff; Gabriel Astruc, *Le Pavillon des fantômes* (Paris: B. Grasset, 1929), p. 151.

22. E. Molier, *Le Cirque Molier, 1880–1904* (Paris: P. Dupont, 1905), p. 10.

23. Paulus, *Trente ans*, p. 149; Maurice Vauclair, "Le Café-concert," *Paris illustré*, August 1, 1886, p. 140; L. Menard et al., *Marseille* (Marseille: Barlatier & Barthelet, 1891), p. 491; Gustave Coquiot, *Les Cafés-concerts* (Paris: Librairie de l'Art, 1896 p. 33; Paulus, *Trente ans*, p. 443.

24. Georges Montorgueil et al., *Les Demi-cabots* (Paris: G. Charpentier & E. Fasquelle, 1896), pp. 41–42; Montorgueil's *Café-concert*, p. 8; Jean Nohain and François Caradec, *Le Pétomane, 1857–1945* (Paris: Jean-Jacques Pauvert, 1967), p. 22; "Les Cafés-concerts," *Paris illustré*, August 1, 1886, p. 2.

25. Montorgueil, *Le Café-concert*, p. 13; Chadourne, *Les Cafés-concerts*, p. 311.

26. Guilbert is quoted in Jean Roman, *Paris, fin de siècle* (Paris: Robert Delpire, 1958), p. 65.

27. Jean de Tinan, a review originally appearing in the *Mercure de France*, November 1897, reprinted in *Noctambulismes* (Paris: Ronald Davis & Cie., 1921), p. 11.

28. Huysmans, *Croquis parisiens*, pp. 24–25.

29. Tristan Rémy, *Les Clowns* (Paris: B. Grasset, 1945), p. 119; Roland Auguet, *Histoire et légende du cirque* (Paris: Flammarion, 1974), pp. 55–58; Franc-Nohain, *Les Mémoires de Footit et Chocolat* (Paris: Pierre Lafitte, 1907), p. 95; *Paris illustré*, August 1, 1886, p. 138—on the Pépinière.

30. Frédéric Passy, *Les Machines et leur influence sur le développement de l'industrie* (Paris: Hachette, 1881), pp. 152–56; d'Avenel, *Le Mécanisme*, 4:182. Madeleine Rebérioux, "Roman, theatre et chanson: quelle Commune?" *Le Mouvement social* 79 (April 1972):273–92; Robert Brécy, "Les Chansons du Premier Mai," *Revue d'histoire moderne et contemporaine* 28 (July 1981):393–432. One of the most famous and politically controversial songs was "En revenant de la revue," sung by Paulus at the Alcazar d'Eté on July 14, 1886, with new words celebrating the ambitious General Boulanger.

31. Josette Parrain, "Censure, théâtre et Commune (1871–1914)," *Le Mouvement social* 79 (April 1972), pp. 327–42. *Le Courrier français*, June 18, 1893, p. 9—for the Neuilly ordinance.

32. Brenda Helms, "The Third Republic and the Centennial," (Ph.D. diss., University of Virginia, 1976), p. 214, citing articles in *La Justice* and *Le Rappel*.

33. Maurice Halbwachs, *La Classe ouvrière et les niveaux de la vie* (Paris: F. Alcan, 1913), pp. 127, 129.

CHAPTER 5

1. *Bulletin officiel de l'Exposition universelle de 1889*, August 7, 1889, p. 2. For numbers of fair exhibits, visitors, and size, see Edmond Labbé, ed., *Paris Exposition internationale 1937, rapport général* (Paris: Imprimerie Nationale, 1938), 1:16ff; Lucien Biart, *Mes promenades à travers l'Exposition, souvenir de 1889* (Paris: A. Flennuyer, 1890), p. 4; Fernand Bac, *Intimités de la IIIᵉ République* (Paris: Hachette, 1935), 1:450.

2. On suggested itineraries and days at the exposition, see Constant de Tours, *Vingt jours à Paris, Guide-Album touriste* (Paris: Quantirs, 1889) and Biart, *Mes promenades*. Receipts are recorded in the *Annuaire statistique de la Ville de Paris* (1890), p. 11.

3. On the reconstructed Bastille, the fullest source is the publicity sheet, *Journal officiel de la Bastille et de la rue St. Antoine*, available in the Bibliothèque Historique de la Ville de Paris, 29381 f°.

4. *L'Illustration*, June 15, 1889, p. 512, with a full-page illustration.

5. J.-K. Huysmans, in the *Revue de l'Exposition universelle de 1889*, May 1888, p. 18.

6. Paul Marguerite, "Le Sourire à l'Exposition," *L'Exposition à Paris de 1889*, September 28, 1889, p. 311. On "le colosse," see Camille Debans, *Les Coulisses de l'Exposition* (Paris: Ernest Kolb, 1889), pp. 70–72. For a perceptive appreciation of the Tower, see Eugène-Melchior de Vogüé, "A travers l'Exposition," *Revue des deux mondes* 49 (July 1889):192ff. Joseph Harriss's *The Tallest Tower: Eiffel and the Belle Époque* (Boston: Houghton Mifflin Co., 1975) is an enjoyable recent treatment of the Tower's history.

7. On the 1889 fair's festivals, see the periodical of the fair *L'Exposition de Paris 1889*, esp. October 12, 1889. See also Alfred Picard, *Exposition universelle 1889 à Paris, rapport général* (Paris: Imprimerie Nationale, 1891), 3:353ff.

8. René Jeanne, *Cinéma 1900* (Paris: Flammarion, 1965), p. 55. For a brief account of the mayors' banquet, see Richard D. Mandell, *Paris 1900: The Great World's Fair* (Toronto: University of Toronto Press, 1967), pp. 86–87.

9. For typical Barnum circus advertisements, see *Le Temps*, November 29, 1901, p. 4, and December 1, p. 3. See also Henry Thétard, *Coulisses et secrets du cirque* (Paris: Plon, 1934), pp. 38–39.

10. *Le Temps*, December 2, 1901, p. 3.

11. Roland Auguet, *Histoire et légende du cirque* (Paris: Flammarion, 1974), p. 165.

12. Picard, *Exposition universelle internationale*, 2:325, 349; Debans, *Coulisses de l'Exposition*, p. 224; and *L'Exposition de Paris de 1889*, June 8, 1889.

13. On the salons de l'automobile, see Rosalind Williams, *Dream Worlds: Mass Consumption in Late Nineteenth-century France* (Berkeley: University of California Press, 1982), pp. 87–90.

14. Emile Tardieu, "Ennui moderne," *Revue bleue* 71 (January-June 1903), pp. 635–56. For a Roman Catholic view, see Henri Chantavoine, "La Tristesse contemporaine," *Correspondant*, March 10, 1889, pp. 935–38.

15. Raoul Ponchon, "La Foire au pain d'épices," *Le Courrier français*, April 15, 1882, p. 2. On peasants watching the train, see Eugen Weber, *Peasants into Frenchmen: The Modernization of Rural France, 1870–1914* (Stanford: Stanford University Press, 1976), p. 235, and Pierre-Jakez Hélias, *Le Cheval d'Orgueil: Mémoires d'un Breton du pays bigouden* (Paris: Plon, 1975), p. 235.

16. George Augustus Sale, *Paris Herself Again in 1878–79*, 8th ed. (London: Vizetelly & Co., 1884), pp. 141, 151.

17. Edmond de Goncourt, *Journal, mémoires de la vie litteraire*, vol. 3 (Paris: Fasquelle & Flammarion, 1956), p. 976, entry for May 18; Biart, *Mes promenades*, p. 57; Emile Monod, *L'Exposition universelle de 1889* (Paris: E. Dentu, 1890), 1:283.

18. André Hallays, *En flânant à travers l'Exposition de 1900* (Paris: Perrin, 1900), pp. xii–xiv.

19. Mandell, *Paris 1900*, exp. chap. 6.

20. Hallays, *En flânant*, p. 225.

21. Biart, *Mes promenades*, p. 58 and p. 9, contrasting the "serious" part, the Champ-de-Mars, with the "amusing" and "picturesque" part, the Esplanade. One can sample the flavor of that exoticism by looking through *L'Illustration* and *L'Exposition de 1889*.

22. Goncourt, *Journal*, 3:1000, 1027, entries for July 25 and August 19. Paul Marguerite, "Gitanes et druses," *L'Exposition à Paris*, October 5, 1889, p. 7. See also Monod, *L'Exposition universelle*, 1:68, admitting that "the rue du Caire has quite certainly constituted one of the most powerful attractions and one of the greatest successes of the Exposition."

23. Henri Chardon, "Souvenirs d'exposition," *Revue bleue*, June 1909, p. 409. Descriptions

of such attractions as the Swiss Village may be found in *Paris Exposition 1900* (Paris: Hachette) and other guidebooks.

24. Jeanne, *Cinéma 1900*, pp. 54–57; L. de Fourcaud, in *Revue de l'Exposition universelle de 1889*, 2:365.

25. *L'Eclair*, November 13, 1900. For other eloquent pessimistic reviews, see Emile Goudeau and Henri Paillard, *Paris-Staff, Exposition de 1900* (Paris: Imprimé pour H. Béraldi, 1902), and Emile Berr, "L'Exposition de

1900," *Le Figaro illustré*, November 1900, p. 232.

26. Jules Claretie, *La Vie à Paris, 1899* (Paris: Charpentier, 1900), pp. 240–41; Vogüé, "A travers l'Exposition," p. 191 (after raising such questions, Vogüé took a less pessimistic position); Goncourt, *Journal*, 3:1026, entry of August 16, 1889.

27. Eugène Demolder, "A travers l'Exposition de Paris: Notes esthétiques," *La Société nouvelle* 5, no. 2 (1889):39.

CHAPTER 6

1. Albert-Emile Sorel, "Les Cirques du Nouveau Monde," *Revue bleue*, March 15, 1902, p. 302. Similar critical response came from circus expert G. Strehly, *L'Acrobatie et les acrobates* (Paris: C. Delagrave, 1903), pp. 51–52.

2. *Le Courrier français*, June 5, 1902, pp. 2–3. The pantomime was written by Jules Roques.

3. Roland Auguet, *Histoire et légende du cirque* (Paris: Flammarion, 1972), pp. 13–20; Henry Thétard, *La Merveilleuse histoire du cirque* (Paris: Prisma, 1947), 1:92–94; Henri Frichet, *Le Cirque et les forains* (Tours: Alfred Mame et fils, 1889), pp. 45ff.

4. Jean Elleinstein, ed., *Histoire de la France contemporaine*, vol. 4, *1871–1918* (Paris: Editions Sociales, 1980), p. 230; Aimée Moutet, "Les Origines du système de Taylor en France," *Le Mouvement social* 93 (October 1975):15–49; Michelle Perrot, "The Three Ages of Industrial Discipline in Nineteenth-century France," in *Consciousness and Class Experience in Nineteenth-century Europe*, ed. John M. Merriman (New York: Holmes & Meier, 1980), pp. 157–68.

5. This theme was regularly reiterated in *Le Tout Théâtre* in columns on cafés-concerts and music halls, 1905–06.

6. Colette, *The Thousand and One Mornings* (New York: Bobbs-Merrill, 1973), pp. 44–46, an article originally appearing in *Le Matin*, November 13, 1913.

7. Georges Montorgueil, *Le Café concert* (Paris: "L'Estampe Originale," 1893), p. 1; *Paris illustré*, August 1, 1886, on the public's preference for being "at ease"; Gustave Coquiot, *Paris, voici Paris!* (Paris: Paul Ollendorff, 1913) pp. 14, 174–75.

8. Roland Barthes, *Mythologies* (Paris: Editions du Seuil, 1957), p. 199.

9. Pierre Sorlin, *La Société française, 1840–1914*, vol. 1 (Paris: Arthaud, 1969), pp. 118–19. Yves Lequin, *Les ouvriers de la région lyonnaise (1848–1914), la formation de la classe ouvrière régionale* (Lyon: Presses Universitaires de Lyon, 1978), 2:202; Michelle Perrot, in *Histoire économique et sociale de la France*, ed. Fernand Braudel and Ernest Labrousse, tome 4, vol. 1 (Paris: Presses Universitaires de France, 1979), pp 473, 481, 489.

10. Auguet, *Histoire et légende*, pp. 127–29; Henry Thétard, *Coulisses et secrets du cirque* (Paris: Plon, 1934), p. 2; Paul Boissac, *Circus and Culture: A Semiotic Approach* (Bloomington: Indiana University Press, 1976), p. 71 and chapter entitled "Circus and Ritual."

11. Jacques Lux, "Divertissements parisiens," *Revue bleue* 7 (April 15, 1907):479–80.

12. Michelle Perrot, in *Histoire économique et sociale de la France*, tome 4, vol. 1, p. 489; Armand Audiganne, *Mémoires d'un ouvrier de Paris, 1871–72* (Paris: Charpentier, 1873), p. 9.

13. *L'Illustré national*, June 21, 1903.

14. Henry Leyret, *En plein faubourg* (Paris: Charpentier, 1895), p. 97; Bernard Legendre, "La Vie d'un prolétariat: Les Ouvriers de Fougères au début du XXᵉ siècle," *Le Mouvement social*,

January 1977, pp. 33–35; Jacques Valdour, *La Vie ouvrière, observations vécues* (Paris: V. Giard & E. Brière, 1909), pp. 70–71.

15. Jules Roques, "A l'Elysée Montmartre," *Le Courrier français*, April 20, 1888; *Paris-Parisien 1900* (Paris: Paul Ollendorff, 1900).

16. Jules Claretie, *La Vie à Paris, 1885*, pp. 258–59—an article dated June 9, 1885; Coquiot, *Paris, voici Paris!* p. 203.

17. Edmond de Goncourt, *Journal, mémoires de la vie litteraire*, vol. 3 (Paris: Fasquelle & Flammarion, 1956), entry for July 24, 1886.

18. Bonnie G. Smith, *Ladies of the Leisure Class: The Bourgeoises of Northern France in the Nineteenth Century* (Princeton: Princeton University Press, 1981), p. 150; Coquiot, *Paris, voici Paris!* pp. 197–203.

19. Georges Bidache, "La Vie passionnée," *Le Courrier français*, March 5, 1889, p. 2; Coquiot, *Paris, voici Paris!* pp. 197–203.

20. Philippe Jullian, *Jean Lorrain* (Paris: Fayard, 1974), pp. 84–85.

21. Edmond Benjamin and Paul Desachy, *Le Boulevard, croquis parisiens* (Paris: E. Marpon & E. Flammarion, 1893), p. 18. Richard O'Monroy, *Coups d'épingle* (Paris: E. Dentu, 1886), p. 3.

22. Jean Beaudemoulin, *Enquête sur les loisirs de l'ouvrier français* (Paris: Jouve, 1924), p. 213; Cl. Geslin, "Provocations patronales et violences ouvrières: Fougères (1887–1907)," *Le Mouvement social* 82 (January 1973):19; Marilyn Boxer, "Women in Industrial Homework: The Flowermakers of Paris in the Belle Époque," *French Historical Studies* 12, no. 3 (Spring 1982):409–17; Theresa M. McBride, *The Domestic Revolution: The Modernization of Household Service in England and France, 1820–1920* (New York: Holmes & Meier, 1976), p. 100.

23. McBride, *Domestic Revolution*, p. 55.

24. On English women in the period, see *Victorian Studies* 21, no. 1 (Autumn 1977), a special issue on leisure.

25. Theresa M. McBride, "A Woman's World: Department Stores and the Evolution of Women's Employment, 1870–1920," *French Historical Studies* 10, no. 4 (Fall 1978):680; Smith, *Ladies*, esp. chap. 6; Louise A. Tilly and Joan W. Scott, *Women, Work, and Family* (New York: Holt, Rinehart & Winston, 1978), pp. 189–190.

26. Jean de l'Etoile, *Le Courrier français*, February 2, 1902, p. 2.

27. Gaston Furalicq, *Trente ans dans les rues de Paris* (Paris: Perrin, 1934), p. 20; Jean de l'Etoile, "La Semaine d'un passant," *Le Courrier français*, March 31, 1901, p. 2; Jules Bertaut, *Les Dessous de la "Troisième"* (Paris: Jules Tallandier, 1959), pp. 187–88.

28. *Pleasure Guide to Paris for Bachelors* (London and Paris: Nilsson, n.d. [ca. 1903]), p. 5; Camille Debans, *Les Plaisirs et les curiosités de Paris, guide humoristique et pratique* (Paris: E. Kolb, 1889), p. 7.

29. Gabriel Tarde, *L'Opinion et la foule*, 2d ed. (Paris: Félix Alcan, 1904), p. 4.

CHAPTER 7

1. J. Elleinstein, ed., *Histoire de la France contemporaine* (Paris: Editions Sociales, 1980), 4:187; Jean Bastié, *La Croissance de la banlieue parisienne* (Paris: Presses Universitaires de France, 1964), pp. 135–36; Norma Evenson, *Paris: A Century of Change, 1878–1978* (New Haven: Yale University Press, 1979), chaps. 1–2.

2. Elie Frébault, *La vie de Paris, guide pittoresque et pratique du visiteur* (Paris: E. Dentu, 1878), p. 49; *1889 Exposition universelle, guide définitif* (Paris: Librairie de la Nouvelle Revue, 1889), p. 355.

3. Curnonsky, "Publicité artistique," *Le Courrier français*, October 22, 1911, p. 2. Prof. Neal Shipley provided information on neon. See also Rudi Stern, *Let There Be Neon* (New York: Harry N. Abrams, 1979), pp. 21–24.

4. Camille Debans, *Les Plaisirs et les curiosités de Paris* (Paris: E. Kolb, 1889), pp. 20–25; *Paris after Dark, Night Guide for Gentlemen*, 13th ed. (Boulogne: J. Boyer, n.d. [1870s]), p. 19;

Emile Bergerat, *Revue de l'Exposition de 1889,* no. 1 (May 1888):6.

5. Jacques Garnier, *Forains d'hier et d'aujourd'hui* (Orléans: Editeur Jacques Garnier, 1968). The details about the fête de Neuilly are drawn from Jules Claretie, *La Vie à Paris, 1884* (Paris: Victor Havard, 1885), pp. 314–15.

6. *Exposition universelle de 1889, Panorama de Tout Paris, peint par Ch. Castellani* (available in the Bibliothèque Nationale, 4°V 2852), an illustrated souvenir book. See also *L'Illustration,* May 4, 1889, p. 374.

7. For entry statistics, see Alfred Picard, *Exposition universelle internationale de 1889, Paris: Rapport général,* vol. 3 (Paris: Imprimerie Nationale, 1891), p. 281. For comparison, note that the Panorama Transatlantique drew 1,100,415 customers in 1889.

8. For the literature of street spectacles, see also the fine collection of essays and Félix Vallotton's prints in *Badauderies parisiennes, les rassemblements: Physiologies de la rue* by Paul Adam, Alfred Athys, et al. (Paris: H. Floury, 1896).

9. For a sample of criticism of "the new need," see the writings of economist Frédéric Passy, *Pages et discours* (Paris: Guillaumin, 1901), pp. 244 ff., esp. a paper read in 1883 to the Académie des Sciences Morales et Politiques. For forceful later criticism, I have in mind Theodor Adorno, "The Culture Industry: Enlightenment as Mass Deception," in *Dialectic of Enlightenment* by Adorno and Max Horkheimer (New York: Herder & Herder, 1972). Debans's remark appears in *Les Plaisirs et les curiosités,* p. 6.

10. Richard Sennett, *The Fall of Public Man* (New York: Vintage, 1978), pp. 213–14; A.-P. De Lannoy, *Les Plaisirs et la vie de Paris (Guide du flâneur)* (Paris: L. Borel, 1900), pp. 21–27.

11. André Warnod, *Les Plaisirs de la rue* (Paris: Editions Française Illustrée, 1920); Louis Huart, *Physiologie du flâneur* (Paris: Aubert, 1841), p. 39.

12. Frébault, *La Vie de Paris,* p. 82.

13. Henry Leyret, *En plein faubourg (moeurs ouv-rières)* (Paris: Bibliothèque Charpentier, 1895), p. 98; Brenda Flo Nelms, "The Third Republic and the Centennial of 1789," (Ph.D. diss., University of Virginia, 1976), p. 265; Paul Pottier, "La Psychologie des manifestations parisiennes," *Revue des revues,* June 15, 1889, p. 571.

14. Huart, *Physiologie du flâneur,* chap. 14, "Conseils à l'usage des flâneurs novices." On Fournel, see Walter Benjamin, *Charles Baudelaire: A Lyric Poet in the Era of High Capitalism* (London: NLB, 1973), p. 69n12.

15. Bastié, *La Croissance de la banlieue,* pp. 147–48; Pierre Sorlin, *La Société française* (Paris: Arthaud, 1969), 1:118–19; Leyret, *En plein faubourg,* pp. 100–101.

16. Jean Beaudemoulin, *Enquête sur les loisirs de l'ouvrier français* (Paris: Jouve, 1924), pp. 226, 240–43; Jacques Valdour, *La Vie ouvrière: Observations vécues* (Paris: V. Giard & E. Brière, 1909); Michael R. Marrus, *The Rise of Leisure in Industrial Society* (St. Charles, Mo.: Forum Press, 1974).

17. Paul Leroy-Beaulieu, *Question ouvrière au XIVᵉ siècle* (Paris: Charpentier, 1872), p. 300.

18. Leyret, *En plein faubourg,* p. 90. Richard O'Monroy [Richard Saint-Geniès], *Coups d'épingle, études parisiennes* (Paris: E. Dentu, 1886), pp. 49–51, 216.

19. Eugen Weber, "Gymnastics and Sports in Fin-de-siècle France: Opium of the Classes?" *American Historical Review* 76 (February 1971):70–98; Jean Foucher and George Michel Thomas, *La Vie à Brest, 1848–1948,* vol. 2, *La Vie quotidienne* (Brest: Editions de la Cité, 1976), p. 77.

20. De Lannoy, *Les Plaisirs,* p. 86; Georges Montorgueil, *Paris dansant* (Paris: Théophile Belin, 1898), pp. 39–40, 53, 81; Jean Richepin, "Petites chronicles," *Gil Blas,* October 28, 1882.

21. Emmanuel Patrick, "Les Bals de Paris," *Le Courrier français,* January 11, 1885, p. 3; Montorgueil, *Paris dansant,* p. 140.

22. Montorgueil, *Paris dansant,* pp. 144, 159, 194. On the hiring of decoy dancers, see Gustave Geoffroy, quoted in P. Bessand-Massenet, ed.,

Air et manières de Paris (Paris: Bernard Grasset, 1937), an excerpt from an article originally appearing in Le Figaro illustré (1893–94).

23. For background information and an interpretation differing somewhat from mine, see Meyer Schapiro, Modern Art: 19th and 20th Centuries (New York: Braziller, 1978), pp. 104–07.

24. G. Tarde, L'Opinion et la foule, 2d ed. (Paris: Félix Alcan, 1904), pp. 11, 59. The essays collected in this volume appeared originally in the Revue des deux mondes (1893) and the Revue de Paris (1898–99).

25. Jean Roman, Fin de siècle (Paris: Robert Delpire, 1958), p. 17.

26. Hughes Le Roux, Les Jeux du cirque et de la vie foraine (Paris: E. Plon, Nourrit & Cie., 1889), pp. 11–18; Jacques Lux, "Divertissements parisiens," Revue bleue 7 (April 13, 1907):479–80; Henry Thétard, Coulisses secrets du cirque (Paris: Plon, 1934), pp. 23–29.

27. René Jeanne, Cinéma 1900 (Paris: Flammarion, 1965), pp. 52–68; Jacques Deslandes, Histoire comparée du cinéma (Paris: Casterman, 1968), 2:16, 28, 209.

28. Deslandes, Histoire, 2:18; Jeanne, Cinéma 1900, pp. 27–28.

29. Paul Hammond, Marvellous Méliès (London: Gordon Fraser Gallery, 1974). For an appreciation of the important contribution of magicians to early film history, see Erik Barnouw, The Magician and the Cinema (New York: Oxford University Press, 1981); Georges Sadoul, Louis Lumière (Paris: Seghers, 1964).

30. Georges Sadoul, Histoire générale du cinéma, vol. 3; Le cinéma devient un art (1909–1920), vol. 1; L'Avant guerre (Paris: Denoël, 1951), chap. 10.

31. Deslandes, Histoire comparée, 2:491–97; Jeanne, Cinéma 1900, pp. 84–85.

32. Jeanne, Cinéma 1900, pp. 44–48.

33. Romi, Petite histoire des cafés-concerts (Paris: Jean Chitry, 1950), pp. 55–57.

34. Anonymous, La Question cinématographique (Lille, 1912), pp. 10ff; Victor Perrot, A Paris il y a soixante ans naissait le cinéma (Paris: Cinémathèque Française, 1955), no pagination. The particularly hostile critic mentioned was Louis Haugmard, "L'Esthétique du cinématographe," Le Correspondant 251 (May 25, 1913):771.

35. Haugmard, "L'Esthétique," pp. 769, 771; Emile Hinzelin, "Les Arts sociaux et la prochaine Exposition des Arts décoratifs à Paris," La Revue 107 (March 15, 1914):168–70; Max Nordau, 'Culture cinématographique," La Revue 107 (April 1, 1914):311–18.

36. All the observers cited above suggested potential benefits of a properly reformed cinema.

37. Haugmard and Nordeau were most eloquent on the popular appeal of cinema, making points summed up in my account. See also André Bazin, What Is Cinema? (Berkeley: University of California Press, 1967), p. 99.

38. The term image factories comes from a film critic known as Canudo whose collection of articles written before the war was entitled L'Usine aux images (Geneva: Office Central d'Edition, 1927); Adorno, "The Culture Industry," pp. 131, 137.

CHAPTER 8

1. Georges Montorgueil in his Vie des boulevards (Paris: May & Motterez, 1896), p. 226, attributes the phrase to M. Joseph Prudhomme, the creation of caricaturist Henri Monnier. Compare, Emile Blavet, La Vie parisienne (Paris: P. Ollendorff, 1890), pp. 21–22.

2. Hyren Nilhoc, Le Courrier français, February 2, 1890, p. 2.

3. Le Rideau de Fer, "Cirque Fernando," Le Courrier français, February 19, 1893, p. 6.

4. On English middle-class leisure, see Victorian Studies 21, no. 1 (Autumn 1977), a special issue on Victorian leisure, and Peter Bailey, Leisure and Class in Victorian England: Rational Recreation and the Contest for Control, 1830–

1885 (Buffalo: University of Toronto Press, 1978).

5. On new Lille Catholic fêtes, see Pierre Pierrard, *Lille et les Lillois* (Paris: Blaud & Gay, 1967), p. 207. On *comités de fêtes* blatantly intended to stimulate business in Bordeaux, mirroring those in Paris, see Louis Desgraves and Louis Dupeux, *Bordeaux au XIXᵉ siècle* (Bordeaux: Fédération Historique, 1969), pp. 442–43.

6. Anonymous, *Le Dix-neuvième siècle* (Paris: Hachette, 1901), p. 234.

7. Hughes Le Roux, *Les Jeux du cirque et de la vie foraine* (Paris: E. Plon, Nourrit & Cie., 1889), p. 28.

8. *La Fin de siècle*, January 17, 1901, p. 3.

9. See Richard Holt, *Sport and Society in Modern France* (Hamden, Conn.: Archon Books, 1981), pp. 128–29, 144.

10. Claude Dohet, *Les Spectacles de la belle époque* (Brussels: S.P.R.L. Sodim, 1976), notes to illustrations 175–76.

11. Luna Park was created by Gaston Akoun Arsenal Library, Paris, *Recueil factice* on music halls and other spectacles, Coll. Ollivie Fol. N.F. 11085. See also *La Nature* 2 (July 1909):75–76. Several years before the war, a second American-style amusement park named Magic City opened on the Quai d'Orsay. Jean Cazeneuve, "Jeux de vertige et de peur," in *Jeux et sports*, ed. Roger Caillois (Paris: Gallimard, 1967), pp. 683–730.

12. Jean de l'Etoile, *Le Courrier français*, January 5, 1902, p. 2.

13. *La fin de siècle*, May 23, 1901, p. 1.

14. Jean-Pierre Seguin, *Nouvelles à sensation: Canards du XIXᵉ siècle* (Paris: Armand Colin, 1959), chap. 5; Camille Debans, *Les Coulisses de l'Exposition* (Paris: E. Kolb, 1889), p. 351; Frederick Brown, *Theater and Revolution: The Culture of the French Stage* (New York: Viking Press, 1980), pp. 113, 130. On the appeal of disaster, see Gerald Mast, *Film/Cinema/Movies: A Theory of Experience* (New York: Harper & Row, 1977), pp. 37–42.

15. Guillaume Apollinaire, *Petites merveilles du quotidien*, ed. Pierre Caizergues (Montpellier: Bibliothèque Artistique et Littéraire, 1979), entry dated February 17, 1910.

16. *La Fin de siècle*, January 10, 1901.

17. Edouard Trogan, "Les Oeuvres et les hommes," *Correspondant* 4 (March 25, 1904):1150–51.

18. Louis Filliol, "Escholiers et etudiants," *Nouvelle revue* 14 (1902):603.

19. Eugen Weber, *The Nationalist Revival in France, 1905–1914* (Berkeley: University of California Press, 1968).

20. Paul Adam, *La Morale des sports* (Paris: La Librairie Mondiale, 1907), p. 243.

21. Ibid., pp. 203, 223.

22. Ibid., p. 12.

23. Holt, *Sport and Society*, pp. 50–52, 100–101, 135–36, 143–44, 182, 215.

24. Maurice Bardèche and Robert Brasillach, *Histoire du cinéma* (Paris: Denoël & Steele, 1935), p. 64.

25. Rosemonde Sanson, *Les 14 juillet, fête et conscience nationale, 1789–1975* (Paris: Flammarion, 1976), pp. 77–79; Eugen Weber, *Action Française: Royalism and Reaction in Twentieth-century France* (Stanford: Stanford University Press, 1962), pp. 86–88.

26. Roger Caillois, *L'Homme et le sacré* (Paris: Gallimard, 1950), Appendix 3.

27. C. Brunschwig, L.-J. Calvet, and J.-C. Klein, *Cent ans de chanson française* (Paris: Seuil, 1981), pp. 385–86.

28. Jean Pierre Azéma and Michel Winock, *La IIIᵉ République, 1870–1940* (Paris: Le Livre de Poche, 1978), p. 378.

29. Pierre Andrieu, *Le Bonheur par le travail—réalisations par le service de travail: Ce qu'il est en Allemagne, ce qu'il pourrait être en France* (Paris: La Technique du Livre, 1943); W. D. Halls, *The Youth of Vichy France* (Oxford: Clarendon Press, 1981), p. 176 and chap. 7.

SELECTED BIBLIOGRAPHY

Some invaluable collections of brochures, posters, local reports on festivals, and newspaper clippings are available only in the Bibliothèque Nationale, the Bibliothèque Arsenal, the Bibliothèque Historique de la Ville de Paris, the Paris Police Archives, and departmental archives (series M). I have cited these and other less accessible or highly specialized sources in the notes.

A. THEORETICAL AND GENERAL

Adorno, Theodor W. "The Culture Industry: Enlightenment as Mass Deception." In Max Horkheimer and Theodor Adorno, *Dialectic of Enlightenment*. New York: Herder & Herder, 1972.

Caillois, Roger. *L'Homme et le sacré*. Paris: Gallimard, 1950.

Caillois, Roger, ed. *Jeux et sports*. Paris: Gallimard, 1967.

de Grazia, Sebastian. *Of Time, Work, and Leisure*. Garden City, N.Y.: Anchor Books, 1964.

Dumur, Guy, ed. *Histoire des spectacles*. Paris: Gallimard, 1965.

Huizinga, Johan. *Homo Ludens*. Boston: Beacon Press, 1955.

Linder, Staffan B. *The Harried Leisure Class*. New York: Columbia University Press, 1970.

Pieper, Josef. *In Tune with the World: A Theory of Festivity*. New York: Harcourt, Brace & World, 1965.

———. *Leisure: The Basis of Culture*. New York: Pantheon Books, 1952.

Thompson, E. P. "Time, Work-Discipline, and Industrial Capitalism." *Past and Present* 38 (December 1967):56–97.

B. FRANCE: FÊTES AND ENTERTAINMENTS

Auguet, Roland. *Histoire et légende du cirque*. Paris: Flammarion, 1974.

Benjamin, Edmond, and Paul Desachy. *Le Boulevard, croquis parisiens*. Paris: E. Marpon & E. Flammarion, 1893.

Bercy, Anne de, and Armand Ziwès. *A Montmartre . . . le soir: Cabarets et chansonniers d'hier*. Paris: Grasset, 1951.

Bercy, Léon de. *Montmartre et ses chansons*. Paris: H. Daragon, 1902.

Braudel, Fernand, and Ernest Labrousse, eds. *Histoire économique et sociale de la France*. Tome 4. Paris: Presses Universitaires de France, 1979.

Caradec, François, and Alain Weill. *Le Café-concert*. Paris: Atelier Hachette/Massin, 1980.

Chevalier, Louis. *Montmartre du plaisir et du crime*. Paris: Robert Laffont, 1980.

SELECTED BIBLIOGRAPHY

Claretie, Jules. *La Vie à Paris*. 20 vols. Paris: E. Fasquelle, 1880–1901.

Deslandes, Jacques, and Jacques Richard. *Histoire comparée du cinéma*. Vol. 2, *Du cinématographe au cinéma, 1896–1906*. Paris: Casterman, 1968.

Esparbès, Georges d', et al. *Les Demi-cabots: Le Café-concert, le cirque, les forains*. Paris: G. Charpentier & E. Fasquelle, 1896.

Garnier, Jacques. *Forains d'hier et d'aujourd'hui: Un siècle d'histoire des forains, des fêtes et de la vie foraine*. Orléans: Jacques Garnier, 1968.

Guilbert, Yvette. *La Chanson de ma vie*. Paris: Grasset, 1927.

Holt, Richard. *Sport and Society in Modern France*. Hamden, Conn.: Archon Books, 1981.

Huysmans, J.-K. "Les Folies-Bergère en 1879." In *Croquis parisiens*. Paris: H. Vaton, 1880.

Isay, Raymond. *Panorama des Expositions universelles*. Paris: Gallimard, 1937.

Mandell, Richard D. *Paris 1900: The Great World's Fair*. Toronto: University of Toronto Press, 1967.

Michelet, Jules. *Le Banquet*. Paris: Calmann-Lévy, 1879.

———. *Nos fils*. Paris: A. Lacroix, 1870.

Montorgueil, Georges. *Le Café-concert*. Paris: "L'Estampe Originale," 1893.

Pillement, Georges. *Paris en fête*. Paris: Grasset, 1972.

Rearick, Charles. "Festivals in Modern France: The Experience of the Third Republic." *Journal of Contemporary History* 12 (1977):435–60.

Romi [Robert Miquel]. *Petite histoire des cafés-concerts parisiens*. Paris: Jean Chitry, 1950.

Sanson, Rosemonde. *Les 14 Juillet, fête et conscience nationale, 1789–1975*. Paris: Flammarion, 1976.

Thétard, Henry. *Coulisses et secrets du cirque*. Paris: Plon, 1934.

———. *Histoire et secrets du turf*. Paris: R. Laffont, 1947.

———. *La Merveilleuse histoire du cirque*. 2 vols. Paris: Prisma, 1947.

Warnod, André. *Bals, cafés et cabarets*. Paris: E. Figuière, 1913.

Weber, Eugen. "Gymnastics and Sports in Fin-de-siècle France: Opium of the Classes?" *American Historical Review* 86 (February 1971):70–98.

———. *Peasants into Frenchmen: The Modernization of Rural France, 1870–1914*. Stanford: Stanford University Press, 1976.

Zeldin, Theodore. *France, 1848–1945*. 2 vols. Oxford: Oxford University Press, 1973 and 1977.

INDEX

Page references to illustrations are in **bold face**.

Adam, Paul, 48, 52, 215; on liberty, 47; on sports, 209, 212, 213

Advertising, 65, 177, 219; by newspapers, 65, 69; by posters, 67, 93; **68**

Allais, Alphonse, 49, 55, 60

Ambassadeurs, 74, 100, 153, 162

Amusement park. *See* Luna Park

Arène, Paul, 53

Automobile: driving as sport, 65, 162; show, 132; **211**

Balls. *See* Dancing

Barnum, Phineas Taylor, 65, 133

Bastille Day, 114; in *1880*, 3–10, 11, 14–18; social and political differences on, 11, 14, 16–18, 22–23; after *1880*, 11, 19–23, 127, 213, 214; as entertainment, 22, 94, 177; **1–2, 8, 12, 13, 20, 21**

Baudelaire, Charles, 36, 176

Belle époque, 32, 202, 209, 215; dating and meaning of, xi, 3, 23, 199

Belly dancing, 78, 138, 139, 186

Bérenger, René, 46, 114, 200

Bicycling, 161, 162, 204, 212; as organized sport, 11, 29, 65, 94, 100, 183, 213; **210**

Bloch, Jeanne, **103**

Boating, 162

Boulanger, General Georges, 22

Bourgès, Paul-Joseph, **104**

Bourget, Paul, 55

Boxing, 204, 213

Brandimbourg, Georges, 48

Bruant, Aristide, 47, 73, 94, 165; career after Chat Noir, 46, 63, 70, 74; at the Chat Noir, 60, 62, 69

Buffalo Bill, 130

Bullfights and runs, 114, 138, 202

Bullier dance hall, 155, 162, 183

Cabarets, 165, 200; artistic, 37, 60, 62, 63–65; audience-performer rapport in, 73, 135; **66**. *See also* Chat Noir

Café-concert, 63, 155, 165, 193; varieties of, 83, 94, 95, 115, 119, 121; appeal of, 84, 91, 153, 154, 183; criticisms of, 101–02, 110, 111

Cafés: 28, 67, 155, 164; activities in, 16, 97, 158, 162, 207; clients of, 48, 96, 97, 161, 182; on Paris boulevards, 170, 173

Cancan, 41, 42, 49, 49n, 78, 186

Caran d'Ache (Emmanuel Poiré), 58, 60

Carnival, 23, 48, 72, 208

Casino de Paris, 67, 204

Censorship, 42, 43, 46, 48, 113; **106–09**

Chaplin, Charlie, 192

Chat Noir, 36; newspaper, 58, 60, 65, 72; attractions of, 58–60, 64; economic success of, 63, 70, 78–79; troubles, 69, 72, 73, 74; **53–54, 56, 57**

Chéret, Jules, 67, 94, 121, 199; **25–26, 87, 128**

Chevrier, Georges, 33, 35

Cinema, 78, 115, 173, 188, 217; at *1900* Exposition, 129, 141, 144; development of, 189–95; and war, 208, 213, 214; **191**

Circus, 115; Fernando (Médrano), 74, 154, 200; acts, 78, 131, 200, 202, 208, appeal of, 91, 93, 135, 153–54, 193; Molier, 101, 149; Barnum, 130–31, 149; traditional, 133, 149–50, 154; and time, 155, 157, 158, 162, 164; **147–48, 151, 156**. *See also* Nouveau Cirque

Claretie, Jules, 63, 83, 96, 97, 158, 174
Clemenceau, Georges, 27, 47
Cockfights, 182, 202
Cohl, Emile, 61, 192
Comédie-Française, 91, 100, 192
Coppée, François, 55
Coubertin, Pierre de, 212
Courrier français, 37, 43, 67, 213; balls, 62
Courteline, Georges, 176

Dancing, 104; on Bastille Day, 11, 17, 18; at
    elite balls, 37, 43–46, 62; popular, 48, 78,
    94, 162, 183; decline of, 72, 183, 186, 215;
    in dance halls, 74, 96, 155, 157, 183; **45, 51,
    184**
Debussy, Claude, 60
Decadence, 32, 145, 146
Donnay, Maurice, 60, 176
Dranem (Armand Ménard), 104, 104n
Dreyfus Affair, 22, 209
Drinking, 96, 97, 124; on *July 14*, 19–20, 23;
    record-setting, 28
Dufay, Marguerite, 102

Eden Concert, 74; **29**
Eiffel Tower, 121, 124–25, 129, 131–32
Eldorado, 74, 84; prices, 95; and movies, 189,
    193, 208
Elite amusements, 100–01, 158, 159, 160
Elysée-Montmartre, 70, 74, 158, 162, 183
Ennui, 37, 199; and entertainment, 132–33,
    166, 186, 194; worries about, 145, 146, 209
Entertainment: admissions, 29, 193; and French
    culture, 115, 133, 174, 176, 199; and war,
    130, 133
Exposition universelle: of *1878*, 5, 119, 134;
    celebrating work, 27; of *1889*, 83, 114, 120–
    21, 127, 134, 144 passim, 174, 177, 207;
    visitors at, 89–90; as entertainment, 119–20,
    129, 138 passim, 145, 146; as fête, 119, 138;
    of *1900*, 127, 129, 132, 134–35, 139, 141
    passim, 190, 207, 208; **117, 122, 123, 125,
    126, 136, 137, 140, 142, 143**

Fairs (fêtes foraines). *See* Street fairs
Ferris wheel (Grande Roue), 129, 214

Festive, the: 214, 219, 221; in entertainments,
    47, 58, 60, 62, 131, 138
Fête: traditional, 6, 14, 48; ideal, 14, 24, 194,
    220. *See also* Bastille Day; Carnival
Fêtes foraines. *See* Street fairs
Feydeau, Georges, 49, 199
Fishing, 157, 182
Folies-Bergère, 74, 78, 101; posters, 67; de-
    scribed, 83–84; audiences, 84, 93, 111; acts,
    84, 132, 153, 189, 202, 204; business prac-
    tices, 95, 162; **81–82, 86, 87, 88, 205**
Footit (George) and Chocolat, 71, 111, 199;
    147–48
Forain, Jean-Louis, 34, 100; **31, 44**
France, Anatole, 35, 48, 49
"Free time," 52; for working people, 29–30,
    115, 155, 157; workers' activities, 157–58,
    182, 213
Fuller, Loïe, 132, 189

Gaiety: and French character, 39–40; and mel-
    ancholy, 47, 71, 199; and war, 214, 215
Galerie des Machines, 121, 129, 134, 149
Gambetta, Léon, 4, 27, 220
Gambling, 29, 113, 114, 159, 206
Games, 11, 17, 18, 97, 158
Gaumont, Léon, 193
Gill, André, 55, 59, 64, 71
Goncourt, Edmond de, 134, 139, 145, 159
Goudeau, Emile, 47, 48, 52, 70; as Bohemian,
    36, 37, 39, 49, 55; later career, 63, 72, 73,
    174
La Goulue, 70, 104, 173, 186
Government (Third Republic): support for, 4–
    7, 14, 19; fear of crowds, 5, 19; and public
    enjoyments, 15–16, 23, 85, 89, 113–16, 153,
    201; opposition to, 17–18, 22–23; censor-
    ship, 43, 48
Gray, Henry, 61
Grille d'Egout, 104, 186
Guilbert, Yvette, 70, 78, 104, 110

Halley's comet, 207
Heidbrinck, Oswald, **98, 99**
Hippodrome, 69, 91, 129, 153, 158, 193
Horloge, 162
Horse racing: betting on, 50, 206; social groups

attending, 90–91, 100, 158, 159, 164; suspended during war, 214
Humor, 49, 102
Hydropathes, 36, 55, 58

Ice skating, 29, 162; at Palais de Glace, 100, 158, 164
Ile de la Grande Jatte, 157, 186
Incoherents, 37, 39, 61; **38**
Isola brothers, 50

Jardin de Paris, 71, 74, 78, 160, 162, 214; **163**
Joan of Arc celebrations, 213
Jouy, Jules, 55, 60, 71, 72, 73
Kropotkin, Pëtr Alekseyevich, 33

Lafargue, Paul, 47, 52; for right to be lazy, 32–34
Leisure, 200, 201. *See also* "Free time"
Lévy, Jules, 37, 39, 48, 61
Lighting, 131–32, 170
Linder, Max, 192
Lisbonne, Maxime, 64
Lorrain, Jean, 159–60, 174
Loti, Pierre, 48
Lowlife entertainment, 62, 91, 93, 96–97
Lumière, Louis, 189, 190, 192
Luna Park, 204, 206
Lunel, Ferdinand, 69, **38**

Mabille dance hall, 41, 186
Mac-Nab, Maurice, 71, 72
Marianne, 10, 14; **9**
Maupassant, Guy de, 48
May Day, 113
Mayol, Félix, 70
Méliès, Georges, 189, 190, 192, 193, 213
Michelet, Jules, 4, 14, 27, 85, 115; on fêtes, 6, 10, 220
Le Mirliton, 63, 64
Monet, Claude, 5
Montagnes russes, 50, 75, 120, 121, 124, 158, 204; **197–98**
Montmartre, 39, 65; as pleasure quarter, 46, 52, 62; and Bohemians, 55, 57, 71–74
Montorgueil, Georges, 93, 102, 174
Montoya, Gabriel, 70

Moulin de la Galette, 91, 183
Moulin Rouge, 50, 160; reputation of, 41, 74; as a business, 62, 70, 91, 95, 214; advertisements for, 67, 94; attractions of, 78, 90, 102, 121, 186; **76, 77**
Musée Grévin, 28, 69, 78, 157
Music hall, 188; business, 63, 74, 78, 83–84, 94, 95, 157, 162, 164, 193; acts, 75, 78, 84, 110, 120, 132, 152–53, 165, 202, 204, 206, 213; revues, 75, 186, 194, 199; audiences, 83–84, 96, 110–11, 135, 158, 161

Nice, 29
Nordau, Max, 194, 195
Nouveau Cirque, 50, 74, 100, 154; attractions, 78, 111, 208; as business, 91, 214; **148, 156**

Oller, Joseph, 50, 52, 70, 78, 95, 153
Olympia, 50, 70, 74, 78, 95, 100, 189, 204
Olympic Games, 212
Opera, 91, 100, 158

Panoramas: scenes featured in, 4, 75, 119, 120, 133, 144, 172–73, 195, 208; business of, 75, 157, 193
Parimutuel, 50, 91
Paris: Commune, 5, 7, 113; as pleasure capital, 40–42; *grands boulevards*, 74, 170, 172–73; transportation, 157, 169; population, 169; social relations in, 173, 181–83; 188
Parisiana, 74, 193
Passy, Frédéric, 111
Pathé, Charles, 190, 193
Paulus (Paul Habans), 70, 102, 104, 165, 173
Pays des Fées, 121; **128**
Pelletan, Camille, 5, 10
Pétain, Marshal Philippe, 215
Pétomane, 70, 75, 102, 190
Phonographs, 188, 190
Pille, Henri, 58
Polin (Pierre Paul Marsalès), 104
Posters. *See* Advertising
Pouget, Emile, 35
Poulbot, Francisque, 34
Privas, Xavier, 73

Rabelais, François, 37, 62, 177
Raffaëlli, Jean François, 176; **167, 171**

Renoir, Pierre Auguste, 219
Rentiers, 160, 181
Resorts, 158. *See also* Spas
Rivière, Henri, 37, 58, 60
Robida, Albert, 60, 141
Rolland, Romain, 220
Rollinat, Maurice, 71
Roques, Jules, 67, 69, 70

Salis, Rodolphe, 73; career of, 46, 58, 63, 69, 70, 71, 74
Scala, 74, 84, 95, 193
Scholl, Aurélien, 37, 72, 176
Scotto, Vincent, 70
Seeth the lion-tamer, 202
Seurat, Georges, 154, 176, 186; **151**
Simon, Jules, 101
Sivry, Charles de, 60
"Slumming," 91, 93, 96–97
Songs, 75, 102, 104, 113, 115, 214, 215
Spas, 29, 159. *See also* Resorts
Sports: new, 28, 65; promotion of, 65, 212–13, 215; participants, 100, 159, 162, 182–83; spectators, 182, 213
Steinlen, Théophile-Alexandre, 34, 58, 64, 69; **21**
Street entertainment, 169–76; **178–79**
Street fairs, 16, 17, 94, 172, 206; under attack, 43, 113–14, 194; specific entertainments in, 90, 110, 194, 199; appeal of, 93, 135, 138, 154–55, 177, 202; modernizing, 115, 188–89, 190; **180, 191**
Swimming pool Rochechouart, 153

Tarde, Gabriel, 165, 188
Taylor, Frederick Winslow, 35, 150, 152
Theater: as a business, 29, 84, 157, 158, 164, 170, 193, 214; performances, 60, 153, 192, 195, 207; audiences, 84, 115, 155
Théâtrophone, 188
Third Republic. *See* Government
Toulouse-Lautrec, Henri de: life of, 35, 69, 74; art of, 61, 64, 67, 69, 94, 154, 176; **112, 210, 211**
Tour de France, 28, 65, 213, 214

Veillées, 29
Viens poupoule, 70, 214–15

Weygand, General Maxime, 215
Widhopff, V. O., 34
Willette, Adolphe, 37, 72, 73; decorated cabarets, 58, 64, 69, 71
Women's wrestling, 110; **185**
Work ethic, 27–28, 215
Work life: agricultural, 6, 7; in urban and industrializing conditions, 7, 154–55, 160, 166, 181, 195, 221; hours and days, 30, 164; women's, 159, 160–61; domestic, 160–61
World's fairs. *See* Expositions

Xanrof, Léon (Léon Fourneau), 69, 70

Zidler, Charles, 70
Zola, Emile, 37, 47